A Gentleman and a Scholar

MEMOIR OF JAMES P. BOYCE

A Gentleman and a Scholar

Memoir of James P. Boyce

by

John Albert Broadus

Solid Ground Christian Books
Birmingham, Alabama

SOLID GROUND CHRISTIAN BOOKS
PO Box 660132, Vestavia Hills, AL 35266
205-443-0311
sgcb@charter.net
http://www.solid-ground-books.com

A Gentleman and a Scholar:
Memoir of James Petigru Boyce

by John Albert Broadus

From the 1893 edition by A.C. Armstrong and Son. *New York, NY*

Published by Solid Ground Christian Books

Classic Reprints Series

First printing October 2004

ISBN: 1-932474-56-0 (hardcover)
ISBN: 1-932474-57-9 (paperback)

Manufactured in the United States of America

TO

MRS. BOYCE AND HER DAUGHTERS,

WITH MANY PRECIOUS MEMORIES IN COMMON,
AND HEARTY PERSONAL FRIENDSHIP.

J. A. B.

PREFACE.

This Memoir has been prepared by request of the family, and through strong impulses of personal affection; for we were of the same age, and had worked side by side for thirty years. But in depicting a character so elevated and sincere, one feels obliged to restrain the natural tendency to eulogium.

I have especially tried to represent the environment and development of Dr. Boyce's early life in Charleston, at Brown University, and at Princeton Theological Seminary, and to bring out his labors as editor in Charleston, pastor in Columbia, and professor in Furman University. The part which he took in the war, and in South Carolina politics, is not overlooked.

As his recognized life-work was the foundation and establishment of the Southern Baptist Theological Seminary, a biography of him could hardly fail to comprise a history of that institution. But this is for the most part thrown into distinct chapters, which some readers can pass over if they like. For the historical sketch of the institution I have carefully used printed and manuscript records, besides recollections which go back almost to the beginning of the movement. If any persons interested in theological education wish really to understand the peculiar plan and operations of this Seminary, they will find a brief chapter of explanation.

The account of Dr. Boyce's ancestry and early life is most of all indebted to Dr. H. A. Tupper, who was his friend from boyhood and married his sister, and who has written copious memoranda and furnished a long series of letters, carefully arranged, from which I drew many facts and impressions, besides the extracts given. Valuable assistance was also afforded by Dr. Boyce's sister, Mrs. Burckmyer, and by William G. Whilden, Esq., Judge B. C. Pressley, and numerous other friends, to whom indebtedness will be found acknowledged at one point or another. The Misses Boyce have carefully selected from their father's letter-books all such as they thought likely to be helpful, and have written notes of his later journeys which they shared, and also personal recollections of his home life and traits of character, which are freely used in the closing chapters. I heartily thank many former students and others who have furnished material for this labor of love.

J. A. B.

LOUISVILLE, KY.,
April 15, 1893.

CONTENTS.

CHAPTER I.

BIRTH AND ANCESTRY.

The Scotch-Irish.— The Boyce Name and Family.— The Grandfather's Services and Adventures during the Revolutionary War.— The Father, Ker Boyce, settles in Charleston as a Cotton-Factor. — Weathering a Financial Storm. — James Boyce's Mother. — Her Conversion, during a Sermon by Basil Manly, Sr.
PAGES 1–9.

CHAPTER II.

THE CITY OF CHARLESTON.

Beautiful Bay, Islands, and Rivers. — The Rich Planters of "Sea Island" Cotton. — The Carolina Aristocracy. — Story of Dr. Jeter. — Population of Charleston at Different Periods. PAGES 10–13.

CHAPTER III.

CHILDHOOD AND YOUTH.

The Namesake, James L. Petigru. — The "Little Guardsman" at Church. — Sketch of the Pastor, Basil Manly, Sr. — James's Early Fondness for Books.— His Archery Club and Debating Society. — His Mother's Early Death. — The Lesson she once gave him in Truthfulness. — His Boyish Care of the Younger Children, and how they regarded him. — Six Months in a Dry-Goods Store. —

Reading the Works of Gilmore Simms. — At Professor Bailey's School, and at the High School with Dr. Bruns. — Timrod and Hayne. — H. H. Tucker his Sunday-School Teacher, and afterwards Judge Pressley. — Hearing Dr. Thornwell. — At the Charleston College under Dr. Brantly. — Tribute of his Fellow-Student, F. T. Miles. — Sketch of Dr. Brantly, the Pastor and President. — Business and Political Activity of Mr. Ker Boyce.

PAGES 14-32.

CHAPTER IV.

AT BROWN UNIVERSITY.

Early Interest of South Carolina Baptists in Brown University. — Sketch of President Wayland, whom James Boyce resembled in Important Respects. — Dr. Wayland's Controversy with Dr. R. Fuller on Slavery. — Professors Caswell, Gammell, Lincoln, and J. R. Boise. — Various Fellow-Students who became famous. — Visit of Adoniram Judson. — Letters of Boyce to H. A. Tupper. — Tributes to him by J. R. Boise and J. H. Luther. — His Conversion, through the Influence of Fellow-Students at Brown, and the Preaching of Dr. R. Fuller in Charleston. — His Zeal on returning to College, and Important Revival there. — His Studies. — Lively Letter to a Charleston Lady. — Continued Religious Labors. — Letters. — Determination to become a Minister. — Disappointment of his Father and some others. — Graduated and licensed to preach.

PAGES 33-54.

CHAPTER V.

MARRIAGE AND EDITORIAL WORK.

How he became acquainted at Washington, Ga. — The Ficklen Family. — The Village, its Schools and Society. — Quickly enamoured, and long persevering. — How prevented from studying Theology at Hamilton. — Marriage. — Editor of "The Southern Baptist" in Charleston. — Characteristics and Success in that Capacity. — Much in Company with Dr. A. M. Poindexter.

PAGES 55-66.

CHAPTER VI.

AT PRINCETON THEOLOGICAL SEMINARY, 1849-1851.

Archibald Alexander and his Famous Sons, James and Addison. — Dr. Charles Hodge. — Fellow-Students, Presbyterian and Baptist. — Very laborious, his Wife aiding by copying Notes.— Preaching often at the Penn's Neck Baptist Church, near Princeton.— The Earliest Sermon that remains.— A Vacation with the Ficklens in Virginia, preaching every Sunday. — Letters to Mr. Tupper, now his Brother-in-law. — Plans on leaving Princeton . . . PAGES 67–83.

CHAPTER VII.

PASTOR AT COLUMBIA, S. C., 1851–1855.

The City, its Surroundings and Beautiful Homes. — Capitol, South Carolina College, Presbyterian Theological Seminary.— The Baptist Church in Columbia, and his Ministerial Labors. — Getting a Strong Hold upon the Colored People. — Setting up a Home. — His Father's Death there. — Closing Estimates of Mr. Ker Boyce. — The Young Minister left as Active Executor. — At the Southern Baptist Convention in 1855 . . . . PAGES 84–99.

CHAPTER VIII.

PROFESSOR OF THEOLOGY IN FURMAN UNIVERSITY.

History of the Furman Institution from 1827, and its Removal to Greenville in 1851, as Furman University. — Boyce elected to its Theological Department in 1855. — Sketches of President Furman and Professors Judson, Edwards, and others. — Boyce's Anxiety to have another Theological Professor. — His Faithful Labors. — Sermon on the Death of Senator A. P. Butler . PAGES 100–110.

CHAPTER IX.

FOUNDATION OF THE SOUTHERN BAPTIST THEOLOGICAL SEMINARY.

Almost every Baptist College began with a Theological Department. — Young Basil Manly and others going to Newton, in Massachusetts. — Separation of Northern and Southern Baptists, in 1845. — Idea of a Common Theological School for all Southern Baptists.— Various Consultations, at Augusta 1845, Nashville and Charleston 1849, in Virginia 1854; in Educational Conventions, at Montgomery 1855, Augusta 1856. — James P. Boyce's Address in 1856 at Furman University on "Three Changes in Theological Institutions." — Copious Extracts from this Epoch-Making Address.— His Views compared with those of President Wayland, Three Years before, in "The Apostolic Ministry."— Proposition of the South Carolina Baptists accepted by an Educational Convention in Louisville, 1857. — Professor Boyce at work as Agent in South Carolina. — Final Convention at Greenville, 1858, organizing the Seminary.— Opening delayed a Year . . . . PAGES 111–154.

CHAPTER X.

THE SEMINARY'S PLAN OF INSTRUCTION.

Its Aim to give Theological Instruction to Men in every Grade of General Education.— How could these work together ?— System of Independent "Schools," like the University of Virginia. — Every Man's Studies completely elective. — List of the Seminary's Schools, or Departments.— Great Stress laid upon the Study of the English Scriptures.— Remarkable Experiences in that Direction.— How the Plan has worked, with even Unexpected Good Results. — Peculiarities as to Graduation. — New Degrees recently introduced, and New Titles. — Wide Range of *Special* Studies.

PAGES 155–165.

CONTENTS. xiii

CHAPTER XI.

THE SEMINARY'S THREE FIRST SESSIONS, 1859-1862.

The Town of Greenville and its Environs. — The Four Professors. — Some of the First Students. — Opening full of Encouragement. — Dr. Boyce's Country Pastorate. — His Kindness to the Students. — Dedicating the New Church at Columbia. — Second Session disturbed by the Great Political Excitement. — Visiting Fort Sumter after its Capture by South Carolina Troops. — Third Session greatly hindered by the War. — Dr. Boyce's Correct Forecast as to Duration of the War. — His Diligence in Study amid so many Interruptions.
PAGES 166–182.

CHAPTER XII.

DR. BOYCE'S PART IN THE WAR.

Opposed to Secession, but went with his State. — Fearing a Long and Bloody War. — Prospect of Heavy Financial Losses. — Chaplain in Confederate Army. — Member of the South Carolina Legislature. — Important Bill and Speech as to helping the Confederate Finances. — Extracts from the Speech. — Aide-de-Camp to the Governor. — His House at Greenville plundered by Union Soldiers.
PAGES 183–197.

CHAPTER XIII.

FIRST SIX YEARS AT GREENVILLE AFTER THE WAR, 1865-1871.

The Seminary reopened, with very Few Students, and Ruined Finances. — Working for the Future. — Dr. Boyce's Personal Losses and Embarrassments, and Great Exertions to collect Support for the Seminary. — Salaries once a Whole Year in Arrears, amid the High Prices. — Southern Interest in Higher Education, and Real Generosity of many. — Boyce refusing Offers of Large Salary. — Number of Students slowly increasing.— Finances improving, and (1869) a Fifth Professor appointed, C. H. Toy. — Dr. Boyce's Sermon at the Funeral of Dr. Basil Manly, Sr. — Extracts. — Professor B. Manly, Jr., goes to be President of Georgetown College, Ky.

PAGES 198–217.

CHAPTER XIV.

SERIES OF EFFORTS TO REMOVE THE SEMINARY.

What had become of the Original Subscribed Endowment. — Necessity for Removal slowly recognized. — Various Suggestions and Propositions, from 1869 onward.— Offer to make Boyce President of Brown University. — Decision in 1872 to remove the Seminary to Louisville. — Professor W. H. Whitsitt elected in 1872. — Dr. Boyce yields the Chair of Systematic Theology to Dr. Williams.— Elected President of the Southern Baptist Convention, 1872–1879. — Removes his Family to Louisville, 1872. — Letters to J. O. B. Dargan and Mrs. Butler. — Grave Difficulties encountered at Louisville, and Opposition of some Excellent Men.— Financial Collapse of 1873.— Boyce's Great Speech before a Meeting in Louisville, and another before the Southern Baptist Convention in 1873. — Remarkable Contributions in Texas, and at the Baptist Anniversaries in Washington City. — Tour of Kentucky. — Long Series of Efforts to secure Endowment in Kentucky and elsewhere.— Preaching much in Louisville. — Work of the Seminary at Greenville. — Failing Health of Dr. Williams, and his Death. — Sketch, and Tribute by Dr. Curry. — Removal of the Seminary to Louisville in 1877 . . . . PAGES 218–250.

CHAPTER XV.

TEN BUSY YEARS IN THE SEMINARY AT LOUISVILLE, 1877–1887.

Extracts from Dr. Boyce's Opening Lecture on History of the Seminary. — Professors cordially received in Louisville. — Dr. Boyce again teaching Theology. — Number of Students much increased. — Resignation of Dr. Toy (1879), and Return of Dr. Manly. — Dr.

CONTENTS. xv

Boyce's Work as a Teacher. — His Method of Instruction in Theology. — His Love of Turrettin, and Class in "Latin Theology." — His Teaching in Church Government, Pastoral Duties, and Parliamentary Practice. — His New Studies in Various Directions. — Seminary's Financial Condition unsatisfactory, and Boyce's Labors and Journeys. — The Institution saved by a Single Gift, in Answer to Prayer, with Further Gifts in Louisville and New York. — More Students. — Assistant-Professor G. W. Riggan. — Need of Ground and Buildings. — New York Hall. — Death of Riggan. — Assistant-Professors J. R. Sampey and A. T. Robertson. — Letters of Boyce to his Sister and others, to M. T. Yates and other Missionaries.
PAGES 251–303.

CHAPTER XVI.

PUBLISHED AND UNPUBLISHED WRITINGS.

Brief Catechism of Bible Doctrine. — Abstract of Theology. — History of its Production. — Adapted to his Method of Class Instruction, but very useful also to Working Preachers. — Highly Favorable Notices in the "Standard" and the "Independent." — Mention of Various Sermons, Lectures, and Essays, which ought to be published . . . . PAGES 304–313.

CHAPTER XVII.

DECLINING YEARS AND DEATH.

Occasional Attacks since 1871. — Overwork. — Co-Professor F. H. Kerfoot in 1887. — Various Letters, one to William E. Dodge, of New York. — Journey with Family to California and Alaska. — Notes of Miss Boyce. — Assault on Dr. Manly, impairing his Health. — Dr. Boyce once more presiding in Southern Baptist Convention, 1888. — Voyage with Family to Europe. — Letters. — Miss Boyce's Notes of their Travels in England and Scotland. — Very ill in London. — Death of two Sisters. — Letters. — Sojourn in Paris, with Failing Strength. — Death at Pau, in the South of France, Dec. 28, 1888. — Funeral from Broadway Church, Louisville. — Memorial Meetings. . . . . . . PAGES 314–344.

CHAPTER XVIII.

GENERAL ESTIMATES OF CHARACTER.

Various Qualities stated, with Numerous Extracts from Memorial and Funeral Addresses, from Letters of Students and other Friends, and from Miss Boyce's Notes . . . . PAGES 345–371

MEMOIR

OF

JAMES PETIGRU BOYCE.

―――◆―――

CHAPTER I.

BIRTH AND ANCESTRY.

JAMES PETIGRU BOYCE was born in Charleston, South Carolina, January 11, 1827. His father, Ker Boyce, had removed ten years before from Newberry District.[1] This large district, or county, lies in the fine central region of South Carolina, which is rolling and healthful, and near enough to navigable streams to have been earlier developed than the upper portions of the State, towards the Blue Ridge. An enthusiastic old citizen is reported to have said: "South Carolina is the garden spot of the world, and Newberry District is the garden spot of South Carolina."

While the early settlers of South Carolina were chiefly English, there were two other considerable elements, which have always been highly influential in the business, politics, and society of the State, — the Huguenots and the Scotch-Irish. These last are a people who have made

---

[1] The term "district" was always used in South Carolina until the Reconstruction legislation of 1866 changed it to "county." The districts near the coast were subdivided into parishes, some of which had separate representation in the State Legislature.

themselves felt in all parts of the world. They went from Scotland centuries ago to the adjacent portions of Ireland, and have continued to occupy all the northeastern part of that island, having Belfast and Londonderry as their chief cities, and keeping themselves mainly distinct from the properly Irish population. They followed the example of their kinsmen in Scotland in becoming Protestant and Presbyterian, and they now constitute an important factor in the possibilities and the difficulties of Home Rule in Ireland.

The father of Ker Boyce was John Boyce, who was born in Ireland. The family name is still common in northeastern Ireland and in various parts of the United States.[1] John Boyce removed to the British colonies of

---

[1] Prof. James R. Boise, formerly of Brown University, and now Emeritus Professor in the Divinity School of Chicago University, in a letter of February, 1889 (after James P. Boyce's death), from which we shall hereafter quote further, says, "I had correspondence with him a few years ago respecting the various forms of our name; and the result may be interesting to some of his relatives and numerous friends. By the aid of encyclopædias and biographical dictionaries we arrived at the following list, showing that the name is found in Greek, Latin, German, Italian, French, and English; and it is quite likely that other forms might be found: Βοηθός, Βοηθόος, Boëthius, Boëtius, Boethe, Boëcius, Boëce, Boëcio, Boëzio, Bois, Boice, Boyce, Boyse, Boise, Boies, Boyes, Boys, Boyis, Boiss, Boöis." There is some reason to believe that all were primarily of Huguenot origin, their ancestors having emigrated, when banished from France, to the north of Ireland, where they found Protestant sympathy. It may be worth while to mention that about 1786 Gilbert Boyce is spoken of as an English Baptist minister, and that a collection of hymns published in England in 1801 contained twenty-one hymns by Samuel Boyse (Dict. Hymn., p. 167). Dr. Rubert Boyce, author of an important medical work, is now a medical professor in University College, London. We learn further, through the researches of Samuel Wilson, of Richmond, that persons named Boyce were early prominent in Virginia. Chyna (Cheney) Boyse came over in 1617, and was of the Assembly of Burgesses in 1629; John Boys was of that body in 1619, both representing Charles City county. Several others appear among the immigrants of that century.

North America in 1765. In 1777 he married Elizabeth Miller, daughter of David Miller, of Rutherford, North Carolina, and shortly after settled in Newberry District, about fifteen miles north of the town of Newberry, in a section which has for many years been called Mollohon. He thus began his married life in the midst of the Revolution. The battle of Fort Moultrie had been fought in June, 1776. On the 15th of January, 1778, the city of Charleston was set on fire, — according to the popular supposition by "partisans of the British," — and lost two hundred and thirty-two houses, valued at half a million of pounds sterling. In the spring of this year the Schophelites, followers of Colonel Schophel, a militia colonel whom Moultrie called "an illiterate, stupid, noisy blockhead," organized in South Carolina and moved across the Savannah River to form a junction with the British troops in St. Augustine, Florida. It was expected that these troops would invade South Carolina, and the military prowess of the Carolinians was greatly aroused. Alexander Boyce, a brother of John not otherwise known to us,[1] obtained a commission as captain; and as a private in his brother's company, John had his first military experience. At the siege of Savannah, Captain Alexander Boyce, on the 9th of November, 1779, in a gallant attempt to carry the British line, fell at the head of his company. John Boyce afterwards joined a company commanded by Captain (subsequently Colonel) Dugan, and was in the battles of Blackstocks, King's Mountain, Cowpens, and Eutaw. After one of these battles he returned home for a brief visit, but had scarcely seated himself to eat when he was startled

---

[1] Nor do we know what kin to John and Alexander was James Boyce, who also came from Ireland to North Carolina before the Revolution, settling near Charlotte. He was an eminently religious man, and highly respected. His grandson is Rev. Ebenezer Erskine Boyce, D.D., of Gastonia, N. C., and the latter's son is Rev. James Boyce, of Louisville, Ky., minister of the Associate Reformed Church.

by the approach of horses. Springing to the door, he found himself confronted by a party of Tories, headed by the celebrated partisan William Cunningham, and another man equally dreaded, named McCombs. Hurling his hat into the faces of the horses, which made them open right and left, he rushed through the opening towards the woods, not reaching them till he had lost three fingers from his uplifted arm, by a furious blow of Cunningham's sabre. When the Tories withdrew, he hurried to the house, that his hand might be bound up; then joined his company, and before night was in pursuit of the murderous marauders. On the Enoree River, near the mouth of Duncan's Creek, they captured eleven or twelve of the party, and among them McCombs. "These were conveyed to the place where the Charleston road crosses the old Ninety-Six road (now Whitmire's), and there a 'short shrift,' a strong rope and a stooping hickory, applied speedy justice to them all. A common grave, at the root of the tree, is their resting-place for all time.

"On another occasion Mr. John Boyce was captured, and tied in his own barn, while a bed-cord was sought for to hang him ; his negro man (long afterwards known as Old Sandy), being hid in the straw, while the captors were absent on their fell purpose arose to the rescue, untied his master, and both made good their escape. . . . These are a few of the hairbreadth escapes which tried the men of that dark and bloody period, when home, sweet home, could not be enjoyed for a moment without danger, and when wife and children had to be left to the tender mercies of the bloody, thundering Tories." The late John Belton O'Neall, Chief-Justice of South Carolina, from whose "Annals of Newberry" the above details are taken, adds: "John Boyce lived long after the war, enjoying the rich blessings of the glorious liberty for which he had perilled so much. He lost his wife in 1797, and died in 1806, leaving seven sons and a daughter, Robert, John, David,

Alexander, Ker, James, Andrew, and Mary." It will be noticed that several of these sons bore familiar Scottish names. It is a family tradition that he and all the seven sons were noted for their wit, and fond of practical jokes; and many anecdotes are preserved which show how the old gentleman, at the age of seventy-five and eighty, still enjoyed getting the best of "the boys." We shall find this characteristic fully inherited by Ker Boyce and by his son James.

Judge O'Neall says that John Boyce was "a well-informed, though not a well-educated, man, who had read much, and exercised a just and wholesome influence in the section where he lived. He was a Presbyterian and an elder in McClintock's church, Gilder's Creek, and his remains rest in the graveyard of that church." His sons all led industrious and prosperous lives, making themselves favorably known in Newberry, Laurens, Union, and elsewhere, and no doubt permanently influenced by the "Let us worship God," heard night and morning in the home of their youth. A son of Robert was Hon. William W. Boyce, a distinguished member of the United States Congress and of the Confederate Congress, and a prominent lawyer, who spent his last years in Washington city in the practice of his profession, and died in 1889.

Beyond the general good influence of the home and the church, we know nothing as to the early life of Ker Boyce, born April 8, 1787, save that he was mirthful and mischievous, so that some imagined he would not succeed well in business, but found themselves very much mistaken. His educational advantages were limited, but he showed a quick and bright intelligence. After some experience as clerk in a store, he established himself as a merchant in the town of Newberry, and steadily prospered. In 1812 the Legislature elected him to be tax-collector for Newberry District over several opponents, and it is related that he showed much electioneering skill in dealing with the members, aided by his contagious good humor and wit. In the year 1813, when the second war with Great Britain interrupted communication by sea with the Northern States, Mr. Boyce began to trade overland with Philadelphia. Cotton was hauled from Newberry to Philadelphia in wagons, which then brought back goods purchased there by the young merchant, who made the journey on horseback. In 1815 he and a friend went on horseback to Amelia Island (off the Forida coast, near Fernandina), purchasing a stock of goods which was there for sale, and transporting it to Newberry by wagons.

In 1815 Ker Boyce was married to Miss Nancy Johnston, of Newberry. She and also his second wife (the mother of James P. Boyce) were sisters of Job Johnston, who was distinguished as a chancellor. The following account of their father was copied from a Family Bible by Hon. Silas Johnston, of Newberry: "John Johnstown [note the spelling] was born in the county of Londonderry, Ireland, and married Mary Caldwell, daughter of Job Caldwell, in the same county, July 2, 1785. The father of John was David Johnstown, whose wife was Mary Boyd, who was the daughter of Thomas Boyd, who served on the side of King William at the siege of Londonderry, in the year 1689. (*Vide* Smollett's History of England.)" So we see that the mother also of James P. Boyce was of a Scotch-Irish family, and they too were Presbyterians. Nancy Johnston was born in Fairfield, S. C., Oct. 9, 1795, and married July 11, 1812. Judge O'Neall remarks, "No more lovely woman ever blessed a husband."

In 1817, two years after the close of the war with England, it became manifest that there were great possibilities for the cotton trade from Charleston to the Northern cities and to Europe. Our far-seeing and enterprising young merchant became dissatisfied with Newberry, as too narrow a field, and too far from the sea. So he and his brother-in-law, Samuel Johnston, formed a co-partnership, and commenced business as merchants in King Street, Charleston. Subsequently they transferred their business to "The Bay," and became factors and commission-merchants. The term "factor," according to its original use, might suggest that such men were only the agents of the cotton-planters, to sell their cotton and buy their plantation supplies. But the leading cotton factors soon began to advance money on the cotton, and themselves furnish the supplies. They would often provide these for the current year, taking the planter's obligation to pay with interest when the cotton should be sold, or taking a lien on the crop, which was sometimes specially authorized by law. Thus the cotton factors frequently became operators on an extensive scale, and men of great business talents had opportunity for large acquisitions of wealth. Judge O'Neall tells us that Mr. Samuel Johnston "was the most perfect man of business" he ever knew. He credits both the young partners with "an excellent judgment," and ascribes to Mr. Boyce "tireless energy and activity." So the firm made large profits, and rose rapidly to financial power. But Mr. Johnston's health gave way, and he died of consumption in 1822. A Mr. Henry had been associated with them, and the firm was for some years Boyce and Henry, and then Boyce, Henry, and Walter.

"In 1823 Mr. Boyce sustained the first great misfortune of his life," in the death of his admirable wife, who lies buried in the cemetery at Newberry. She left three children, — John Johnston, Samuel J., and Mary C., who became Mrs. William Lane.

In 1825 occurred one of the great periodical revulsions in trade and finance. At such times cotton factors are exposed to peculiar danger, when from the beginning of the year they have made large advances in supplies to planters, expecting to borrow money as needed, and replace it all when the cotton should be sold the next winter. When the banks shut down, and private loans become impossible, the cotton factor of large connections is apt to go under. Mr. Boyce's firm is said by our authority to have accumulated by this time fifty thousand dollars. He put the whole of it in requisition to save his business, but this would by no means have sufficed. Mr. Blackwood, president of the Planters' and Mechanics' Bank, had closely observed Mr. Boyce's business talents and character, and told him that the bank would furnish him funds to any needed extent. In all pursuits and relations, personal character tells. We learn (from an obituary) that at this time Mr. Boyce also upheld various other men, in whom with his remarkable insight he put just confidence, and enabled them to tide over the time of danger.

In the latter part of this year, Oct. 25, 1825, Ker Boyce formed a second marriage, with his previous wife's younger sister, Amanda Jane Caroline Johnston, born Dec. 3, 1806. Her children were five; namely, James, Nancy (Mrs. H. A. Tupper), Rebecca (Mrs. Burckmyer), Ker (or Kerr), Elizabeth (Mrs. Lawrence). This young wife, the mother of James, is described as singularly attractive and admirable. Thus Dr. H. A. Tupper says: "A more gentle and lovelier Christian woman never lived. Her person had the frail beauty of the lily; her character, the rich fragrance of the rose. The writer, as a little boy, knew her well and admired her greatly. Tristram Shandy says a man's history begins before his birth. The almost womanly gentleness and amiability of James P. Boyce may be clearly traced to his mother, — just as his hard common-sense, great executive ability, and deep vein of humor may be with equal readiness traced to his father and his paternal grandfather."

It cannot be ascertained under what precise circumstances Mr. Boyce and his wife, though both reared in Presbyterian families, began to attend the ministry of the young Baptist pastor, Basil Manly (see below in chapter iii.). In November, 1830, the pastor felt bound, for some highly important reason, to attend the Baptist State Convention, though one of his children was very ill. He and his wife prayed for direction, and decided that he must go; and all matters at the convention were satisfactorily arranged. Returning, he found that the child, named John, had died and been buried. It was hard for him to preach on the following Sunday; but under a similar sense of duty he did preach, taking as his text Genesis xliii. 14: "If I be bereaved of my children, I am bereaved."[1] Through that sermon Mrs. Ker Boyce was converted; and others were known to have been specially blessed, as well as the preacher himself. In after years he would sometimes tell of these events, as showing that it is always best for us to subordinate personal and family affection to the claims of duty in the service of Christ. And who would have thought that Mrs. Boyce's little boy, near the same age as the one he had lost, was in the course of Providence to preach Basil Manly's funeral sermon, with grateful recognition of the good done by that day's discourse?[2]

[1] The notes made in preparing are still in existence, and are singularly interesting and suggestive. Every thought comes right out of the text or the occasion, and the tone is healthy and uplifting.

[2] In October, 1891, the venerable and greatly beloved widow of Dr. Manly recited the circumstances of her child's death in a letter to a bereaved young mother, and added: "The Lord was with us both, and strengthened us for our duties. I can truly say He comforted us, and has ever been to us a tender, loving Father. Never doubt His tender mercies, my child, but trust in Him, and He will sustain and comfort you."

CHAPTER II.

THE CITY OF CHARLESTON.

CHARLESTON has always been the most important city on the southern Atlantic coast. Its harbor is not so extensive as that of Port Royal, farther south in the same State, but was far better adapted to defence against assaults from the sea. Its advantages in this respect attracted world-wide observation during the War of Secession. The principal channel across the bar has some sixteen feet water at ebb tide, which sufficed for the largest sea-going vessels until recent times. Since 1891 jetties have been built by Congressional appropriations, which are beginning to wash out the bar; and it is hoped they will so deepen the channel as to receive the largest ocean steamers of to-day, and thus greatly increase the prosperity of this ancient seaport. The site of the city is beautiful. The Ashley and Cooper rivers, as they approach the sea, run a parallel course for nearly six miles, at no great distance apart, but somewhat widening towards the point at which they flow into, or in one sense constitute, the bay. On this peninsula between the rivers the city is built. The lower end, fronting the bay, is known as the Battery,— doubtless because (as in New York) batteries were early placed there for defence against hostile ships. The Cooper River, on the northeastern side of the city, and the Ashley,[1] on the other side, are pleasing

---

[1] The rivers of South Carolina mostly retain their Indian names, as Santee, Pedee, Wateree, Congaree, Enoree, Edisto, Ashepoo. Saluda, etc. So the two rivers here mentioned were called Etiwan and Kiawah, but

streams, and after their union the bay winds its way out for some seven miles southeastward to the ocean, with islands on either side that produce a picturesque effect, besides affording great facilities for defence. Sullivan's Island, on the northeastern side of the bay, has long been the seat of summer homes for some of the citizens. Here is situated Fort Moultrie, successor to that palmetto fort which in 1776 resisted the bombardment of the British fleet, and fairly drove it away. The cannon-balls might penetrate into the palmetto logs, but their peculiar toughness of texture received and held the iron masses, without weakening the fortification. On the other side of the harbor lie James's Island and Morris Island, which became so famous during the recent war. Between Morris and Sullivan's Island, upon a shoal in the harbor, and covering the main channel, is Fort Sumter, which was first built when James P. Boyce was a child, but in fact was not entirely completed when it became the theatre of the celebrated bombardment and defence.[1] On a smaller shoal and much nearer to the city is the little fort called Castle Pinckney. The two rivers, the inner harbor, and the narrow straits that separate the islands from the mainland and from each other, are admirably adapted to boating and fishing; and all the coast region formerly abounded in game, attracting the vigorous huntsman, with his gun and dogs. The city is very healthy, for those who are acclimated, as the heat in summer is delightfully tempered by the sea-breeze. The average mortality is far less — as also in most of the cities on our southern coast — than in the great cities of the North. Occasional outbursts of

afterwards received the two names of Sir Ashley Cooper. Gilmore Simms has a novel called "The Cacique of Kiawah."

[1] See "The Defence of Charleston Harbor (1863-1865)," by Rev. John Johnson, who was Confederate Major of Engineers in charge of Fort Sumter, and has given us an admirable book. Charleston: Walker, Evans, & Cogswell Co.

yellow fever, brought from the West Indies, impress the imagination of people at a distance like some great railway or steamboat accident, while yet travel by steamer or rail is on the average far safer than by private conveyance. The diseases produced by extreme cold in northern regions are much more destructive to life than those produced by extreme heat, — a fact which reminds us that all the earliest seats of civilization were in hot countries. The wealthier people of Charleston and all the adjacent coast region could in summer cross at pleasure to Sullivan's Island and other cool spots on the bay, or could journey in their private carriages to Cæsar's Head, Flat Rock, or Asheville, in the mountains of North Carolina, or far away to the White Sulphur and other springs in the Virginia mountains, where South Carolinians used to be very numerous, or could go by sea to Saratoga and Newport, or across to Europe. Thus they possessed a rare combination of advantages for health and every higher gratification. The planters who produced "sea-island" cotton, the long staple of which was so much better adapted than "uplands" to the manufacture of all the finer fabrics, and thus commanded a greatly higher price, were better off than the owners of a gold-mine. Besides the summer journeys above mentioned, many of them would spend part of the winter in spacious and hospitable establishments which they maintained in Charleston, or in Columbia, the capital of the State, where they formed a ruling element in legislation and government. Every low-country parish had its separate senator, and the districts a much larger proportionate representation in the lower house than had been assigned by the old and still unchanged legislation to the up-country districts. In a word, the wealthy planters around and the wealthy citizens of Charleston constituted an aristocracy, with all the good and ill attaching to such a social condition. It is the fashion now in our country and in most countries to have only words of scorn for aristocratic institutions; yet, as often seen in America as well as in England, they certainly afford very great opportunity for developing and exalting individual character, and furnishing noble leaders of mankind. Many of these Charleston and low-country homes gathered large and carefully chosen libraries, with a growing preference for English editions, and often bound in English tree-calf. These books were read, and high discussion of history and literature, as well as philosophy and politics, prevailed in domestic and social gatherings, besides clubs and societies formed for the purpose, and conducted with great spirit. Charleston was long the chief seat of culture at the South, as Boston was at the North. Dr. J. B. Jeter, a celebrated Baptist minister of Virginia, from whom a thousand sayings are repeated, once visited Charleston, having previously spent some time in Boston. One day he asked a friend in Charleston, "What do you think is the difference in the look of a Boston man and a Charleston man?" The friend referred the question back to him, and he said: "A Boston man looks as if he thought, 'I know everything;' and a Charleston man, 'I know everything that it's worth while for a gentleman to know.'" It was a palpable hit, and might repay a good deal of reflection.

The population of Charleston in 1830, when James P. Boyce was a child, was 30,289, of whom 12,828 were whites. In 1840 the whites were 13,030, and the blacks had fallen off a little, being probably more in demand on the plantations, so that the total was 29,261. After this the white population gained more rapidly. In 1860 the total was 40,519, of whom 23,373 were white. In 1870 it was 48,956, of whom the whites were 26,207; but it is understood that the blacks in that census were often quite incompletely enumerated. In 1890 the total was 54,955, of whom 23,919 were whites; and the blacks were again largely in the majority.

CHAPTER III.

CHILDHOOD AND YOUTH.

THE oldest child of Ker Boyce's second marriage, born Jan. 11, 1827, was named after James L. Petigru, a highly distinguished lawyer of Charleston, a man of brilliant wit and other attractive qualities, and Mr. Boyce's cherished friend. He was of mixed Scotch-Irish and Huguenot ancestry, and born and reared in Abbeville District, adjoining Newberry. Mr. Boyce and he were of nearly the same age, and removed about the same time to Charleston. Ere many years Mr. Petigru had no rival at the Bar. In 1822–30 he was attorney-general of the State, and exceedingly popular. This popularity was greatly diminished by his opposition to the Nullification movement of 1830–32, which doubtless prevented his rising into the highest political distinction. In later years he was also steadfastly opposed to the Secession movement; but (as we shall see) was so highly esteemed for personal character, and legal abilities and attainments, that a Legislature bitterly hostile to his opinions treated him with marked consideration. Mr. Petigru's wife was quite a musician, and one of their daughters was an artist; but he does not appear to have been himself much acquainted with music, whatever other artistic gifts he may have possessed. The story is told that once when Ole Bull came to Charleston, at the height of his reputation, and, appearing on the platform, began to tune the violin a little, Mr. Petigru turned to his wife and said, "My dear, isn't that superb!" "Hush, Mr. Petigru!" she replied, "he is only tuning the instrument; you'll disgrace yourself." The great lawyer

CHILDHOOD AND YOUTH. 15

subsided in humiliation, and a good while afterwards, when Bull was in the midst of one of his noblest passages, Mr. Petigru timidly touched his wife's elbow and said, "My dear, will the man never get done tuning his violin?" Mr. Petigru long outlived his early friend, surviving until 1863, when his namesake had become a man widely known and honored.[1]

The earliest glimpse we get of Jimmy Boyce, as he was familiarly called, is in connection with public worship. In the old First Baptist Church of Charleston, not many squares from the Battery, the beloved Thomas P. Smith, long a cotton factor in the city, recently pointed out to the writer the Boyce pew. It is a long pew, rather near the pulpit, extending from the centre aisle to the side aisle, and having only space enough for one seat between the side aisle and a large wooden column. In this space the rotund boy, with his fine head, could be seen regularly every Sunday, absorbed in a book until the service began; and people called him "the little guardsman," always at his post. In this slight incident are already revealed several distinctive characteristics,— punctuality and self-reliance, love of reading, interest in public worship.

The pastor at that time, as already indicated, was Basil Manly the elder, who became one of the most eminent Baptist ministers in the whole country. He was born in Chatham County, North Carolina, 1798; his elder brother, Charles, became governor of that State, and his younger brother, Matthias E., became a Justice of the Supreme Court of the State. Basil graduated at the College of South Carolina in 1821, with the first honor, his fellow-students including many gifted men. After preaching some years at Edgefield Courthouse, he removed to Charleston in March, 1826, and remained till 1837. Then for nearly twenty years he was president of the State Uni-

[1] See a Biographical Sketch of J. L. Petigru, by W. J. Grayson. New York: Harpers, 1866.

versity of Alabama, showing extraordinary talent for administration as well as instruction. But he always loved the pastorate best, and returned to Charleston in 1855. He spent his last years of failing health with his son and namesake at Greenville, S. C., where he died in 1868. It was among the marked advantages of James P. Boyce's childhood to attend on Dr. Manly's ministry, and be brought in contact with such a pastor. His preaching was always marked by deep thought and strong argument, expressed in a very clear style, and by an extraordinary earnestness and tender pathos, curiously combined with positiveness of opinion and a masterful nature. People were borne down by his passion, convinced by his arguments, melted by his tenderness, swayed by his force of will. James Boyce was only ten years old when this honored pastor moved away; but we might be sure he received from him in public and in private many a wholesome and lasting impression.

Nor are we left to conjecture as to this matter. Witness the following extract from Dr. Boyce's Funeral Discourse upon the death of Dr. Manly in 1868: "Indeed, I do not know how a people could be more attached to a pastor than they were to Mr. Manly. He made himself accessible to all, manifested deep interest in their welfare, readily advised them according to his best judgment, and above all showed a cordial sympathy with their joys and sorrows. Especially was this true in spiritual matters. No one ever understood better how to console a suffering soul, or dealt with it more tenderly. And his people loved him with a depth of devotion seldom equalled. Nor was this confined to the members of the church. The presence of no one conferred more pleasure upon any family. The little children felt him to be their own, and spoke of him as such. And he loved them, and never forgot the word of kind exhortation, or admonition, or sympathy, suited to their case. The elders found in his genial intercourse a true copy of that of his Master, who mingled with men everywhere, entering into the ordinary social festivities of life, yet ever ready to utter the warning words of wisdom or counsel. It was his peculiar *forte* to say a word in season, and from his lips things unseasonable from others would be acceptable, because of the way in which he spoke them. . . . After a lapse of more than thirty years I can yet feel the weight of his hand, resting in gentleness and love upon my head. I can recall the words of fatherly tenderness, with which he sought to guide my childish steps. I can see his beloved form in the study, in the house in King Street. I can again behold him in our own family circle. I can remember the very spot in the house, where the bands which he was accustomed to wear with his gown were laid on a certain Thanksgiving Day on which he dined with us. I can call to mind his conversations with my mother, to whose salvation had been blessed a sermon preached on the Sunday after the death of one of his children upon the text, 'If I be bereaved of my children, I am bereaved.' And once more come to me the words of sympathy which he spake while he wept with her family over her dead body, and ministered to them as it was laid in the grave."

James's boyhood and early youth were not fruitful of events. He entered, we are told by a comrade, into few of the games that prevailed among boys. He did not "shoot marbles," "play shinny," or engage in games of ball or "prisoner's base."[1] As a bigger boy, he was not given to running, swimming, rowing, sailing, horseback-riding, or gunning. He was even averse to most of these sports, and through life never felt at ease on horseback. The explanation of all this is not found in any lack of sportive

[1] Another schoolmate writes to the same general effect, but says that he joined with great zest in such games as ball and shinny. In this conflict of authorities the Muse of History can only leave the question undecided.

disposition, for he was the very quintessence of fun and jollity, but chiefly in the fact of his unusual size, which did not qualify him for sports requiring much activity or involving risk, and to which he sometimes referred in later years as having materially conditioned his early life. For the same reason, he never indulged in boxing, fencing, or fighting, — a not uncommon amusement of Charleston boys in his school-days. But this negative view of his youthful likes and dislikes makes only more prominent his fondness for archery. He organized a company of archers on the spacious grounds about his home in George Street, and was quite enthusiastic in the sport. Some of his friends find significance in this early desire for a definite object to aim at and hit. And his occasional liking for the more complicated aims and movements of the billiard table, with the great delight in chess which he developed at a later period, could hardly fail to suggest the skill and mastery of his combinations in after life. A friend of about the same age who knew him well adds the testimony that he was scrupulously temperate, and that the most searching scrutiny of memory does not recall a single act which stained his youth or young manhood with the slightest dishonor.

From early childhood, James was an excessive reader. While his companions were in the "city square," or on the "citadel green," engaged in their physical sports, he would be lying flat on the "joggling-board," in his father's piazza, absorbed in some story-book, novel, or history. He would often drive down town with his father, on the way to the bank of which Ker Boyce had become president, and return with a pile of books on the front seat of the carriage, brought from the Charleston Library and other places; and these books he would devour in an incredibly short time. His voraciousness only increased by gratification; and the number and variety of books that he read, all through life, was a marvel to his family and

CHILDHOOD AND YOUTH. 19

intimate friends. Besides his archery club, he organized at home a debating society. The "hall" was the room over his father's carriage-house. He was a leader then, as he became afterwards in the college societies and in denominational gatherings. Some of the lads who stood with him in that "upper room" have ranked, or rank now, among the foremost men of the Southern country. It is evident that the wide reading, which was thought excessive by his home folks and teachers, would serve him a good part on the floor of the debating society.

When James was ten years old, his mother died, leaving four children younger than himself, of whom she charged him to take care; and this he often recalled in after life when thanked for any kindness. Her life and character made a great impression on Mary also, the daughter of the first marriage, then fourteen years old; and she and James would try very earnestly in the years that followed to carry out all her rules in the home life. The oldest now surviving daughter can remember but little of their mother, except that she was very particular about truthfulness, as James also was through life. It is related that she once gave the lad a hard lesson in this respect. He remarked one Saturday morning that he would spend all his Saturday money on candy, and eat it all himself. When he returned, and, with his usual hearty generosity, wanted to distribute his candy, he was required to eat it all himself, because he had said he would. He took one of the little girls aside, and begged that she would ask mother to let him give her some; but no. Such was Mrs. Boyce's extreme solicitude as to truth; for there was no thought of James's being stingy. At that time and through life he was not only generous, but very considerate towards others, and seemed to have as much delicate tact and intuitive perception of the situation as women have. He was also very grateful for any present or any slightest attention, — a rose, a book, or anything; and would tell his little sister how kind somebody had been. The younger children were very fond of James, and felt that they could depend on him. He seemed to be an "all-round" person, ready for everything. It is said that the four boys and four girls of the household gradually fell into couples; James and Rebecca being special cronies, John and Mary, Samuel and Nanny, Kerr and Lizzie. Yet James showed no unpleasant favoritism in any way, and was always sympathetic, not only towards the other children, but to everybody. A friend states that the family housekeeper of those days, who cared for the children, was in after years uniformly visited by Dr. Boyce when in Charleston, and we learn from his business agent in Charleston that he regularly supplied her wants as long as she lived, and provided for her funeral.

At home, as well as elsewhere, James was fond of fun, delighting in all manner of jokes, and never at all vexed when made the butt of a joke himself. This sportive turn of mind was clearly inherited from his father, who overflowed with amusing stories of his own youth. James liked when a lad to go out at Christmas to the plantation homes of his father's friends, where they often dispensed a magnificent and delightful hospitality; and when somewhat older, he was quite fond of being with girls. His father required the boys to be scrupulously polite and attentive to their sisters, and himself always treated his daughters with marked courtesy and consideration. If one of them was out at evening, she must not come home in the carriage alone, but one of her brothers must go after her. Through life their father would give a son almost anything that one of his sisters asked.[1] The beginning of James's library was made with a gift of five hundred

---

[1] In like manner Patrick Henry, as we learn through his brother-in-law, was always the advocate of his sisters "when any favor or indulgence was to be procured from their mother" (Wirt Henry's Life of Patrick Henry, vol. i. p. 9).

dollars, handed him in New York after he graduated at college, at the special request of Nanny, as a gift to her. James was remarkable for being easy to please as to bodily comfort, and this continued through life, in all his wide travelling; he would be sometimes quite solicitous about a companion's comfort, and not seem to think of himself. It is also remembered that he appeared to his sisters a brave boy, while gentle and tender, and that he was singularly kind to animals. Those who knew him in later life would see in all this how "the child is father of the man."

Mrs. General Dickinson, of Florida, *née* Mary Elizabeth Ling, on a visit to Louisville in 1890 told that when a little girl at the dancing-school in Charleston she was always glad whenever Madame Feugas told her to waltz with Jimmy Boyce, because he was so springy and strong, and they went whirling. This exercise served to make some amends for the lad's disinclination to schoolboy sports. We know that his "barrel-shaped" figure — as several have described it — finally developed into a very symmetrical specimen of "episcopal dimensions," and his movements were always remarkably light and graceful.

In his earlier school-days James was hardly a student, in the common acceptation of the term, but seemed to neglect his text-books through devotion to general reading. Dr. W. T. Brantly, Sr., who was pastor of the First Church from 1837–1844, called Mr. Boyce's attention to this defect in the lad. He was not then old enough to enter Charleston College, though he had been over the requisite studies. The father, who had a remarkable knowledge of men, as shown throughout his business career, had tried a successful experiment on an older son, which he now repeated. Samuel, who was seven years older than James, had said much about a desire to go to sea. His father finally secured him a cabin passage from New York around Cape Horn; and after an absence of two years, he never spoke again of going to sea. In like manner, James was taken from school and put in the wholesale drygoods store of Wiley, Banks, & Co., in which his father was a partner. This new life would give excellent training of a certain kind until he grew old enough for college. James himself once told the writer in later years how his father gave express directions, both to him and to the men in the store, that he was to perform his full share of all the roughest and hardest work done by other boys of the same age. He must rise at six in the morning, go down and help to sweep out the establishment, and at any time be ready to help bring out the heaviest boxes, and in general must stand back for nothing. All this exactly suited his energetic temperament.[1] Many a rich man's son might feel in after life, as was felt in this case, that such a boyish discipline had been very helpful. However, six months of it sufficed for the lad's wishes, and he was quite willing to return to school. He had always stood fairly well in his classes, as a classmate testifies. The fact is, he acquired the appointed lessons with wonderful rapidity; and then threw aside his school-books to revel in his favorite authors, — never, however, of evil or doubtful character, the books he read being always open to the inspection of the family. But returning now to school, he turned over a new leaf as to the lessons, and applied himself with such diligence as to have an excellent standing in his classes, both at the well-known private school of Professor Bailey, at the High School, and at the Charleston College.

Yet, while the lessons now received regular attention, the wide reading continued. Apart from the books com-

[1] The early familiarity with elegant dress-goods also helped to develop his remarkable talent and taste in that respect. In after years his wife and sisters and daughters not only sought his advice in such matters, but would often commission him, when visiting Charleston or New York, to make the most important selections.

mon to all well-furnished boys of that period, — those great classics of literature for the young which are at the present day in danger of being neglected for the immense multitude of current and transient books, — and besides the novels of Cooper and Marryatt, we can see that the eager young reader would find much to attract him in the early history of Charleston and of South Carolina. He would often notice a fine statue of William Pitt (Earl of Chatham), "erected by the Commons House of Assembly of South Carolina," in gratitude for his procuring a repeal of the Stamp Act in 1766. It was placed in 1769 at the intersection of Broad and Meeting Streets. The right arm was destroyed by a cannon-ball from the English batteries on James Island during the siege of Charleston in 1780. After 1808 it stood in front of the Orphan House until a recent time. This fine statue would kindle the lad's curiosity about the causes of the great American Revolution. William Gilmore Simms published in 1840, when James Boyce was thirteen years old, a "History of South Carolina, from its first European Discovery to its Erection into a Republic," designed avowedly for the young, and suggested by the wants of his own daughters. Written in the author's flowing and agreeable style, and detailing the early settlement of South Carolina, the three attacks of the British upon Charleston, including the famous story of the Palmetto fort and Sergeant Jasper, and the stirring adventures of Marion and Sumter, we may be sure that this book was eagerly seized upon by a lad so fond of reading. Mr. Simms was a native of Charleston, and spent his life there (1806 to 1870), though usually giving half the year to his country home in Barnwell District. Before the appearance of this history he had published numerous volumes of poems and romances, including the "Yemassee," which is considered his best novel, and the "Partisan," which is a romance with Marion as the chief hero; many others appeared while James Boyce was still growing up in Charleston. Mr. Simms, like some other famous novelists, wrote too rapidly and hurriedly, and thus fell short of doing justice to his noble powers. Yet Edgar A. Poe pronounced him "the best novelist America had produced, after Cooper," and his books of every kind were exactly suited to delight an enthusiastic Charleston youth. It is worth while to notice that his History of South Carolina ended with the close of the Revolution; and the phrase in the title, "to its Erection into a Republic," is an amusing indication of the type of political opinion which was so popular in the State.[1] Besides the works of Simms and others, "Horse-shoe Robinson" was at that time a favorite Southern romance. James was too young to be much interested in the brilliant and powerful "Southern Review," published in Charleston from 1832 to 1840, and edited by the famous Hugh S. Legaré and others; but he read the volumes as he grew older, and was not a little stirred by the presence in the city of several gifted and eminent men who had contributed to it essays seldom equalled in even the great English Quarterlies.

Professor William E. Bailey, who was young Boyce's first teacher after he returned to school, was a man of classic tastes and aspirations, and evidently became much attached to this now diligent pupil; for when James P. Boyce opened the Theological Seminary at Greenville in 1859, it received Professor Bailey's library, specially bequeathed by him for that purpose, and comprising, among the thirteen hundred volumes, many of the most elaborate and costly editions of the great classic authors, as well as the histories of Prescott and Motley and many others, and a complete edition of Gilmore Simms's novels, which have doubtless many a time relieved the ever-arduous labors of theological students.

[1] After this was written appeared the Life of William Gilmore Simms, by W. P. Trent (Houghton, Mifflin & Co.). It is an interesting book, but the author seems curiously incapable of understanding the Carolina people of that day.

CHILDHOOD AND YOUTH.   25

The Charleston High School had been organized in 1839. The venerable Dr. Henry M. Bruns, who still resides in Charleston, at a great age, was principal at the time when James Boyce was for six months a student there. Among the teachers was Andrew Flynn Dickson, who is said to have been a remarkably gifted man, specially zealous about distinguishing between words, and always using exactly the right term. It is quite likely that in this respect he made a definite impression on his pupil, who was through life solicitous to get the right word, and was thereby frequently retarded in extemporaneous utterance. Dr. Bruns recently told the writer that young Boyce was fonder of mathematics than of classics, and received at the Commencement a silver medal for solving an original problem in algebra. He was a good, sensible lad, conscientious in preparing his lessons, jolly, and quite popular with the students. The Commencement mentioned was held at the Lutheran church, the pastor of which was the celebrated Dr. Bachman, whose works on natural history (some of them in association with Audubon, with whom he was also closely connected by marriage) did not begin to appear until 1850. Bachman was already a great promoter of education. Coming originally from New York State, he continued pastor of this church from 1815 until his death in 1874. He was a friend of Ker Boyce, and was always regarded by his son with great pride as an honor to Charleston. Other medals were taken at this Commencement by Bazile E. Lanneau, afterwards a Presbyterian minister and theological professor (and brother of Rev. Charles H. Lanneau), whose kinsman and namesake is Basil Lanneau Gildersleeve, the famous Professor of Greek in the University of Virginia and Johns Hopkins University, himself a native of Charleston; by Charles H. Simonton, now United States Judge for the District of South Carolina, and one or two other men who became well known. The venerable principal remembers that the poet,

Henry Timrod, was also his pupil at the High School, and that he recited at Commencement a passage from Moore with beautiful effect. Timrod was a native of Charleston, two years younger than James Boyce, and is said by Mr. W. G. Whilden to have been one of Boyce's intimate friends. He afterwards studied law in the office of Mr. Petigru, as Boyce would no doubt have done had his father's cherished wish been carried through. Paul H. Hayne, another distinguished Carolina poet, was also a Charlestonian, three years younger than James Boyce, and resided there during the greater part of his life. After Boyce had spent some time at Charleston College, and designed to enter Brown University, Dr. Bruns gave him some special lessons by way of preparation. It is said that at the memorial services held in the Old First Church after Dr. Boyce's death, this aged teacher was present, and showed deep emotion. A life-long instructor can have no truer, deeper joy than in surveying the noble character and useful career of those whom he helped to mould in their youth. Mr. Whilden states that while at the High School James was frequently a peacemaker among the boys, because of the confidence felt in his justice and equity; also that his amiability and courtesy won him friends among all classes, rich and poor; and though all knew that his father possessed large means, it was no barrier to general sociability. This was the more remarkable in the case of one who already had very decided views, and a very earnest way of expressing them.

In the Sunday-school he was at one time taught by Charles H. Lanneau, Sr., a man of excellent talents and noble character, other members of the class being J. L. Reynolds, Basil Manly, Jr., William Royall, William J. Hard, and T. W. Mellichamp, all of whom became ministers. When twelve years old his Sunday-school teacher at the First Church was Henry Holcombe Tucker, who became one of the most distinguished Baptist preachers and educators in the Southern country. He was a native of Georgia, but spent most of his early life in Philadelphia, where his grandfather, Dr. Henry Holcombe, was pastor; he graduated in 1838, at the Columbian College, in Washington city (now Columbian University); and the next year, at the age of twenty, was residing in Charleston, as "clerk" in a bookstore kept by his uncle, Mr. John Hoff, in Broad Street. It was a great privilege for young Boyce to be brought even for a short time under the influence of that singularly acute and powerful mind, that enthusiastic and inspiring instructor. We shall have occasion towards the close of this Memoir to quote from Dr. Tucker's striking address at the memorial services held before the Southern Baptist Convention after Dr. Boyce's death.

At a somewhat later time Dr. Brantly formed a Sunday-school class in the Greek Testament; and being greatly burdened with duties as pastor, and professor in Charleston College, he afterwards turned over the class to B. C. Pressley, Esq., a member of the church. Judge Pressley remembers as belonging to the class, James P. Boyce, H. Allen Tupper, James K. Mendenhall, and R. Furman Whilden, who all became ministers. He says that young Boyce seemed anxious to get the exact meaning of the Greek, and that he thought him likely to become a strong and clear thinker. When some fifteen years old, James was enamoured of a girl belonging to one of the Presbyterian churches. He went one Sunday morning to that church, and so placed himself in the gallery as to command a full view of her family pew. There came a stranger into the pulpit, and preached, more than an hour, a sermon abounding in deep thought and strong argument. When it was over, the lad felt positively ashamed of himself, for he had been so busy listening as hardly to look at his girl. The preacher turned out to be the great Dr. Thornwell, who probably never received a higher tribute to his powers.

It is also clear that the entranced hearer was no ordinary youth.

From 1843 to 1845, James Boyce was a student at the Charleston College, passing through the curriculum of the Freshman and Sophomore classes. This institution had been founded in 1787, and though lacking sufficient endowment to support a large faculty, it had some able teachers. Dr. Brantly, the Baptist pastor, an able and scholarly man, was now president of the college. One of the professors was Edward R. Miles, a student of Sanskrit and learned in various languages, who afterwards became an Episcopal clergyman. At college the youth was increasingly studious; but no study suppressed his exuberance of spirits, which occasionally overflowed in some "college prank," never injurious to any one, and always regarded among his comrades as venial, because clearly the result of mere humor and merriment. Dr. Brantly formed a high estimate of his abilities, but had some misgivings on the score of his jollity, with which the grave and stern president could not readily sympathize. Once when engaged in some practical joke on the campus, James ran behind a tree which was not big enough to hide him, and Dr. Brantly, looking out of a window, said, "There is Boyce, who will be a great man, if he does not become a devil." Yet he stood well in every class, especially in Latin and mathematics, and in history. And no one was more popular, in the class-room, in the debating society, or on the campus. Several fellow-students state that James's utter loathing of everything mean, and the brave and manly stand he always assumed when any principle was involved, together with his uniform regard for the feelings and wishes of others, made him a general favorite in the college. At a time when many students were hostile to the president, young Boyce stood up for him, even when almost alone. On one occasion he slapped a student in the face for some reason; but that evening waited for him and begged his pardon. James's ringing laugh could be heard afar, and was contagious. He would sometimes purposely mistranslate a Latin phrase, and when called to account would justify it by a joke, which worthy Dr. Hawkesworth, the Latin professor from Dublin, did not always appreciate. Among his classmates was Francis T. Miles, a native of Charleston, and now a distinguished physician and medical professor in Baltimore. In a letter of February, 1889, to Dr. Tupper, he speaks concerning Boyce as follows: —

"It was my good fortune during my college career in Charleston to have for a friend and classmate James P. Boyce; and although ever since we have been widely separated in life, I have always carried with me a strong and affectionate remembrance of him.

"He was conspicuous among his class and the students of the college by his talents and the strong, rapid grasp of mind, which not only enabled him to master with ease the studies of the curriculum, but caused him to push his reading, thought, and inquiry quite beyond the circle of required recitations. But it is not only as the clear, original thinker, the quick, cogent reasoner, that I remember him. I recall him as the genial, amiable, affectionate companion, who was never tempted (how rare a quality among young men!) to give pain or annoyance by a jest, nor, standing as he did on the high ground of a very pure morality, to scorn or animadvert upon those on an inferior level.

"I believe his subsequent life was the bright day of this clear dawn; and he now rests from labors which endeared him to those who admired him."

In March, 1845, the pastor and college president, Dr. Brantley, died. Born in North Carolina in 1787, he was graduated with distinction at the South Carolina College in Columbia, and early became remarkable for his fine classical culture and his eloquence as a preacher. His pastorates of eight years at Beaufort, S. C., of seven years at Augusta, Ga., — where he founded the church, and was at the same time rector of an academy, — and of eleven years at the First Baptist Church in Philadelphia, were all surpassingly popular and successful. His health beginning to fail in Philadelphia, he returned southward, succeeded Dr. Manly in Charleston in 1837, and soon after became president of Charleston College., Such combined labors, though often performed by eminent ministers, are necessarily apt to be exhausting. It was a great blessing for young Boyce, and several others destined to become eminent ministers, to attend upon the ministry of this great man.

Dr. Richard Fuller said of Brantly that "his characteristics were grandeur of conception, and reverence for divine revelation." Dr. Manly said: "He seemed ever to come fresh from communion with his Saviour, mellowed and enriched by hours of prayerful seclusion. I must regard him as the most uniformly engaging, instructive, and inspiring preacher that it has ever been my good fortune to hear." Dr. Sprague in his "Annals" says in regard to some of Brantly's published writings: "They were read and re-read, and laid up among the selectest treasures of memory."[1]

It was no doubt partly in consequence of Dr. Brantly's death that Mr. Boyce determined at the close of that session, which was James's Sophomore year, to send him to Brown University. The father's penetrating insight into character must have already begun to discern in the youth of eighteen years no ordinary possibilities. There was in many respects a striking resemblance. James inherited his father's large frame, fine head, and strong features; also in a remarkable degree his business talent and force of will, together with his cheerfulness even in times of special adversity and trial. It was Mr. Boyce's fond hope

[1] See H. A. Tupper's volume, "Two Centuries of the First Baptist Church in South Carolina (1683–1883)." Baltimore: R. H. Woodward & Co.

that his son would become an eminent lawyer, perhaps a distinguished statesman, and at the same time would conserve and carry forward his own great business undertakings, and care for the financial interests of his numerous children.

While his son was growing up, Ker Boyce had lived a very laborious life, for some years adding political activities to his ever-enlarging business engagements. When the great Nullification struggle began, in 1830, we are assured by Chief Justice O'Neall, from personal knowledge, that Mr. Boyce was opposed to the dangerous experiment; but in the political combinations that arose, and through the skilful tactics of General James Hamilton, he was induced to act with the Nullification party, as practically the wisest course. The Chief Justice, who was on the opposite side, says that this "secured the triumph of Nullification;" for Mr. Boyce's many business friends, scattered all over the State, "took very much his lead." He was subsequently a representative in the Legislature for the parish of St. Philip's and St. Michael's, and State Senator during two terms (1840–1848). When the Bank of Charleston was started, Mr. Boyce took a large amount of the stock, which he found very profitable; and some time afterwards was president of the bank for several years. This was at that time the largest bank in the South, having a capital of three millions. S. Y. Tupper, Esq., of Charleston (who died in 1891), being in Washington city in 1840, had a conversation with President Van Buren, in which "the President said he had read Mr. Boyce's bank reports with much interest and instruction, and that they were the most able and intelligent papers on finance and banking he had ever read, and had been of service to him in his messages to Congress."[1]

Mr. Boyce was also actively concerned in the leading

[1] Mr. Tupper wrote down these words soon after leaving the President, and gave them in a letter of January 9, 1889.

improvements of the city, such as the erection of the Charleston Hotel and the Hayne Street buildings; and two important wharves still bear his name. In 1837 he passed through a second great commercial revulsion. But though popularly supposed to be much shaken, he had learned from the former experience, and was now in no real danger. He had to pay out large sums for his friends and customers, but he had habitually taken pains to become liable for no man who had not more than the corresponding amount of visible property. Many an eminent business man has from some early experience of severe struggles and losses — sometimes even temporary failure — acquired the prudence necessary to temper his enterprising spirit, and enable him to steer safely through all the financial storms of subsequent life. After this period of trial in 1837, Mr. Boyce retired from the factorage and commission business, and employed his great and increasing wealth in other ways. He was one of the founders of the Graniteville Manufacturing Company, which established near Aiken, S. C., the most extensive cotton factories in the Southern States. This great establishment is still prosperous, and stock in it is still held by some of Mr. Boyce's heirs. He also united with a friend in establishing a wholesale dry-goods house in New York city which did a very large Southern business, and of which we shall afterwards hear, in the course of his son's history. Soon after the period we have reached, he began large investments in coal lands around Chattanooga, and a furnace, foundry, etc., in that rising city, which were afterwards developed and made extremely profitable by James, as his father's executor. Mr. Ker Boyce never became a church member, but he was for many years president of the board of trustees of the Baptist church to which his wife belonged, and a generous financial supporter.

CHAPTER IV.

AT BROWN UNIVERSITY.

THE Baptists of South Carolina had from the beginning taken an active interest in Brown University (originally called Rhode Island College), founded at Providence, R. I., in 1765, and generous contributions were sent by them towards its support and endowment. This being the first American college founded by Baptists, it awakened interest among the churches of that denomination throughout the colonies. The movement for its institution began with the noble old Philadelphia Association, and was heartily taken up in Rhode Island; and it is doubtful whether anywhere else the zeal for it was as great as in South Carolina, where the leading Baptists were already quite pronounced in favor of an educated ministry. In fact, it was at first a question whether the proposed institution should be placed in Rhode Island or in South Carolina; and the former is said to have been preferred [1] because the principles of religious liberty which Roger Williams had infused into that Colony made it easy for a Baptist institution to obtain a charter, while in South Carolina there was a religious establishment, namely, of the Episcopal Church. Among the honored presidents of the University had been Jonathan Maxcy, D.D., who afterwards went South for his health, and was for sixteen years president of the College of South Carolina at Columbia, where his extraordinary eloquence was greatly admired by such men as Mr. Petigru and Judge O'Neall.

---

[1] So Dr. Boyce stated in an address before the alumni of Brown University in 1871.

He died there in 1820, and his tomb is conspicuous on the campus.

When young Boyce entered Brown, in 1845, the president for eighteen years had been Francis Wayland, who was one of the most distinguished of all American educators, and who made a more potent impression upon the character, opinions, and usefulness of James Boyce than any other person with whom he came in contact. Dr. Wayland's famous sermon on "The Moral Dignity of the Missionary Enterprise" had been preached in Boston as early as 1823. His "Elements of Moral Science," published in 1835, was already widely used, and is believed to have become the most popular of all treatises on the subject in our language, including a revised edition in 1865. The "Elements of Political Economy" had appeared in 1837. From the nature of the subject, and the necessity of taking sides upon some questions involving heated political discussion, this treatise gained no phenomenal circulation, but it has been very widely used, and regarded as a remarkably good introduction to political economy as then held and taught. Dr. Wayland was already giving a full course of original lectures on Intellectual Philosophy, but his treatise on that subject did not appear till 1854. It is a notable epoch in the life of many a gifted young man when he first makes systematic study of psychology and logic, of ethics and sociology. This must have been in a very high degree the case with young Boyce when studying these subjects under the lead of a man so able in general, so impressive as an instructor, and (as we can now see) so like in many respects to the type of character and abilities which the young man himself was destined to develop. For we can perceive that each possessed sound practical judgment, combined with love of abstract thinking, and intense but quiet religious fervor; each showed great force of will and personal dignity, united with humility, considerateness, and benevolence; each was eminently truth-loving in studious inquiry and in statement, promptly indignant at any exhibition of insincerity or dishonesty, and yet forbearing, and in all personal matters ready to forgive; each was cheerful and sometimes merry, yet full of serious aims and purposes. In style also, both men were clear in explanation and strong in argument, and used excellent English. These similarities may help to account for the profound and permanent impression made by Dr. Wayland upon this pupil, who throughout his life delighted in every grateful expression of obligation, and in supporting his own views by reference to any similar opinion of the great college president. And if this instance was conspicuous, it was far from being singular; for no pupil of Dr. Wayland can have failed to receive benefit, and very many, including men of great distinction in various callings, have accounted their contact with him as the highest educational privilege of their life. Mr. Boyce adopted, when he became a teacher of theology, President Wayland's method of analytical recitations, without questioning; and some other pupils, probably many others, have done likewise. Hon. C. S. Bradley, Chief Justice of Rhode Island, stated to the writer some years ago that the alumni of Brown were proud of the very large proportion of eminent lawyers included in their number; and he believed it to result from Wayland's method of teaching, since the main thing for a lawyer is the power of making a clear and complete analysis of the case.

Dr. Wayland's studious fairness and moderation in argument had just been strikingly exhibited in a newspaper discussion with Dr. Richard Fuller, then of Beaufort, S. C. (afterwards of Baltimore), on "Domestic Slavery considered as a Scriptural Institution." The articles on both sides were afterwards published in a volume. The sympathizers with each of the disputants generally considered their champion to have had the best of the argument; but it was universally agreed that both conducted the discussion in a good Christian spirit and with good taste. This was notable, for it was a day of grievous political bitterness, and the controversy as to slavery was swelling higher and higher towards the terrific outburst of fifteen years later.

Among the other professors during Boyce's two years at Brown University were several men of marked ability and distinction. Dr. Alexis Caswell, Professor of Mathematics and Natural Philosophy, was an able and earnest teacher, an agreeable preacher, and remarkable for his courtesy as a gentleman, and the strong hold he took upon the respect and affection of young men. William Gammell, Professor of Rhetoric and English Literature, was a man of fine literary taste, and the author of some well-written books. John L. Lincoln, son of the famous Boston publisher, had just become Professor of the Latin Language and Literature, after a course at Brown and Newton, and several years as a student in Germany, and was already a pleasing and inspiring teacher; he afterwards published very good and popular editions of Livy and Horace. James R. Boise had also recently become full Professor of the Greek Language and Literature, which he has ever since continued to teach, in various institutions, with uncommon exactness of scholarship and skill as an instructor, and with the high respect of all who know him. He is now Emeritus Professor of New Testament Interpretation in the Divinity School of Chicago University; besides "Exercises in Greek Composition" and other text-books for school and college, he has published several small and excellent volumes explaining the Greek text of certain Epistles of Paul.

The Junior class of 1845–1846, which James P. Boyce entered, contained thirty-five men. Several of these must be here mentioned; and there are doubtless others whose names would attract the attention of persons more thoroughly acquainted with New England and the Northwest. Frederic Denison became a Baptist minister, pastor of several churches in Rhode Island and Connecticut, and chaplain in the Union Army for three years, and has published a large number of pleasing and popular works. George Park Fisher afterwards studied theology at Yale and Andover and in Germany, and is the well-known Professor of Ecclesiastical History in the Yale Divinity School. Besides numerous elaborate articles in the reviews, he has published quite a number of valuable books, including "The Beginnings of Christianity," "History of the Reformation," "Outlines of Universal History," "Faith and Rationalism," "The Grounds of Theistic and Christian Belief," and "History of the Christian Church." Reuben Aldridge Guild has spent his life as librarian of Brown University, becoming one of the eminent librarians of the country. He has produced several books of great interest, including a life of James Manning (the first president of the university), a Biographical Introduction to the Writings of Roger Williams, a History of Brown University, and "Chaplain Smith and the Baptists." He and Boyce formed a special friendship, which was maintained with ever-increasing cordiality through all the years. Whenever Dr. Boyce was able to attend annual meetings of his class he was the guest of Dr. Guild; and a visit of the latter to Boyce in Louisville is remembered by many with special interest. John Hill Luther graduated at Newton in 1850, and has ever since lived in the South, as teacher and Baptist minister, — in Georgia and South Carolina, in Missouri and Texas. He edited the "Central Baptist" of St. Louis for ten years, was long president of Baylor Female College at Belton, Texas, and is now one of the editors of the "Baptist Standard," Waco. He delivered an address at a memorial meeting after Dr. Boyce's death. Amos Fletcher Spaulding was afterwards graduated at Newton, and spent his life as a Baptist pastor in Canada and New England, much respected and beloved. Ambrose P. S. Stuart became a distinguished Professor of Chemistry in New England and Illinois, afterwards residing in Nebraska. Benjamin Thomas went to Burmah as a missionary, and has been called "the Apostle to the Karens." From a class report forty years after their graduation it appears that thirteen of the class became ministers, eight lawyers, and five presidents or professors, and four are set down as poets.

According to the class system, which at that time was rigorously observed, a student had but little association with members of other classes than his own. But it ought to be mentioned that among the Seniors of Boyce's Junior year were Samuel Sullivan Cox, — the celebrated "Sunset Cox," — and Francis Wayland, Jr., now the distinguished Professor of Law in Yale University. Among the Sophomores of that year were James Kirk Mendenhall, of Charleston, who was a friend of Boyce from boyhood, was afterwards with him at Princeton, and has been very useful as a Baptist minister in South Carolina; James Wheaton Smith, who graduated at Newton, and was long an eminent Baptist pastor in Philadelphia; and Adin B. Underwood, who was Boyce's roommate, and an earnest Christian, who became a prominent lawyer and a brigadier-general in the Union army; and the two had a joyful reunion at Providence some years after the war. The Freshman class of that year included James Burrell Angell, now president of the University of Michigan, and Heman Lincoln Wayland, now editor of the "National Baptist;" and in the Freshman class of Boyce's senior year was George Dana Boardman, now Baptist pastor in Philadelphia.

In May, 1845, James P. Boyce had been present at the Baptist Convention in Augusta, Ga., which formed the Southern Baptist Convention, — though he was not a member of that body, being not yet a church-member. But although a division then took place between Northern and Southern Baptists as to their missionary work, those of the South felt, and have always continued to feel, a deep interest in the work of their Northern brethren, and especially in Adoniram Judson. So it cannot have failed to impress the young student when, in November, 1845, Judson came to Brown University, of which he was an honored graduate, and remained some time as a guest of Dr. Wayland. Some persons of like age remember to have been profoundly impressed by even the reports of persons present at the Southern Baptist Convention in Richmond the following spring, who saw the great missionary, and could repeat the few words he was strong enough to speak.

Concerning Boyce's life as a student in Brown University, the testimony on all hands is that he did his work thoroughly and well. Take, for example, the following extract from a letter of James R. Boise, the Professor of Greek, written in February, 1889: —

"He was a pupil of mine in his college course, and I have a very distinct recollection of him as he appeared in the class-room. He was always attentive, scholarly, and a perfect gentleman. He was one of that type of students whom a teacher does not soon forget. Though more than forty years have elapsed since that time, and though I have had classes, often very large, through the entire intervening period (excepting a year and a half spent in Europe), yet there is no one of the many who have been in my class-room whom I have loved and respected more than James P. Boyce."

We begin now to find letters from the young student to his friend and future brother-in-law, H. A. Tupper, of Charleston. They are at first chiefly occupied with matters pertaining to their young friends in that city, and the experiences of a beginner at Brown, together with plenty of the gay *badinage* which is natural in the intercourse of young fellows at the age of seventeen or eighteen. It will be remembered that Boyce had excelled in mathematics during his Charleston studies, but here he found that this branch was completed within the Sophomore year. His father urged him to enter Junior, if possible,— wishing him to begin promptly the study of law; but he had done nothing in analytical geometry, and a letter tells of the severe and desperate exertions he made to work up this subject in time for the entrance examination, sometimes tempted to give it up as too difficult a task, but finally knowing every proposition Professor Caswell called for. A month after the session began, we meet something of a new student's usual summary and sharp judgment of one or another professor. Some young man had said in Charleston that the students at Brown were not gentlemen; but Boyce finds it far otherwise. "There are some as noblehearted fellows here as you would find anywhere; only one or two in college with whom I would not wish to associate, and these are gentlemen's sons, though not themselves what I call gentlemen." This favorable judgment came from one who through life was extremely sensitive to every point of propriety and honor. In another letter he says it was reported that to a student who had greatly misbehaved, Dr. Wayland said, "My son, go home; and if you can make anything of yourself, do try and do so." Boyce thought this a fine combination of paternal kindness and strict discipline.

Catalogues show that at this period the Junior class studied Physics, Chemistry, and Physiology, something in Greek and Latin poetry, Modern Languages (in Boyce's case the French, which he acquired in a very short time, and through life read with great ease), Logic (which brought him in contact with President Wayland), and Modern History, in Smythe's Lectures,— a book to which he not unfrequently referred in after life. Our student soon begins to glorify his literary society, the United Brothers, which has most of the Southern students, and in general the best men of the University, admitting a few exceptions. Did n't we all talk so, especially during the first session, about "our society"? He supposes his friend has "heard of the secret societies which are generally attached to the Northern colleges;" and mentions in confidence that he has just been initiated into one of them, the Delta Phi. He thinks these societies are something similar to the Odd Fellows and Masons, though held for different purposes. It is believed that the college secret societies were at that time just beginning their somewhat checkered career. In one letter he gives some account of the Senior speaking, saying that S. S. Cox was the best, having " in reality a splendid piece. He is by far the best writer of his class. His speech was well written, well delivered, and was filled with some of the most splendid imagery." One can't help wondering whether already the imagery included a gorgeous "sunset," such as afterwards gave to the admired statesman his familiar sobriquet.

College students are not at the time fully aware to what an extent they are influencing each other, intellectually and morally. Yet every one who looks thoughtfully back upon his own life when prolonged, and around upon current and recorded examples, will be likely to perceive that a young man's fellow-students are hardly less important to him than his instructors. Even the memory and fame of those who studied there in other days, and have since achieved something honorable in the world, becomes to susceptible young minds a powerful incentive. There is thus great advantage in attending an institution which has a large number of students, gathered from far and wide, and possesses an inspiring list of distinguished alumni.

The glimpses we catch of James Boyce in his association

with fellow-students at Brown, reveal the same character and disposition we have heretofore observed. Dr. J. H. Luther, in an address after Boyce's death, speaks as follows: —

"Little did we once think that the central figure of a group that nightly met in a well-furnished room in University Hall would be chosen of God to be a leader in theological thought, and the founder of a school of the prophets. That group was composed of noble spirits, — Stoddard, Ellis, Robert, Garnsey, — not one then a professor of religion; but they were all true gentlemen. A happier set of fellows I have never met since. They enjoyed the good will of their professors, and the respect of the entire class. But 'Jim' was the leading spirit. There was a magnetism in his humor, a nobility in his presence, and a manly expression in his language, which made him attractive to all. Blessed with a generous allowance from his father, he took a lively pleasure in helping a poor student to bridge over a crisis in his college course; and when he had once made a gift, he would never suffer the recipient to return it."

It is remembered that at the end of a session, when James submitted a statement of the year's expenditures, his father expressed some surprise at the gift of a large sum to a fellow-student, and was evidently inclined to disapprove. But one of his daughters said, "You know, Father, that if James had spent it in buying a horse or the like, you would not have objected." And so the matter was dropped.

At the approach of Christmas vacation, Boyce was sent as ambassador to Dr. Wayland, and obtained leave for the Southern students, who could not go home, to continue occupying their rooms, and get their meals down town. He had thought of going to Boston; but it was "so tremendously cold that were I in Boston I hardly believe I'd budge a foot from my lodgings." Students from the far South of course felt the difference of climate.

In March, 1846, he lets his correspondent know that he

has been chosen to take part in the Junior speaking, by an amusing extravagance of complaint as to a professor's corrections of his address: "Confound it all, here have I been called away just at this moment by the old prof., to examine my exhibition piece; and as a matter of course have more work to do. But wait, I will tell you when I come back. . . . As I thought, more corrections, dubitations, and scratchations (if I may manufacture a word), than I would have thought it possible for one man to make in a year, and he has had it but a day and a half. Alas, alas, wretched being that I am! These confounded profs. are the hardest to please. If you don't curse, they tell you your piece is too tame; if you do, they tell you it is profane. It is absolutely impossible to tell what they do want. Now, here I have one half my piece to write over, and the whole to copy over, just for those inquisitive women who must be coming up here to see us make fools of ourselves. Oh, how I wish they were all sunk in the bottom of the sea!" He is evidently proud of the distinction, and extremely anxious to please both the professors and the rather dreaded audience from the city. The little outburst reveals a lively and exuberant nature.

We come now to a highly important event in James P. Boyce's life,— his conversion to Christ. It is known that Dr. Wayland earnestly longed and labored for the conversion of all his students, and often greatly impressed them by private conversations as well as public addresses and sermons. In this he was seconded by other professors and by devout students. The class to which Boyce belonged contained up to its Junior year many who were not Christians. In 1889 Dr. R. A. Guild, the librarian, published in the "Watchman" a series of articles entitled "Revivals in Brown University," from one of which we extract. It is stated that many students below the Senior Class of 1846 were not professors of religion.

"This was a source of anxiety to Dr. Wayland, who in his familiar talks to us frequently alluded to the subject, and urged upon Christians the importance of earnest prayer and special effort in behalf of the impenitent. Meetings for prayer and conference were for a time held every evening, and there were several conversions. In September, 1845, James Petigru Boyce, whose recent death is so deeply deplored, especially throughout the South, entered the class as a student from Charleston College. He was a fine scholar, very popular in his ways, and the heir-presumptive to large wealth, his father being the richest man in Charleston. His classmates at once became deeply interested in his spiritual welfare, and made him a subject of special prayer, that his wealth and gifts and graces might all be consecrated to the Master's use. Several of the class who were thus interested had 'power in prayer.' I might mention one especially, whom, on account of his piety, we named 'St. James,' and another, the sainted Thomas, whom we know now in missionary history as the Apostle to the Karens.

"The usual college fast for the last Thursday in February was a day of great solemnity, and was attended by the students generally, including Boyce, who appeared to be deeply interested. The meeting in the morning was conducted by Dr. Wayland, who made the opening prayer. He was followed by Dr. Caswell, who spoke upon the necessity of religion in college, and dwelt upon the influence exerted by pious students. Professor Gammell enlarged upon the importance of cultivating our spiritual natures as well as improving our intellectual faculties. In the afternoon, Dr. Wayland preached an eloquent and practical discourse, addressed mainly to the impenitent. Shortly after this occurred the spring vacation for 1846."

James K. Mendenhall tells that he and Boyce went at that time by steamer from New York to Charleston. The voyage was in a rather small sailing-vessel, and extremely protracted. He noticed that Boyce kept his state-room a great deal, and supposed he was reading a novel or the like; but at length found that he was reading the Bible. They had then much talk together, and before arriving at Charleston he was deeply under conviction of sin. We learn incidentally from a subsequent letter that some two years before this he had been a good deal moved, but the feeling had passed away. On reaching the city they were met by the news that their friend H. A. Tupper had just been received into the church, and that one of Boyce's sisters was deeply concerned. That wonderful preacher, Dr. Richard Fuller, had come from Beaufort, and was preaching every day, and a mighty religious movement was pervading the community. The appeals of Allen Tupper to James and his sister deepened his impressions. This sister, on the occasion of Dr. Boyce's funeral, recalled an expression used at the time in regard to her brother, which shows his high reputation for morality, and her imperfect conception at that time of the nature of the Gospel. She said, "But James has not been so bad as the rest of us." He, however, felt himself a ruined sinner, and, like the rest, had to look to the merits of Christ alone for salvation. On the 22d of April he was baptized, Dr. Fuller's meetings being still in progress. The Charleston pastor at this time (1845–1847) was N. M. Crawford, from Georgia, who afterwards became quite distinguished as a college professor and president. Let us pause to notice that young James Boyce had thus, by the age of nineteen, been brought under the special influence of six of the most notable Baptist ministers in America, — Manly and Brantly, Tucker, Wayland, Crawford, and Fuller.

Writing from Brown University on May 15, Mr. Boyce speaks with great interest of the previous Sunday, which he and Mendenhall spent in Philadelphia on their way back. They attended in the morning Dr. Ide's church, and heard from some visiting minister "a most excellent sermon," which is reported at considerable length. At the afternoon observance of the Lord's Supper —

"We spent a delightfully solemn hour in commemorating the death of our Redeemer. It seemed so delightful thus among strangers to join in recalling that event which makes us brothers and sisters. As I looked around I was almost ready to go up and speak with those around me as to our hopes of meeting in heaven. I am sorry now that I did not; I think it would have been better for me if I had done so."

The letter continues: —

" There has been no revival here. The work has been going on among a great number of the colleges, but we have none here. Pray for us, Allen, pray for us; pray that God may shower down his Spirit among us, and bring sinners to repentance. There is a strong feeling among those of the college who have professed Christ, and they I believe are praying earnestly for a revival. But what though we pray forever, and use no means of exhortation, can we expect our prayers to be answered? Surely not; and yet that is just our case. . . . The members of the First Baptist Church are interested for us. They have a prayer-meeting every morning from eight to half-past eight o'clock, and at two o'clock on Sundays; and while praying for the youth of the church they are also kind enough to remember us, and to offer up prayers for a revival here. I hope their prayers may be answered; I am sure they are needed."

The letter concludes with loving messages and exhortations to the recent converts in Charleston.

With this letter accords the further narrative of Dr. Guild: "He returned to college a changed man. He at once joined the religious society, and with characteristic energy and zeal engaged in efforts to promote a revival, of which his conversion may be regarded as the beginning." His subsequent letters show similar fervor and zeal. He proposes to join by letter the First Church, and begins to teach a class in the Sunday-school. He is glad to hear that his correspondent has decided to be a minister. He speaks with much interest of some devotional tracts and books he has been reading, and of the Foreign Mission Journal just started by the F. M. Board of the Southern Baptist Convention at Richmond. He tells of a serious fellow-student, reared under Unitarian influences, whom by prayerful effort he has convinced of the divinity of Christ, and the need of atonement. An address was given at Brown just before the close of the session by J. L. Shuck, a missionary to China, — now connected with the Southern Board, — and made quite an impression.

"Those who are accustomed to call all nations barbarian and ignorant except some two or three, Mr. Shuck's remarks must astonish. To those also who put education before Christianity as a means of civilization, what a lesson must his account furnish! To think that a nation should be so literary, should have advanced so far in the arts and sciences, and yet present such a picture of degradation in morals! . . . I only wish there were more to go to carry the news of salvation to the ends of the world. I am rejoiced to hear of the efforts being made in Charleston for the cause of missions."

In the summer vacation (1846) he made a long trip for recreation and improvement. The letters speak with enthusiasm of the Catskill Mountains and of Niagara. From Montreal he returned by Lake Champlain and the Hudson steamer. Before railways made us so eager for speed, the great river-steamers probably afforded the most delightful mode of travel ever known on earth.

Mr. Boyce's Senior year (1846-1847) demanded closer work than he had ever before known. The Senior class gave some time to Plato, and studied astronomy and geology, continuing also the modern history, but devoted its principal attention to intellectual and moral philosophy, with Christian Evidences and Butler's "Analogy," and to rhetoric and political economy, and the American Constitution. In this year he was brought constantly in contact with Dr. Wayland, and received from him those lasting and powerful impressions which have been already mentioned. With subjects so congenial and a teacher of such power he was stimulated to great exertions. He also took a very large share in the religious interest which had come over from the former session, and was now deepening. He taught a Sunday-school class with regularity, and found time for a good deal of devotional reading, as appears from the books recommended in his letters.

Besides the correspondence with Mr. Tupper, he corresponded with Miss Mendenhall, of Charleston (now Mrs. Scott), a friend of the family, and whose brother James was his fellow-student and room-mate; and he was of course much interested in the accounts she gave of all that was going on in the city he loved so well. One of his letters has been preserved, written Dec. 11, 1846, when James Mendenhall had returned home for a time on account of some trouble with his eyes. She had informed Boyce of a visit to Charleston by two young ladies. So he overflows with gratitude at the outset: —

"I can hardly express the pleasure I experienced at receiving your letter. The fondest hopes I had dared to entertain were that Jimmy would now and then favor me with a paper. But when in the place of a paper there comes a letter full of news, and everything pleasing, you cannot imagine my pleasure. You write me that —— is in Charleston, and also ——. This is news; I had not heard of it before. Pray remember me to my old sweetheart, and tell her I regret that I am not now at home, that I might do the honors of the house. I suppose —— is as lively as ever. I often look back upon the pleasant days I have spent in her company,—days which will never be forgotten so long as I have the power of memory, or of experiencing pleasure in the events it brings to mind. Do remember me to ——; tell her I often think of her, and that it is by no means seldom that my prayers ascend to God for his blessings upon her and hers."

He then sends an imploring and vehement entreaty that she will use all possible influence for the salvation of one of his near relatives, and ends the paragraph by saying:

"Dear ——, God bless her! She has ever reminded me of my mother. May she be as faithful a Christian, and be preserved to eternity!

"Another term has closed, and the Senior class now rest upon their well-earned laurels. Not a single man has been unsustained in a single study. During the whole of yesterday a blaze of glory surrounded as with a halo the members of our venerable class. Symptoms of gratification ever and anon broke forth from the examining committee and strangers present while we proceeded in stately dignity to enlighten their ideas, and teach their withering minds to blossom with new vigor. Tell Jimmy, would for his sake I could say the same for the Juniors! With their usual luck, they came out with two unsustained, both in rhetoric. All the Sophs and all the Freshmen were sustained.

"The students are mostly all gone. A few of us retain our rooms during the vacation. This morning I laid out as the business of the day the mending of my carpet[1] (no small job, I assure you, and so can Jimmy) and the writing of two letters, — this for the morning, and the arranging of my books for the afternoon. All this, I am happy to say, will be accomplished. Tell Jimmy that I am going to board at the eating-houses. However, to-day we will have a private dinner, — that is, Mabbitt and I will; Mabbitt is cook, and I am to help him eat.

"We had a heavy fall of snow last night, and the snow now lies some ten or twelve inches deep. This afternoon and to-morrow we shall have fine sleighing. Don't you wish you were here?

"I expect to study pretty hard this vacation. I have laid out about three or four thousand pages to read. First there is Plato; then Mill's Logic; then the Republic of Letters; while on the

[1] His skill with the needle was well known to his friends. When a small boy he went to a dame's school and learned to sew, becoming soon so proficient as to make a complete outfit for his little sister's doll. In after years he would tell his children of this with great glee, explaining that he made "leg of mutton" sleeves for the doll in imitation of what he saw worn by the young ladies. Once, when he was President of the Southern Baptist Convention, a brother had the misfortune to tear his pantaloons; and various gentlemen, dropping in at the President's room in the hotel, were much amused to find him mending the rent. The owner — whose name has not been kept in memory — differed with Dr. Boyce on some theological points; and upon warmly thanking him, received the good-humored reply, "Ah, Brother ——, I only wish I could mend your theology as easily."

moral and religious side come Wayland's Discourses, Milton's Paradise Lost, Bunyan's Pilgrim's Progress, interspersed with other books occasionally. So you see I have my hands full."

He proceeds to narrate at length how two students had been recently expelled, and then taken back. One of these, who became a famous Baptist minister, was expelled for lecturing on temperance during study hours. The other was expelled for striking a student during the rush for library books. By the intercession of one of the professors, both were restored. It is evident that the young Southerner relates with considerable gusto the circumstances of this personal rencontre; but it has to be admitted that the parties concerned were both from New England. The letter ends: —

"I suppose ere I receive your answer, Christmas, with its eventful times, will have passed. Would that I were home on that day!"

Even in this lively letter of the gay young student to a lady friend we see that his religious earnestness shows itself. In letters to Mr. Tupper, during the early part of 1847, he is full of devout fervor, and longing for the salvation of friends, both in college and at home. On March 5 he says that for five or six weeks he has been greatly occupied and deeply impressed. A revival has now begun in the college, and there are three converts, including two of his special friends. "Everything seems to indicate a great work about to be accomplished." Near the close of the spring term he tells that the revival has made a great change in the moral tone of the college, putting an end to profanity and other forms of irreverence.

"There was not a particle of excitement. Not a single man, as far as my knowledge extended, seems to have been converted under excitement. Many, I know, took works on the Evidences of Christianity, and, reading with a determination to learn the truth, were convicted of their sins, and taught to cry out, 'What shall I do to be saved?' Several, myself among the number, who had unconverted room-mates, have been gratified by seeing them turn to the Saviour. Two or three who had been brought up in the doctrines of Universalism were convinced that these were unscriptural and absurd, and taught to look to Jesus as the author and finisher of our faith. Nor do we expect it to end here; we are determined, with the aid of God's Spirit, to continue this work during the next term, and not to rest until not a soul can be found here who has not felt and known the pardoning grace of God. Many of those who have recently become converted will labor among their impenitent friends at home, and return, we trust, strengthened in the faith of Jesus Christ. Never have I felt until this revival what a blessed privilege it is to save a soul. May my prayer evermore be to God that he may make me instrumental in his hands in the salvation of many! It is indeed a glorious and blessed privilege to labor in the vineyard of my Master."

Dr. Guild tells us that the revival went on throughout the session, with much earnest prayer and effort on the part of devout students, and constantly fostered by the conversations and discourses of President Wayland. Before the close of Boyce's Senior year the converts included George P. Fisher, James B. Angell, H. L. Wayland, Rowland Hazard, and in all twenty-seven of the students. Probably few people consider how much a revival at a college may amount to. Among these quiet but bright-eyed young men there are almost sure to be some who will be a great power in the land. Not only on set days, but often, in public and in private, ought Christians to pray for those who teach and those who learn in colleges and universities, in theological seminaries, and all educational institutions.

The spring vacation (1847) was spent by Mr. Boyce as the guest of his room-mate, Adin B. Underwood (afterwards General Underwood), at Milford, Mass. Writing to Mr. Tupper from Milford, on April 17, he refers to the approaching Commencement, saying that the Senior class is reputed the very best that has ever graduated at Brown, and speaking of a subject for the Commencement address, of which he has been thinking. In a postscript to this letter comes an important statement, for which an extract from a former letter has prepared us: "I believe I have never told you my intention to study for the ministry. I will tell you all about it another time." Two weeks later he writes: "As to my profession, I think at present that I shall study for the ministry. That seems to me the only subject in which I could have any interest; and it seems to me a theme so glorious, and one so much needed by mankind, that I should love to proclaim it." In June we find that he has written to his father about his desire to be a minister, and to study at some theological school. His father suggested that he should wait till he comes home. He is now hesitating whether first to spend a year in general reading (as a resident graduate at Brown, or at home in Charleston), or to go next fall to a theological seminary. August 2 he writes from New York that he has been sick some days, and is barely able to sit up. He was doubtless broken down by the hard study of the session, accompanied by intense religious zeal and effort. Later we learn that his grade was seven (in a class of thirty-four); he had hoped to be fifth. The Commencement would occur in September, and his graduating address was to be on "International Charity, a New Thing in the Civilization of the World."

When Boyce returned home after being graduated at Brown in September, 1847, it became increasingly manifest to those who knew him well, not only that he was thoroughly earnest in the religious life, but that he was developing great intellectual power. His mind was full of questions which he was anxious to have solved. On one occasion, in company with Allen Tupper, he approached a distinguished divine at Charleston, and immediately after the exchange of salutations the minister said, "I am very glad to see you, James; but please do not ask me any hard questions." He was equally pleased to have hard questions asked him. He delighted to unravel any knotty matter, whether a conundrum, a philosophic paradox, or a social difficulty. He would be merry in positions wherein others were perplexed. His father, as we are told, was now very proud of James, and expected him to become a man of distinction. The young man, for his part, was burning with ambition for profound scholarship and the widest possible mastery of knowledge. One indication of this was in the character as well as number of the books he began at once to procure, at large cost. He was laying a broad foundation for life-long acquisition. While circumstances, during the greater part of his subsequent life, largely denied him the benefit of studious quiet, he did become a very remarkable combination of scholar and business man, such as one rarely sees. But his youthful ambition for vast attainments and profound scholarship was sadly hindered and thwarted throughout his busy years; and those who loved him best will appreciate the statement of Dr. Tupper, made from personal knowledge, that Boyce *regarded this as the greatest sacrifice he made for the theological seminary.*

It was a sad disappointment to Mr. Ker Boyce when he found, during the summer and autumn, that James was immovably resolved to be a minister. Besides a natural ambition that his son might become distinguished as a lawyer, and perhaps as a statesman, — for both of which pursuits the father's insight discerned in him peculiar qualifications, — he began already to hope, as we have heretofore observed, that James would be the man to take charge of his large estate, and carry on his great business undertakings, for the benefit of the whole family. While a strictly moral man, and a generous supporter of the church he attended, the father had no great sympathy with the claims of the ministry; and, as in many other such cases, it was hard for him to acquiesce in the youth's determination to "throw away" all his practical powers and possibilities upon the work of a minister. There were of course others who took a similar view. His namesake Mr. Petigru said, "What a lawyer he would have made!" We hear of an old merchant in Charleston, one of his father's partners in the dry-goods house, who, being told that Jimmy Boyce meant to be a parson, said, "Well, well, why don't he follow some useful occupation? If he would only have stuck to business, he would have made one of the best merchants in the country." Young men of no remarkable talents or worldly advantages often have to pass through similar opposition and reproach in entering upon the ministry of the gospel. A surviving sister testifies that their father was already proud of James's talents, and became so more and more; and we shall find him gladly affording every possible advantage for the prosecution of ministerial studies.

On the 14th of November, 1847, H. Allen Tupper and James P. Boyce were licensed to preach by the church in Charleston. Two weeks earlier, Boyce had written to his friend from Aiken, the summer home of the family, where he was teaching his young brother Kerr, preparing him for boarding-school. In this letter he greatly laments his decay of spirituality. When he offers a prayer, it "often seems to be the discord of the lips, and not the music of the heart." A fortnight after the licensing he writes again, "Rejoice with me, for my joy now is not exceeded by that which I felt when I first entered on Christ's delightful service." Such changes of feeling are neither rare nor strange. He was already beginning to preach on Sundays, and writing some articles for the South Carolina Baptist.

CHAPTER V.

MARRIAGE AND EDITORIAL WORK.

AMONG James Boyce's classmates at Brown University, and for a while his room-mate, was Milton G. Robert, of Robertville, S. C., belonging to a family which has produced several distinguished Baptists. In visiting his brother, Rev. L. J. Robert, pastor at Washington, Ga., this young man made a marriage engagement with Miss Colby, of that place, and he still lives in the vicinity. After their graduation he took James P. Boyce with him to Washington, as one of the "waiters" at the wedding, Dec. 9, 1847. One of the bride's attendants, though not his partner, was Miss Lizzie Llewellyn Ficklen, daughter of Dr. Fielding Ficklen, of that village. It is related by a resident that the young man became quite enamoured that evening. The next day, when the wedding party were going into the country to dine, he was reproached by the bridegroom for asking to accompany Miss Ficklen instead of his partner. Things went so fast with his feelings that in returning from the country dinner he asked her to marry him, but without success. In fact, it cost the ardent youth several months of repeated visits, to say nothing of numerous letters, before he could gain any promise of marriage.

Dr. Ficklen had come from Virginia, where his brother, George Ficklen, was an eminent citizen and leading Baptist of the famous Gourd Vine Church, in Culpeper County, and another brother, Burwell Ficklen, was an honored citizen of Fredericksburg; while the family connection includes a number of well-known men in different parts of that State. The Fickleus were of Welsh origin, and one fancies that they exhibit some of the better Celtic traits of character. Dr. Ficklen's wife was Miss Frances Ann Wingfield, whose grandfather came from Albemarle County, Va., the name showing an English family. The doctor did not give his whole attention to the practice of medicine in Washington, but turned more and more towards planting, in which he was quite successful. In middle life he became a Christian, and afterwards a greatly honored deacon of the Baptist church in Washington,— a man of frank and manly bearing, "transparent candor, scrupulous conscientiousness, and Christian probity," and notably strict in his ideas of Christian life and of church discipline. Miss Lizzie had been educated in a very remarkable school at Washington, which had been built up especially through the efforts of Adam Alexander (father of the Confederate general, now railroad president), whose numerous daughters, there educated, became the wives of distinguished men in Georgia and South Carolina. The lady principal at the time when Lizzie was educated was Miss Bracket, who had come from the North, and afterwards married Dr. Nehemiah Adams, a well-known Congregational minister of Boston.

Washington is a pleasant village in Northeastern Georgia, eighteen miles north of the Georgia Railroad, and not far from the South Carolina line. It is the centre of a rolling and healthy country, which the Wingfields compared to Albemarle, very fertile in grain and cotton. Here the famous Jesse Mercer was the first Baptist pastor, and started here, in 1833, "The Christian Index," which is still the Baptist paper of Georgia. Here lived the celebrated Senator Robert Toombs, and Alexander H. Stephens went to school here, — in a square wooden building which still stands, — but made the home of his life at Crawfordsville, in an adjoining county. Thus the village and surrounding country presented good society as well as good schools. To these advantages of family and education were added rare personal attractions, great kindness of heart, and extraordinary brilliancy in conversation; so that our young collegian, with all his ardor, may be defended as not having lost his head when he so quickly lost his heart.

We cannot venture to quote the letters written to his friend and future brother-in-law during the next few months. On one occasion whole pages are filled with outpourings of a lover's wretchedness when rejected, but winding up with the steadfast purpose to try again. A loving sister brings to bear upon the case a certain feminine clairvoyance, and comforts him with the hope that he may succeed at last. Then the correspondence fails us, as a well-behaved correspondence should do; but in May we learn, from an allusion to plans for the future, that an understanding has been reached, and definite hopes are permitted.

In April, 1848, Mr. Boyce and Mr. Tupper went to New York, on their way to Madison University, at Hamilton, N. Y.,—now called Colgate University,—for the purpose of entering the theological department. After arriving in New York city, they heard from Dr. T. J. Conant, then Professor of Hebrew at Hamilton, that three months of Hebrew had to be made up in about three weeks, in order to enter the theological course at the point they desired. Mr. Tupper accomplished this, and went through the course at Hamilton. Mr. Boyce found his eyes so weak and suffering at the time that it was evidently unwise to attempt the Hebrew. On April 28 he wrote from New York to his friend at Hamilton a very sad letter. The celebrated Dr. Delafield had ordered that he should stop study for a year, and advised that he should abandon altogether the idea of a studious life. "I shall therefore adopt the latter advice. I regret much that we cannot pursue our studies together, but more that I am compelled to give up that profession towards which I have so long looked. I shall return to-morrow week to Charleston." A week later he writes again that he is not going to give up the study for the ministry. The physician thinks that by leading a very active life during the summer, together with certain medical treatment, he may recover the use of his eyes for study. The doctor has said that a trip to Europe would of itself be sufficient to cure him. But he shrinks from making this journey without a certain companionship, on which he may not count.

We learn from others that his return voyage to Charleston was protracted by bad weather; and through the consequent nautical experiences he was relieved of extreme biliousness, and this contributed to the cure of his eyes. Throughout the summer he found it necessary to be careful, but his eyes finally recovered strength. He often suffered through life from severe bilious attacks, but we never again hear of any trouble with the eyes, though he read so widely, at all hours, on railway trains and everywhere. A like trouble from study at college led Richard H. Dana, Jr., to a voyage to California in 1834–1836, described in his famous book, "Two Years before the Mast;" and the biographer states that he also never afterwards suffered from weak eyes.

In the autumn we find Mr. Boyce in much better health, and preaching with great zeal at Aiken, at Washington, Ga., and other points, and at length undertaking important duties in Charleston, to which we shall presently give attention. The marriage occurred at Washington, Dec. 20, 1848, and the young couple went at once to live in Charleston. But he delighted in visiting the pleasant village where he had found his wife, and easily made himself a place in the family circle. Some time after her marriage the bride told his sister, in her sportive way, that her mother always took sides with James rather than with her. So glad he was to have a mother again! In one of the subsequent visits, it is stated by Capt. J. T. Wingfield, Mrs. Boyce's cousin, that the young minister preached, at the time when he was ordained deacon, a sermon an hour and a half long, which the captain quaintly declares to have been "the shortest long sermon" he ever heard. Some years later, Mr. Boyce's brother-in-law, Rev. H. A. Tupper, became pastor at Washington, and remained there nearly twenty years, taking great delight in his charge, and resisting many invitations to go elsewhere.[1]

[1] The following was published not long ago in the "Washington [Ga.] Gazette:" —

"GENERAL LAWTON AND WASHINGTON.

"The unforeseen consequences of our actions are often the subject of comment. On a November day of 1845, Gen. A. R. Lawton came to Washington on a very interesting occasion ; namely, to be married. He doubtless felt very pleasantly disposed to the little up-country town in which he found his wife. On one of his trips he was accompanied by a bachelor friend, Mr. Milton Robert, who fell in love with another Washington girl, and married her. There came to this wedding another bachelor, Rev. James P. Boyce. He, too, married a Washington girl. From these two marriages Washington has derived many advantages besides the blessing of good husbands to her daughters. The children and grandchildren sprung from them form a large circle of excellent and desirable citizens. But this was not all the good derived from General Lawton to Washington. In consequence of the marriage of Rev. James P. Boyce, Dr. Tupper, who married his sister, was invited here. The good Dr. Tupper did is untold. His influence on religion, and his thousand kindnesses, will never be forgotten while a single person remains who knew him. Now, General Lawton, though not the cause, was certainly the occasion, of all this good to Washington. . . . This is a good deal to owe to General Lawton ; and running it up, it seems as if we ought to present the general with a silver service. But it occurred to us just here that General Lawton owes a good deal to Washington, for the town furnished Mrs. Lawton. In detailing all this to the general, we asked him, did he not think he and Washington were even ? 'Yes,' he said, 'more than even. I owe Washington

In May, 1846, there had appeared in Charleston "The Southern Baptist," a weekly paper which was continued till the beginning of the War of Secession. For more than two years it was "edited by a committee of brethren of the Baptist churches in Charleston." The pastors of the First Baptist Church at that period were the famous Georgian, Dr. N. M. Crawford, from 1845 to 1847, and from 1847 to 1854 Dr. J. R. Kendrick, of the distinguished Baptist family in New York State. No doubt each of these took an active part in the editing, and they were aided by James Tupper, Esq., a leading lawyer and Baptist, and others whose names are not known. On Nov. 22, 1848, the heading reads, "James P. Boyce, Editor." A notice of the change, signed "The late Editors," says: "Mr. Boyce is a graduate of Brown University, a licentiate of the First Baptist Church in Charleston, and possesses qualities of mind and heart which give promise of distinction and usefulness in the new field of labor he has entered." The new editor's salutatory mentions that the paper has been going into three thousand families, thinks that in excellence "it has been surpassed by none of our Southern Baptist papers," and very earnestly asks for increased patronage and continued contributions. In fact, their high standard of intelligence and taste had caused the brethren to make a better paper than could at that time be supported in a comparatively small State, where the great mass of the Baptists were in the middle and up country, — and railroads did not then extend above Columbia.

The young editor threw himself earnestly into the undertaking, and produced a paper of real value. To a much greater extent than was then common in religious weeklies, it is seen to have given copious and well-collated

boot, — large boot.' And come to think of it, it was in fact Mrs. Lawton who brought the general here, and set the ball rolling in the first instance."

news, foreign and domestic, secular as well as religious. There are many notices of books and periodicals, with special interest in the four British Quarterlies, and "Blackwood's Magazine," which were republished in this country by Leonard Scott & Co., and at that day represented the very cream of good reading. Many a young man of that period can remember the instruction and inspiration derived from these great British periodicals. Remarkable space is given in the paper to foreign missions, those of the Missionary Union in Boston, as well as those of the Southern Baptist Convention, organized three years before. No opportunity is missed for commending institutions of learning, or discussing questions of education. The editor's writing consisted largely in brief paragraphs, such as have now become common in the best papers. Among the leading editorials, such general topics as "Purity of Heart," "Faith an Antidote to Trouble," "The Blessedness of Affliction," are discussed in a readable and helpful fashion. Under the head of "State Schools and Teachers," great earnestness is shown in urging improvement of public instruction. Under "Southern Baptist Literature," it is said: "We trust the day is not distant when Southern Baptists will be extensive *producers* as well as consumers of religious reading." Under "Missions among the Southern Slaves": "No planter, we contend, should rest satisfied until he has taken measures either to provide a religious instructor for his negroes, or to instruct them himself;" and favorable mention is made afterwards of the way in which this was managed by B. C. Pressley, Esq. (now Judge Pressley), on his plantation. An editorial in the first number for 1849 refers quite impressively to the European revolutions of the preceding year. On March 28, 1849, a leader of unusual length favored the establishment of a "Central Theological Institution" for all Baptists of the South, — a subject which had been broached two or three years before, and with which this Memoir must largely concern itself in later chapters.

Meantime, on March 7, Rev. A. M. Poindexter, who had the previous summer come from Virginia to Charleston to be Corresponding Secretary of the new Southern Baptist Publication Society, gave the following notice in the paper: "The Depository of the S. B. P. S. has been removed to 40, Broad Street, and Rev. James P. Boyce has been appointed Depository Agent." From that time the advertising columns contain long lists of religious books as kept for sale at the depository, with his name as agent. The editor and incipient theologian found great delight in the intimate friendship thus begun with Dr. Poindexter, one of the strongest theological thinkers in the country, and destined to a highly influential co-operation with him in the future establishment of the theological school. His own *penchant* for theology, even at this early period, appears in his allowing the paper to be for many weeks weighted down by two distinguished brethren with long and elaborate articles on the doctrine of "Imputation," in which comparatively few of the readers could be expected to take much interest.

On April 11 the editor in three several instances defends himself against personal attack. The "Christian Index" had severely complained of the "Southern Baptist" for publishing a misleading account of action taken by the trustees of Mercer University in regard to the question of a general theological institution, and declared that statements given in quotation marks were utterly different from what had been actually said in the report of the trustees. Mr. Boyce replies: "*Strictures of the 'Christian Index.'* — We regret very much that errors such as the 'Index' notices in the piece quoted below should have been found in any article in the 'Southern Baptist.' We copy the entire strictures of the 'Index,' purposely to manifest our regret. And yet we are not to blame." He goes on to explain that his account of the matter had been derived from another paper, and the quotation-marks referred to that paper's statements. The defence is ample, and the opening expression of regret is characteristic of a man so frank and candid. It is said that some one connected with the paper censured this expression, on the ground that a newspaper cannot well afford to admit that it has made a mistake. This idea does appear to be entertained in some editorial offices; but one can imagine that James P. Boyce must have been not a little vexed at the mere suggestion. Following this editorial is another, in reply to the criticisms of a correspondent. These had included an utter misstatement of something the editor had said, and he replied very sharply: "We said no such thing; and how a man of common sense and common honesty can assert it, we know not. This may seem strong language, but . . . it is enough to irritate any man to have his language perverted in this way." A third editorial replies to an anonymous "Subscriber" who grossly misrepresents the editor, and upon the strength of this misrepresentation announces that he will cease to be a subscriber when the time expires for which he has paid. The editor in reply tries to be calm in pointing out the misrepresentation, but adds: "In conclusion, we say to a 'Subscriber' that if he will but forward his name, it shall be immediately stricken from the list. We would not for ten times the sum of his subscription be again subjected to so much impertinence and injustice."

The number for May 2d ends the third volume of the paper. The editor calls attention to that fact, and says: "Our own connection with the paper is to close with the present number. We opened its editorial charge at the solicitation of our brethren, and with no expectation of retaining it beyond a few months. We feel a deep interest in the 'Southern Baptist,' and the prosperity of the Baptists of South Carolina, and this interest alone induced us to consent to occupy our present post." He states that the former editing committee will resume their task, but that the paper is still in debt, and the receipts not sufficient to pay the expenses; and so he appeals for payment of subscriptions in arrear, and for efforts to procure new subscribers. In resuming the editorship, on May 9, the committee state that "during five months the paper has been gratuitously and efficiently edited by Rev. James P. Boyce."[1] In the editorial that follows they speak of the fact that editors must expect at times to have "their motives misapprehended and rudely impugned, their honest opinions perverted and unkindly assailed." This goes to show that the young editor had keenly felt the injustice done him, especially by the writers he had replied to on April 11. He was a man so thoroughly honest, candid, and just that he felt surprise at first, and then indignation, at any cases in which the opposite qualities appeared to be manifested; and few men of twenty-two would have been quite patient under such provocation. Had he felt bound by some high sense of duty to pursue the editorial career, he would have learned to bear quietly such unjust assaults, even as he afterwards did learn in other relations that any servant of the public must expect to be now and then misrepresented, and to have some speech or action of his perverted and seized upon as the occasion for exploiting personal views. But Mr. Boyce had not at all undertaken to make editing his life-work. The discussion of religious topics would only deepen the desire for regular theological education, which he now determined to seek at Princeton in the autumn. The close of the paper's third year was a convenient time for ending his connection with it, and the recent assaults perhaps made him impatient to throw

---

[1] The number of subscribers had increased while he was editor, but the receipts had been five hundred dollars less than the expenses of publication.

the task aside without delay. All this may remind us that truly great and useful men have seldom escaped early struggles with impatience, and have never been without strong feelings which it was difficult to control. A great man has an ardent nature, or he would not be a force in the world. Those who see men of eminence silently bearing undeserved reproach, or explaining with quiet dignity, frequently have little conception of the discipline which has been needed to make this possible.

For one so young, with little experience in preaching, and no regular study of theology, Mr. Boyce had done remarkably well as an editor. Had he thought proper to continue in that line of work, his great administrative talent, wide and eager reading, special interest in the practical enterprises of missions and education, and rapidity of composition, would sooner or later have made his editorial life a marked success. Years afterwards he more than once intimated that if the Seminary could become fully established and allow some leisure, he would like to conduct a religious quarterly or monthly.

Until the end of July, 1849, he continued to act as depository agent for the Publication Society, and sometimes wrote for the paper over his initials.

During the summer he hesitated whether to take a theological course at Hamilton, where Mr. Tupper was, or at Princeton. There was much talk at the time of removing the theological school from Hamilton to Rochester, and he did not fancy being there in a time of dissolution and reconstruction. He inquired particularly about the extent and value of the library at Hamilton, in which respect Princeton then doubtless greatly excelled. Few patrons of higher education appreciate the value of a great library in attracting the more aspiring students and in promoting breadth of culture.

In April, 1849, Mr. Boyce's eldest brother, John Johnston Boyce, died in Florida. He had married his cousin, the daughter of Chancellor Johnston. His father had established him on a plantation in Florida, with the vague hope of stopping the ravages of consumption. An obituary in the paper which James was editing says that he died "in the hope of a glorious resurrection."

CHAPTER VI.

AT PRINCETON THEOLOGICAL SEMINARY, 1849–1851.

IN September, 1849, Mr. Boyce went to the Presbyterian Theological Seminary at Princeton, and remained there as a student for two years. This famous seminary had, like all the rest, its small beginnings. It was founded in 1812, and for one year Archibald Alexander was the sole professor. In 1813 Samuel Miller was added, and in 1822 Charles Hodge. By 1849 Princeton and Andover were the two leading theological schools in America. The whole number of students during Mr. Boyce's first session was one hundred and thirty-six, and for the second session one hundred and forty-seven. The division of the Presbyterian Church into Old School and New School was by this time thoroughly established, and Princeton was recognized as the great bulwark of Old School theology.

When our student entered, in 1849, Dr. Samuel Miller had just been made Emeritus Professor, and he died in January of the next year. His numerous practical writings on ecclesiastical questions and ministerial duties must have been quite in demand among the students. The author of "Clerical Manners" was somewhat formal in his own deportment, but proved quite cordial when visited at his home. The active professors at this time were Dr. Archibald Alexander, his two sons, James and Addison, and Dr. Charles Hodge.

Archibald Alexander had in 1840 turned over the department of Didactic Theology to Dr. Hodge, and was Professor of Pastoral and Polemic Theology. Though now seventy-seven years old, and taking but a limited part in the instruction, this gifted and charming man left a lasting impress upon his students, and Mr. Boyce often spoke of him with gratitude and affection. He was a sort of pastor for the young men, with whom they found counsel and sympathy.[1] His numerous works gained a wide circulation, and his "Moral Science," "Religious Experience," and "Sermons to the Aged" may still be particularly commended. The memoir by his son James is a delightful book. Dr. Alexander excelled in the somewhat difficult matter of helpful criticism upon sermons preached by the students before the class. His general kindness and sympathetic appreciation gave keener edge to the caustic remarks which sometimes appeared needful. Dr. Boyce used to relate that on one occasion a student took as his text, "Let there be light, and there was light," and launched into a magnificent description of the creation of light, with great splendor of diction and vehemence of delivery. The aged professor sat with his chin on his breast, quietly listening throughout the performance, and then, lifting his head, said, in the piping tones characteristic of old age, "You're a very smart young man, but you can't beat Moses." A few years earlier, a student of very imposing talents and bearing, a Presbyterian then, but who afterwards became a High Churchman and a bishop, made a grand discourse upon the religious instincts. He represented that every man's character and life will depend simply upon which of his instincts gets the upper hand,

---

[1] It was probably at an earlier date that we must place a story which theological students might find suggestive. An old negro was accustomed to attend a church some miles from Princeton, and often praised the "high larnt" young preachers who came out from the seminary. One day he looked glum on returning home, and being asked whether he had had a good sermon, said, "No, sir; no, sir. There did n't none of them high larnt young gentlemen come to-day, but jes' a old man, and he stood up and jes' talked and talked." The preacher was Archibald Alexander.

and everything human was made to turn on a battle of instincts. When he finished, and the time came for critical remarks by the students, they seemed afraid to venture, and were silent. Dr. Alexander simply said, "My instincts are not sufficient to comprehend, much less to criticise, that discourse." In these cases the severity was no doubt well deserved, and ought to have proved beneficial. But professors of homiletics, and even unofficial critics of preaching, doubtless often err, and sometimes gravely and hurtfully err, in bestowing their causticities as well as their commendations.

Dr. James Waddell Alexander this year succeeded Dr. Miller as Professor of Ecclesiastical History and Church Government, and the next year took over from his father the subject of Composition and Delivery of Sermons. He resigned in 1851, and it was Boyce's singular good fortune to hear his only course of lectures on this latter topic,— the notes of which lectures the student always greatly valued. From 1851 to 1859 Dr. Alexander was pastor of the Fifth Avenue Presbyterian Church of New York city, which he did much to strengthen and train, and which, under the pastorate of Dr. John Hall, is now recognized as one of the leading churches of America. He published a large number of popular and useful books, of which the "Sermons on Consolation," the biography of his father, and the "Forty Years' Familiar Letters of J. W. Alexander," are of particular interest and value. His now venerable mother was the daughter of James Waddell, the "blind preacher," whom William Wirt heard in a church near Gordonsville, Va., and described in an often-quoted passage of "The British Spy." James's wife was also a Virginia lady, a sister of the famous medical professor, Dr. James L. Cabell, of the University of Virginia. These two ladies naturally took a special interest in Southern students, and the elder once said that she knew the Baptist students better than the Presbyterian, because they were more inclined to be sociable. Her daughter and namesake, Miss Janetta Alexander, is also remembered as particularly cordial and agreeable towards the wife of a student.

The younger son, Dr. Joseph Addison Alexander, among the foremost of American Biblical scholars, was still Professor of Oriental and Biblical Literature, which two years later he gave up for Biblical and Ecclesiastical History. His great work on Isaiah had appeared in three parts in 1846, 1847, and "The Psalms Translated and Explained" came out in 1850. Addison was by no means a patient teacher of the elements of Hebrew. He learned languages himself with marvellous facility, and could not sympathize with, or patiently endure, the slow mental movements of the ordinary student. One day, when some fellow had made a very bad out of his Hiphil forms of the verb, the professor threw down his Hebrew grammar on the table, and angrily said, "Gentlemen, I can't spend any more time on these elementary matters. Learn them for yourselves. I shall begin lecturing on Genesis to-morrow." For three years before this, his students had enjoyed the help of William Henry Green as instructor in Hebrew, who resigned that position in 1849, and in 1851 succeeded Dr. Alexander in the chair which he still occupies with so much honor. In 1850, when the professor had worked alone for one year, it was found advisable to appoint another instructor in Hebrew. It is somewhat frequently the case that a great linguistic or mathematical genius proves ill-suited to elementary instruction in the subjects he masters with such facility; and a teacher, in whatever department or grade, must constantly strive to maintain intellectual sympathy with his pupils. As a lecturer on exegesis, Dr. Alexander made a great impression. He did not teach the students how to make exegesis for themselves, but he set them a noble example, by his complete mastery of the requisite learning, his honest and unwearied pursuit of truth, and the clear and convincing fashion in which his results were stated. He was particularly fond, as his works also show, of reconciling antagonistic views, not simply by the easy method of taking an intermediate position, but often by rising to some higher principle, which comprehended them both in its unity; and he would often startle by the felicity with which he converted objections to the truth into arguments for its support. A few years later, as Professor of Biblical and Ecclesiastical History, his course for the Junior class consisted really of lectures on the English Bible, and awakened great enthusiasm, so that Presbyterian pastors in Philadelphia would run out to Princeton to hear them, and students of that period have often dwelt upon their extraordinary interest.

Dr. Chalmers had in his Lectures in Theology, a few years earlier, urged upon his students a thorough study of the English Bible. But these lectures by Alexander are the earliest known instance of making the English Bible the text-book on a large scale in a theological seminary, — a plan afterwards much more extensively and systematically pursued in the Seminary which James P. Boyce founded, and of late years beginning to be adopted in various institutions. In his last years, Addison Alexander published Commentaries on Acts, Mark, Matthew (chapter i.-xvi., interrupted by his death in 1860), which are admirable specimens of penetrating and judicious exposition, and must long continue to be necessary to a minister's library. The memoir by his nephew, Dr. Henry C. Alexander, is a work full of inspiration for any minister or student for the ministry who values high scholarship, and appreciates rare and varied gifts. It is said that Princeton students were greatly impressed by Addison's occasional sermons, and many of these have been collected in two volumes of great value. His intellectual power seized upon a truth with the most vigorous grasp, his imagination threw over it the chastened splendors of a genuine illumination, and his wealth of choicest English fitted itself to every phase of truth like a garment to him that wears it. A shy and recluse student, he was never a pastor, and was not widely known as a preacher; but others besides the students have testified that when inspired by some great theme he would at times read one of his noble discourses with overmastering and seldom-rivalled power. Dr. Hodge once said to Dr. J. W. Warder that Addison had the finest mind he had ever known. It may be a useful warning to add that this admirable man presumed on his always vigorous health, and devoted himself to incessant reading and writing, with an almost total neglect of exercise; and so, at the age of fifty, there came a sudden collapse, and the world lost all those other noble works which he might have been expected to produce, and which some of us were so eagerly awaiting.

But the most influential of all Boyce's instructors at Princeton was Dr. Charles Hodge, now fifty-two years old, and at the height of his powers. A graduate of the seminary, and professor there since 1820, he had spent 1826-1828 as a student in Paris and Germany. He had founded in 1825 the "Biblical Repertory," afterwards called "Biblical Repertory and Princeton Review," which he was still editing, and which as a theological quarterly had no rival in America save the Andover "Bibliotheca Sacra." Two years before this he had collected from the review his two volumes of "Princeton Theological Essays," and much earlier (1835) had sent out his famous "Commentary on Romans," abridged in 1836, and enlarged in 1866. Other works had also appeared from his busy pen, including an excellent practical treatise called "The Way of Life." The Commentaries on Ephesians and on First and Second Corinthians came out some years later, and his *magnum opus*, the "Systematic Theology," three volumes 8vo, did not appear till 1871. But already in Boyce's time this great theological course was mainly developed, and laboriously dictated to the students. Dr. Hodge was a singularly clear and consecutive thinker. Dr. Manly remembered it as a saying of the students, "His thoughts move in rows." Even in the most familiar address, every thought would bring with it the related thoughts. In the Sunday afternoon meetings, when his turn came to speak upon the practical topic which had been chosen, he would first lead up to the subject, then discuss it, and finally draw inferences or lessons; and this not in the way of formality, but through the habit of his mind. He was also a man of marked Christian earnestness and fervor, with whom the great doctrines were living facts. James Boyce was more powerfully impressed by Dr. Hodge than by any other Princeton professor, and probably more than by any other teacher except President Wayland. Dr. Manly also felt satisfied that he learned more from Hodge than any of the others. It was a great privilege to be directed and upborne by such a teacher in studying that exalted system of Pauline truth which is technically called Calvinism, which compels an earnest student to profound thinking, and, when pursued with a combination of systematic thought and fervent experience, makes him at home among the most inspiring and ennobling views of God and of the universe he has made. Dr. Hodge was at this time in quite poor health, and suffered great and long-continued distress at the death of his wife, Dec. 25, 1849; but his work was faithfully done.

We have thus seen that, except the lack of Dr. Green's help in Hebrew, our student was greatly favored in his Princeton professors. Hodge and Addison Alexander were at the height of their great powers. Archibald Alexander was still giving, in the class-room and in private, the fruits of his eminent gifts and rich experience, and these were the last two years of his long life. James Alexander was an inspiring teacher and friend, and his professorial work was limited to Boyce's two years.

His fellow-students also comprised a number of superior men. Among the fifty-two members of the entering class, even persons little acquainted with Presbyterian history can point out several who afterwards became distinguished. R. F. Bunting, D. D., was long pastor at San Antonio and Galveston, Texas, and at Nashville, Tenn., and in 1876 became editor of the Texas "Presbyterian." W. C. Cattell, D. D., was Professor of Greek and Latin in Lafayette College, Pa., 1855–1860, and in 1863 became president of the college. J. M. Crowell, D. D., was long pastor in Philadelphia. Caspar Wistar Hodge, D. D., son of Charles Hodge, was teacher and pastor for some years, and in 1860 became Professor of the New Testament in the seminary, having succeeded Addison Alexander, who had held that position for one year; Dr. C. W. Hodge died in 1891. George McQueen was a missionary in Western Africa from 1852 to his death in 1859. Robert Price, D. D., a Mississippian, was long pastor in Vicksburg. Robert Watts, D. D., a native of Ireland, was pastor in Philadelphia for ten years, and in Dublin for three years, and since 1866 has been professor of Systematic Theology in the Assembly's College at Belfast, Ireland. He is the author of numerous works in support of Presbyterianism or of general orthodoxy, of which the best known are "The Newer Criticism" (1881), "The Rule of Faith and the Doctrine of Inspiration" (1885), and "The New Apologetic."

Among the students who entered a year later than Boyce we may mention Edgar Woods, who was Presbyterian pastor at several places in Virginia and Ohio, and after 1877 a teacher at Charlottesville, Va. There was also quite a group of Baptist students from the South who entered that year, the division between Northern and Southern Baptists making many reluctant to attend Newton or Hamilton. Alfred Bagby has spent a very useful life as pastor of Baptist churches in King and Queen and adjacent counties of Virginia. Andrew Fuller Davidson was

AT PRINCETON THEOLOGICAL SEMINARY. 75

also a beloved pastor of churches in Virginia for a good many years till his death. James K. Mendenhall had been Boyce's friend in Charleston, and his fellow-student at Brown University. He became pastor of various Baptist churches in South Carolina and Florida, and since 1875 has labored as missionary and evangelist in South Carolina, residing in Greenville. Richard Furman Whilden had studied at the Furman Institution in South Carolina, and was admitted to the middle class in Princeton, thus becoming Boyce's class-mate. He was graduated in 1852, was pastor and teacher at various points in South Carolina, and since 1864 has resided in Greenville County, teaching and preaching.

Of those who had entered a year earlier than Boyce at least a few ought to be mentioned. Robert G. Brank, D. D., was long pastor in Lexington, Ky., and since 1869 has been a well-known pastor in St. Louis. S. S. Laws, LL.D., was for some years president of Westminster College, Mo., and then president of the University of Missouri from 1875 to 1890. Joseph W. Warder, D. D., of Kentucky, had been two years a student at Newton Institution, near Boston, and came to Princeton for his third year. He was Baptist pastor at various points in Kentucky and Missouri, and of the Walnut Street Baptist Church in Louisville, 1875–1880. Since that time he has been Corresponding Secretary of the Executive Board of the Baptist General Association of Kentucky. Of those who composed the Senior class when Boyce entered, L. G. Barbour, D. D., has been a teacher at various points in Kentucky, and is now professor in the Central University at Richmond, in that State. Basil Manly, Jr., of Alabama, after one year at Newton, had entered Princeton in 1845, and been graduated in 1847. This was two years before Boyce entered; but it is mentioned because they had been boys together in Charleston, and were destined to be colleagues for many years.

Almost every student is more interested in one or two subjects than in the rest of his appointed course of study. Mr. Boyce had at Brown University become a thoroughly earnest student; and the conviction that it was his duty to be a preacher, together with his brief experience as an editor, must have deepened the desire to become acquainted with all the leading departments of a theological course. He worked faithfully in all directions. He also gave unusual attention to the library, steadily accumulating that general knowledge of books for which he was remarkable through life. Observe the plans indicated in a letter written a few weeks after his arrival at Princeton: —

"I am now pursuing, in connection with lectures on that subject, a full course of reading in Mental Philosophy, designing to extend it from that of the Greeks down to the present day. At the same time I am pursuing Hebrew Exegesis in Genesis, and Greek in Romans, and am carrying on a course of reading in the biography of the great and the good who have shed lustre upon the Christian name."

But his favorite study from beginning to end was Systematic Theology. He was naturally inclined to reflect upon principles and causes, and had a facility in organizing the results of reading and talk which was akin to his unusual talent for organizing and administering business affairs. These natural capacities had been no little developed by Dr. Wayland's instructions in psychology and ethics, and by his familiar association with Dr. A. M. Poindexter, who delighted to draw every young minister into the deepest theological inquiry and the most animated discussion. The leading subject at Princeton has always been Theology. Thus the whole atmosphere of the place united with the great powers and influence of Dr. Hodge and the native tendencies and previous training of this student to make him especially earnest in the study of Systematic and Polemic Theology.

During the second session he took his regular part in the appointed preaching and in the prayer-meeting; but Mr. Whilden says he was not prominent in the debating society. This must have arisen from the pressure of his studies, for he was naturally fond of discussion, and through life his powers always worked to better advantage in debate on the floor than in pulpit discourse. During the second session, when Mr. Whilden was there, Boyce was overwhelmingly busy, for he determined to carry on the studies of the Senior class together with those of the Middle class, to which he belonged. He obtained from some fellow-student the full notes of Dr. Hodge's course in Theology, as dictated in previous years; and these were patiently copied by the young wife, thus saving him a great deal of time and toil. Add to this that he had an extraordinary power of application and endurance, — he could work for weeks, when under any special pressure, with five hours a day of sleep, almost no exercise, and well-nigh incessant application to study. His recreation was found in cheery talk at meals, in the occasional drives of which he was fond, and the somewhat frequent visits which he and his wife paid to his sister Mary, Mrs. William Lane, of New York city.

In December he writes to Mr. Tupper that they have a delightful place of boarding, with the widow of an eminent physician. The Georgia wife is "in perfect ecstasies with the to her somewhat unusual sight" of a heavy snow. Two of his sisters have just been married in Charleston to Mr. Tupper and Mr. Burckmyer, and in sending congratulations he speaks most enthusiastically of his own wife. He is exceedingly pleased with Dr. James Alexander, — a handsome man, with beautiful dark eyes, and the bearing of a Christian gentleman, and in the department of sacred rhetoric "the most delightful lecturer I have ever heard." He thinks Addison Alexander "the most gifted, but by no means the most admirable, member of the Faculty," having seen him display "an ungovernable temper,"— probably with reference to the Hebrew. Dr. Archibald Alexander is fast declining in years, and does not seem " as gifted as his sons, but has a very clear, logical mind." Dr. Hodge " is one of the most excellent of men; so modest and yet so wise, so kind and fatherly in his manner, and yet of so giant an intellect, he is a man who deserves a world of praise." In February Boyce has been to New York, and finds the Lane family about to build a home on Madison Square, and attending the ministry of the famous Dr. William R. Williams. He expresses much fervent solicitude, and again and again proposes special prayer for the conversion of various relatives. He affectionately urges Mr. Tupper, who has become pastor at Graniteville, S. C. (near Aiken), to be very faithful in pastoral visiting, which he thinks a good many ministers comparatively neglect.

On Feb. 17, 1850, Mr. Boyce preached the first sermon that remains to us, and it is indorsed as written in January. It was given at a Baptist church called "Penn's Neck," a few miles from Princeton. The text is Acts xxvi. 28: "Almost thou persuadest me to be a Christian." It is thoroughly practical, and intensely earnest, abounding in pointed address to different classes of hearers, and fervent exhortation. You feel in reading that you are dealing with a man of strong intellect, great force of character, and large heart, a man full of Christian love and zeal, and consumed with desire to save souls. The sentences are often wanting in symmetry, and show the hurried negligence from which his style never wholly recovered; but the thoughts are made entirely clear, and are expressed with vigor and force. Written when he was just twenty-three years old, it is a notable sermon.

We learn from his wife that he frequently preached at "Penn's Neck" during this and the following session. Dr. C. W. Hodge, who was his fellow-student, in a letter after Boyce's death spoke of "his high reputation for eloquence and strength in the pulpit," and says he "was in request for supplying pulpits out of town." It is well that seminary students should preach somewhat frequently, not for practice and criticism before a class, but as actual preaching to a real congregation. They can thus add greatly to the evangelizing and pastoral work of the city and vicinity, and in this day of fast trains can go to distances of a hundred miles or more. In every theological school there are doubtless some students who spend too much time in preaching, especially when they become pastors, and must hold protracted meetings. But on the whole it is believed that students should be encouraged to preach, for they may do good to others, and gain benefit to themselves. The religious fervor in which a young man gave himself to the work of the ministry will often be best maintained by actual preaching, or at any rate by teaching in mission Sunday-schools and the like. Theological studies ought to be pursued throughout as having a practical aim; and this aim is best kept in view by the student who is doing some actual ministerial work. Besides, the pecuniary compensation which is sometimes received will enable a man to continue his studies without depressing want or extreme dependence upon the generosity of others. Mr. Boyce's means are well known to have been ample; but through life he welcomed, and indeed required, suitable compensation for ministerial service, because he would have just that much more to give away, and because he was not willing to encourage a church in the neglect of its own duty to support the ministry.

The vacation in the summer of 1850 was spent by Mr. and Mrs. Boyce with her relatives in Virginia, chiefly with her uncle, Burwell Ficklen, in Fredericksburg, and her uncle, George Ficklen, at Thompsonville, in Culpeper County, and her aunt, Mrs. Brown, who lived in the same neighborhood. These were all families of high standing and large hospitality, where many agreeable acquaintances were to be made, besides the circle of kinsfolk. It was a delightful way to spend vacation. The Piedmont Counties of Virginia, east of the Blue Ridge, are a singularly healthy region, half way between North and South, half way between sea-coast and mountain. In summer weather, to ride or drive over beautiful hills and vales, gazing at will upon the deep-blue mountain range on the west, and to visit the large country houses and large-hearted country folk, must be healthy in every sense. Our young couple were both remarkably adapted to enjoy such a series of visits, and to brighten life for all with whom they met. Few men so promptly win and so permanently hold the confidence and affection of others as did James P. Boyce. Highly cordial in manner and manifestly sincere, big-hearted and considerate, overflowing with vitality, and yet full of gentle courtesy and abounding in delicate tact, he seemed perfectly at ease, and made all around feel at ease, alike in the palaces of the rich and in the cottages of the poor. One fancies there must still be persons in Culpeper and in Fredericksburg who remember that summer visit of their gifted and charming young cousins as an epoch of rare enjoyment.

This region was full of Baptist churches. A sermon remains, indorsed by Boyce as first preached at Mount Lebanon church, Rappahannock County, Va., August 11, and at Fredericksburg, August 25, 1850. It contains glowing expressions about the beauties of Nature, which leave little doubt that it was written in Culpeper, amid the beautiful hills and in sight of the beautiful mountains; for Princeton, with all its celebrity and advantages, lies in a flat and dull country. It is always pleasant when the thoughts of poet or speaker take shape and color from the immediate surroundings. This sermon is on John iii. 16, "For God so loved the world that he gave his only begotten Son," etc. The introduction is excellent, and the plan good.

There is perhaps too much of theological discussion about the divine nature and purposes, and the relations of the Father to the Son, for a discourse meant to be thoroughly practical. It often requires considerable experience before the ministerial student can avoid carrying unchanged into the pulpit the thoughts and methods which have deeply interested him in the lecture-room. But the fault in this case is at any rate not serious. The sermon is earnest, and aims at practical results; and it can hardly have failed to have been heard with great interest, when read in the sonorous and musical tones, and with the impressive and engaging aspect, of the young preacher.[1] After leaving Virginia he visited New York city, and attended a meeting of his class at Brown University, introducing his wife to his classmates.

Through his first letter from Princeton in September we learn that this summer travelling had occupied more than four months. On every Sunday but three he had preached, and had enjoyed much time for general reading. His health was now excellent. He had decided to carry on the third year's work together with that of the second year, and was beginning to plan for the next summer, when he should leave Princeton. If no immediate opening for usefulness should be found in South Carolina, he thought of going to Halle, in Germany, especially to study German and Hebrew; or, to avoid separation from his wife, he might spend several months in some Northern city, and there

[1] He must have left Culpeper for Fredericksburg about August 20. Ten days later, the writer of this memoir, having been graduated in June at the University of Virginia, and gone to visit his kindred in Culpeper, attended a meeting of the Shiloh Association at a place only four or five miles from Mr. George Ficklen's, and was frightened by being asked to preach. If Boyce had remained a little longer he would have attended also, for he was fond of Associations, and two, who were destined to toil so long together, would have met years before they did meet. Hawthorne has a quaint story to illustrate how often things come very near happening, and do not happen.

study the same languages. Two weeks later he is still considering where he shall settle as a minister. If there is no available place in South Carolina, he would be willing to labor near Providence, R. I., or else he will go West, having had already an informal invitation to St. Louis. His present studies (probably meaning especially Theology and Homiletics) have impressed on him afresh the great importance of the ministry. He feels deeply unworthy to be an ambassador for God, not competent to speak words on which must depend men's happiness or misery, according as they shall believe them. He envies his correspondent the ministerial usefulness already attained, and longs to equal him, — yea, wishes he could do more than man ever did, in saving souls through the grace of God. He is engaged in anxious self-examination as to the reality of his call to be a minister. In December he expresses great regret at learning that all the pamphlets, etc., he left at home have somehow been destroyed. He was through life very solicitous to preserve every pamphlet or periodical, and bequeathed to the Seminary a very large and valuable collection of these, along with his theological library. This early loss included all his college addresses, and some sermons, with valued letters, etc. He is rejoiced to hear that Mr. Tupper has been preaching on Sunday afternoons to the negroes, including a large number of hired men engaged in building a railroad, and urges him to continue this, if his health will possibly allow. "The Lord will bless your labors to them. Teach them as well as preach to them. You know I have long thought that for such congregations there should be given a great deal of exposition, such as is suitable to explain and cause them to remember the sacred text. I should delight to preach to them myself. I think that while we from the South should support our mission to Africa, we should also remember Africa at home. Let us teach them, preach to them, bear with them, explain to them, though they may be slow of heart to believe. May God bless your efforts, and those of all who attempt to preach the gospel to these poor of our land."

Mr. Boyce left Princeton somewhat before the close of the session, May 1st. As a matter of course he received no diploma, since he did not remain till the end of the course. He was always satisfied that he learned more by the plan pursued than if he had entered the middle year (making up the Hebrew by private work), which would have given him the regular graduation. He spent two or three months in New York, devoting himself to a thorough review of his theological studies. He considered the question of going to study in Germany, but concluded that he must now begin ministerial work. Writing to Mr. Tupper in March, he expresses a deep sense of unworthiness, but a strong desire to be the means of saving souls and glorifying Christ.

In July we find him at Washington, Ga., considering an invitation to become pastor of the Baptist Church at Columbia, S. C. The church records show that, August 9, they received a letter from him accepting the pastoral charge, to take effect 1st October.

In the summer of 1851 Mr. Ker Boyce made a trip to Europe, accompanied by his youngest children, Ker and Lizzie; but we have no details. The desire to visit Europe grew upon James through all the years, but had to be denied till near the close of his life,— one of the many sacrifices he made for the work of theological education.

CHAPTER VII.

PASTOR AT COLUMBIA, 1851-1855.

COLUMBIA, the capital of South Carolina since 1790, is one hundred miles northwest from Charleston, on the Congaree River. This river is formed by the junction of the Broad and the Saluda, and is navigable to the rapids which lie just below the junction. Hence the location of the city, and marked advantages in the way of water-power, never realized till recently. The population in 1851, when Mr. Boyce became pastor, was about seven thousand. There was a railway to Charleston, which presently made a junction with a railway leading northward by Wilmington, N. C., and lower down with another leading westward by Augusta and Atlanta. Of late years Columbia has become quite a railroad centre, and there has been a marked growth in manufacturing and in population.

The city is in a healthy region. The ridge of sand and pines, which near Augusta has become so famous at Aiken, the home of consumptives, extends northeastward so as to include the neighborhood of Columbia. The sand absorbs moisture so as to dry the atmosphere, and the pine-trees take out malarious elements, so that in this region persons having weak lungs in early years have lived a comparatively long and vigorous life.

Columbia was already quite a handsome Southern town. The spacious streets were well shaded, some of them having not only trees along the sidewalks, but a double row along the centre, with a walk between, as in Augusta, Savannah, and other Southern cities, and in Commonwealth Avenue, Boston. There were many handsome residences, built in the Southern style, with large rooms and ample windows, and with broad porticos or verandas, sometimes on all four sides of the house, and even repeated for the second story. The principal dwellings were surrounded by extensive grounds filled with trees, shrubbery, and flowers. It is difficult for one who has not seen them to imagine the delightsomeness of these Southern abodes, found often in the country as well as in the town. From the blazing sun you passed into an atmosphere of delicious coolness, delicately perfumed by the odor of growing flowers that entered at every window. The family were often highly educated, and always had in a high degree the charming manners of an aristocratic society. The hospitality seemed perfect. The memory of even brief visits to those noble Southern homes bears now a touch of romance, like the history of the old French *noblesse*, and something like the stories of the Arabian Nights. Probably the most notable residence in Columbia was the famous Hampton House, built by the second Wade Hampton, whose father was colonel in the Revolutionary army, and general in the War of 1812, who was himself *aide* to General Jackson at the battle of New Orleans, and whose son, of the same name, is the Confederate general and United States Senator, — all three celebrated for skilful horsemanship, all gifted and gallant soldiers, all capital specimens of the Southern gentleman, and born leaders of men. The Hampton House and its grounds are said to have cost $60,000, which was then a large sum of money. Around Columbia in various directions are low and pleasing hills, which, with the river scenery, make fine drives, such as Boyce delighted in.

The Legislature of South Carolina possessed unusual powers, electing not only governor and judges and senators, but the electors for president, and also appointing all manner of county officials. This gave dignity to the post of State representative or senator, and so the Legislature included many of the leading planters. These, with the governor and other members of the State government, who were apt to be wealthy, constituted every winter a very attractive social circle in Columbia, often occupying handsome dwellings of their own, and dispensing a lavish and refined hospitality.

The State sustained in Columbia a military school, called the Arsenal, for the first and second years of study, the two higher years being taken at the Citadel, in Charleston. Here also was the South Carolina College, founded in 1804. We have seen that among its alumni were J. L. Petigru and Basil Manly, and may add that they included by 1851 a great many men of whom South Carolina is justly proud, in every leading pursuit of life. Among them was the celebrated William C. Preston, who in the United States Senate and elsewhere was recognized as almost unrivalled in oratorical splendor and passion (not strange in the son of Patrick Henry's sister), and who was just ending in 1851 a term of six years as president of the college. His wide popularity, and the charm of his personal influence, had attracted many students; and though not remarkable for teaching power or general administrative talent, he had given to the college great celebrity and a commanding influence. The famous James H. Thornwell, D. D., one of the most eminent Presbyterian ministers and educators in America, was also an alumnus of the college, and had for thirteen years been professor, at first of Logic and Metaphysics, and afterwards of Sacred Literature, with the additional and influential office of chaplain. He had resigned in May, 1851, and gone to Charleston to be pastor, but was destined soon to return.

There was also at Columbia a Presbyterian Theological Seminary, which had been twenty years in existence, and was in a prosperous condition. Among the professors was Dr. George Howe, a good Biblical scholar and a very gifted teacher, of whom Mr. Boyce often spoke with admiration in subsequent years; and from 1853 Dr. B. M. Palmer, who since 1856 has been pastor in New Orleans, and one of the most eminent preachers in America. As a matter of course, the city had a very flourishing Presbyterian church. The Scotchmen and Scotch-Irish, who had been so influential among the early settlers of the State, were generally faithful to Presbyterianism, and so were many of the Huguenot families; others of the Huguenots, together with the leading English families among the early settlers, attached themselves to the Episcopal Church. These retained the social prestige brought over from the English Establishment, as Presbyterians still held the educational and social influence which they had brought from Scotland. Both of these important religious bodies have endeavored in America to confine their ministry to men regularly trained for the purpose. This has prevented their taking hold upon the American people at large, — even as the lawyers and doctors of this country have necessarily included a very large proportion of men irregularly trained; and the great popular denominations have been those that encouraged every man to preach who felt moved to do so, and whom the people were willing to hear. But the fact that Presbyterian and Episcopal clergymen were regarded as an educated class added to the influences above mentioned in giving those religious denominations a powerful hold upon American cities and towns, which continues to the present day. About the middle of this century, just at the time when James P. Boyce began his work as a pastor, we can see signs of a marked advance among Methodists, Baptists, and other denominations, in the way of having a larger proportion of their ministers to be men thoroughly trained for that calling. The Baptist ministry had always included some such men, in South Carolina and in all the States; but about this time there was a definite forward impulse.

The Baptist church at Columbia comprised in 1851 but

few members, none of them possessing much of social influence or wealth. The house of worship was a small brick building, presenting a very plain gable front. When young men reared in Baptist families came from the country or from Charleston to reside in the capital, there was everything to draw them away from the Baptist church to the other denominations of whom we have spoken; and yet far-seeing men could perceive that it was wise to bestow special labor upon this little church. If a minister of ability could manage to live there, faithful work would tell; for the Baptists were numerous in some parts of the State, and beginning to grow almost everywhere. Mr. Boyce's predecessor, Rev. H. A. Duncan, was a man of talents and worth, but doubtless found it impossible to sustain himself on the meagre salary. Mr. Boyce had the advantage of a large private income, and also of personal acquaintance and influence in the Charleston Association, to which the church at Columbia belonged, and which might be induced to give aid and comfort. It was understood before he accepted the call to be pastor that an effort would soon be made to erect a better house of worship, for which it was believed that he could obtain assistance in other parts of the State.

So we find our young minister entering upon his duties as pastor in Columbia, Oct. 1, 1851. Two weeks after, he writes that he is much pleased with the work. The congregations are very small, but he hopes, by the blessing of God, to be useful. In November he was ordained, the presbytery comprising J. R. Kendrick (of Charleston), John Culpeper, John M. Timmons, and the famous Dr. Thomas Curtis, whom we shall meet later in these Memoirs. Dr. Curtis asked the candidate for ordination if he proposed to make a life-long matter of preaching; and he answered, "Yes, provided I do not become a professor of theology."

These early years of ministry present, as frequently happens, but little to record. As he is now near to Mr.

Tupper and they often meet, the letters between them are few. We may be sure that he was diligently studying theology, reading widely in his own already large collection of books and in other accessible libraries, and faithfully preparing his sermons. Besides the Seminary, the College library was one of the best in the South. Boarding at the principal hotel, he had opportunity for making pleasant acquaintance with legislators and other leading men. His father being known as the wealthiest man in Carolina, and he himself being uncommonly attractive and agreeable, while his wife possessed like qualities in a remarkable degree, he would rapidly gain consideration in important quarters. Yet these things did not at all hinder his visits to the humblest homes of his congregation, nor his personal influence over all who attended his ministry; for he had rare power of making himself easy and agreeable among all, and he was deeply earnest in the desire to be useful as a minister of the gospel. In December Colonel Preston left the presidency of the college, on account of ill health, and Dr. Thornwell yielded to much urgency, and, giving up again his cherished desire to be a pastor, returned to Columbia and became president. As a graduate of Princeton, the son of Ker Boyce, and an attractive gentleman, the young Baptist pastor must have early become acquainted with this great man, whose sermon in a Charleston pulpit had so charmed him in boyhood, and whose influence must have conduced to the promotion of profound thinking, wide reading, and great earnestness in the gospel ministry.

On May 13, 1852, the church, as its meagre records show, granted the pastor three months, or longer if necessary, to visit other churches in the State, and solicit contributions towards building a new house of worship. The pulpit was to be supplied by his early friend and fellow-student, Rev. J. K. Mendenhall. We know that in his private carriage Mr. Boyce drove over large portions of the State.

The contributions pledged do not seem to have been sufficient at that time for the purpose, as the new church was not built till several years later. In the summer of this year he was thinking of purchasing a certain house and fitting it up for his residence. In April, 1853, various letters to Mr. Tupper in Charleston contain nothing but requests to select this article, and order that, for his house. It was his fancy that the dwelling should be completely finished and furnished when his young wife first entered it; and those who knew him well can imagine the pleasure he took in arranging all details and perfecting all preparations for their home life. Here they lived for more than two years, delighting to entertain their friends and kindred. In the summer of 1853 Mr. Boyce went northward. He had stipulated with the church in the beginning that he should have one month of vacation every summer, such definite arrangements being at that time rare in Southern churches. During this trip to the North he attended the meeting of his class at Brown University, now six years after their graduation, and took the degree of A. M. in course.

On Jan. 11, 1853, the church records show that the pastor succeeded, after months of persuasion, in introducing a melodeon to help the singing; and the next year he secured a choir-leader, at a salary of one hundred dollars *per annum*. It requires time and patience to alter any fixed usage of a Baptist church; and this respect for established custom is, on the whole, a beneficial check upon the action of a thoroughly free organization in a period enamoured of progress.

Throughout these four years of pastoral work at Columbia, the young minister was encouraged by a steady growth of the little church. We have seen that the white people of the city were mainly attached to other churches, and so the material available for him was not large. But there was a marked increase in numbers, and still more in liberality and other Christian graces. It must have been especially gratifying that he was enabled to get a strong hold upon the colored people. We have seen him dwelling upon this subject when editor, and exhorting Mr. Tupper, in one of his letters from Princeton, to work faithfully among the negroes, giving them much oral explanation of the Scriptures. He doubtless pursued this course himself, striving not only to touch their religious susceptibilities, but to give them helpful instruction in the way of salvation and the fundamental duties of a Christian life. A wealthy and highly educated young minister was fitly employed in such labor for the benefit of the slaves. Nor was this a singular case. While the reading world was just then becoming fascinated and enkindled by the high-wrought pictures of "Uncle Tom's Cabin," published in 1852, and deeply impressed with the real and supposed evils of slavery; while events were rapidly moving towards the great and awful conflict of ten years later, numerous ministers throughout the South, chiefly Baptist and Methodist, were faithfully laboring to convert and instruct the vast multitude of colored people among whom they found themselves called to the work of the ministry. By no means all was done that ought to have been done; when and where has this been the case about anything? But thousands and ten thousands of Christian men and women did feel the burden of these lowly souls laid upon themselves, did toil faithfully and often with great sacrifice to bring them to the Saviour, and lovingly to guide their weak and ignorant steps in the paths of Christian life. Certainly there was among them, in some respects, a very low standard of Christian morality, as is usually the case with ignorant converts of any degraded race. But there are many still living who can testify, from personal observation and effort, that not a few of these negro Christians gave real and gratifying evidence of being Christians indeed. They were not black angels, as some romantic readers of romance half imagined, nor yet black demons, as some who hated them then and now would have us believe; they were and are simply black men, from among the lowest races of mankind, yet by no means beyond the reach of saving Christian truth and loving Christian culture. Some of us remember them with strange tenderness of feeling, like that of foreign missionaries for their lowly converts, and find it painful to see them grossly misrepresented, either by fanciful eulogy or foolish censure. And now that the long conflict is long past, and we are facing the most remarkable problem that any civilized nation was ever called to attempt, — the problem of slowly and patiently lifting these people up to all they can reach, — it were well if mutual misjudgments could be laid aside, if the faithful work of many Christians in those trying years could be on all sides appreciated, and the whole undertaking before us could be estimated in part by its best results, and not simply by its worst difficulties.

From this ministry of four years there remain notes of several sermons, and a good many sermons written in full. He usually prepared by making a rather extended sketch, — what lawyers call a "brief," — which he kept before him when speaking. Most of these were allowed to perish in the course of years. From the outset we find him grasping with decided vigor the thought or several thoughts of the text, explaining and strongly vindicating the great doctrines of Scripture, applying the truth to his hearers with direct and fervid exhortation. There is still not much of illustration, but now and then an expanded figure that shows imaginative powers worthy to be oftener employed. The style is sometimes negligent, but rarely fails to be lucid and vigorous. Above all, the sermons show a man very anxious to do good; they belong to "an earnest ministry." In later years we shall meet several sermons that will require our special attention.

On March 19, 1854, occurred the death, at Columbia, of Mr. Ker Boyce. He had for some years made his home at Kalmia, not far from Aiken and Graniteville, where he had a delightful residence, shared with him by Mr. and Mrs. H. A. Tupper, until they removed, in 1853, to Washington, Ga. Going to Columbia on a visit to James, he was taken ill with heart-troubles, and after lingering ten days he died on a Sunday at midnight. His children had all gathered, and it is said that they "confidently expected his recovery; but he was persuaded of his approaching death, and in view thereof he spoke calmly and with resignation, expressing his hope and trust in the mercy of Christ." Dr. Tupper says that during their residence together at Kalmia he showed great love of the Bible, and special interest in the family worship. Numerous letters to the Tuppers during 1850–1854 have been preserved, and not only abound in the warmest expressions of fatherly interest and affection, but often speak in a distinctly religious tone.

Obituaries in numerous papers of South Carolina and other States, and personal recollections of various friends, all go to show that Ker Boyce was a man of remarkable abilities and character. His achievements in the business world would necessarily imply this; for causes have to be equal to effects, and he who has through a long life achieved great things must necessarily be at least in some respects a great man. Mr. Boyce was especially noted for his insight into the character and abilities of men. To an extent quite unknown before that time in Charleston, he trusted his business associates and employees. People observed that notwithstanding predictions to the contrary, the enterprises in which he was interested almost always proved successful; and it slowly dawned upon them that he was safe in trusting men, because he selected men who could be trusted. We have already seen that he was a man of great nerve and pluck, who in time of commercial panic never feared, but held up things. It is said that he had an extraordinary memory for business matters, keeping details in his head, and never forgetting his business engagements. A marked peculiarity was the ease with which he left all business anxieties behind him at the close of the day. He sometimes said that in shutting the doors of his bank he shut in all his worries; and when in the family circle you could hardly have imagined that this was a great financier, daily engaged in large transactions, for he seemed as lively and gay as the children. This power of completely throwing off one's cares, and heartily enjoying the cheery and humorous side of life, has been observable in many of those who have endured great labors and carried through great undertakings in the world. After the death of James P. Boyce, his colleague, Dr. Basil Manly, wrote as follows in a newspaper article: "My memory, as a child, of Mr. Ker Boyce, is of a most dignified, vigorous, commanding figure. The cast of his countenance and the peculiar compression of his lips indicated settled conviction and determination, while his penetrating eye showed the intelligence and inquiring mind which made him a power in the city and the State." Portraits show that James strikingly resembled his father in personal appearance; and his friends are well aware, as his whole career shows, that there was also a marked resemblance in many admirable points of character.

Mr. Ker Boyce bequeathed $20,000 to the Orphan House in Charleston,— an institution highly esteemed in the city, — and $30,000 to the College of Charleston. The income of this latter fund was to be used in aiding needy students, who were chosen by his son James as long as he lived, and are now chosen by one of the sisters. His large estate was left under the control of a son only twenty-seven years old, and a busy and faithful minister of religion. The associate executors, Judge John Belton O'Neall, Arthur

G. Rose, Esq. (who afterwards went to live in England), and James A. Whiteside, of Tennessee, are said to have never taken any part in the management, fully sharing the father's confidence in his son. This confidence was the more remarkable, as much of the estate was to continue in the hands of his executors for many years, the final division not to be made till the youngest grandson should come of age. Through all the trying losses of the war time, and all the solicitudes of the years that followed to the end of his life, the executor bore these burdens of weighty responsibility.

It was inevitable that he should need some time for undivided attention to the settlement of so large an estate. Accordingly, the church records show that on April 8, 1854, he asked and obtained leave of absence from pastoral duties until October, "at which time he hoped to be able to resume them," his salary to be used in securing a supply. The letters of that summer to H. A. Tupper are almost entirely occupied with business details. Indeed, from this time forward he had to write so many business letters that there was seldom opportunity for speaking of general matters such as would interest the readers of a Memoir. In November he was chosen moderator of the Charleston Association, thus for the first time called to exercise his remarkable powers as a presiding officer, which we shall have frequent occasion to observe hereafter. In that year Rev. Edwin T. Winkler became pastor in Charleston, having previously served two years as Corresponding Secretary of the S. B. Publication Society, and editor of the "Southern Baptist." The frequent meeting thus occasioned with one so gifted and cultured and lovable must have been a great pleasure to the Columbia pastor.

At the end of the year came out Dr. Thornwell's "Discourses on Truth," a small volume of sermons which had been delivered in the chapel of South Carolina College. These made a profound impression on some young pastors of that day, which might well be deepened in the case of Mr. Boyce by his personal acquaintance with the author.

During that winter or spring there were probably negotiations as to the idea of Mr. Boyce's becoming Professor of Theology in Furman University at Greenville, S. C., the health of Professor Mims having hopelessly failed ; for the church records show that on April 29th Boyce tendered his resignation, to take effect October 1st. The church earnestly sought to prevent this dissolution of the pastoral relation, but on May 6th they accepted his resignation, with unusual expressions of regret and affection. They had indeed unusual cause, apart from the pastor's personal worth ; for he showed his interest in the struggling church of which he had for four years been pastor, by proposing to contribute $500 towards a salary of $1200 for his successor.[1] We know also of a promise on his part to contribute $10,000 towards a new house of worship for the church, whenever they should be prepared to build,— a promise duly carried out a few years later. It was probably in the autumn of 1854 that he also promised to aid in building a new church on Citadel Square, in Charleston. Mr. Burckmyer, who had married his sister, was about to be baptized, and consulted James Boyce and B. C. Pressley, Esq., as to whether he should join the First Church, or the newer church on Wentworth Street. Pressley said he should do neither, but took them out to Citadel Square, and showed the point at which a new and elegant church building ought to be erected. James approved the idea, and said they could put him down for $10,000. The movement soon began, and others of the Boyce family gave $30,000 more towards erecting what was for a long time, and is perhaps still, the noblest Baptist house of worship in the South. Let it not be imagined that our young minister was thoughtlessly giving away his ample

---

[1] These extracts from the records have been kindly furnished by Rev. W. C. Lindsey, D.D., now pastor of the church at Columbia.

inheritance. He gave with reflection and foresight, as we shall find him continuing to do through life.

In May, 1855, just after his resignation had been accepted, Mr. Boyce attended the Southern Baptist Convention (which then met once in two years) at Montgomery, Ala. Some of us were on the long journey of three or four days from Central Virginia, by way of Wilmington and Augusta. At a point some hours west of Augusta, a branch road came in from Washington, Ga., and several passengers came aboard the train, among them a young man of large figure and smooth, youthful face, at whose entrance the Foreign Mission secretaries, Dr. James B. Taylor and Dr. A. M. Poindexter, both rose eagerly, and met him with great cordiality. Presently Poindexter came and sat down by a young minister of the company, and said, "Yonder is a man I want you to know. He is a minister of ability and thorough education, and full of noble qualities. His father was a man of great wealth, and he is now very generous in his gifts. He is going to be one of the most influential of all Southern Baptists. I want you to know him." At the introduction, it is remembered that his marked heartiness seemed somehow a little clouded by a certain reserve. It was not thought by the person introduced, though sometimes thought by others in after years, that this reserve was due to hauteur. All who knew him well soon came to understand that he had simply such a contempt for all *affected* cordiality as sometimes to go just a little towards the opposite extreme, and thus be slightly misunderstood. He was in fact, from youth to age, the soul of cordial kindness. At Montgomery the Convention appointed a Committee to investigate some controversy between the Foreign Mission Board and Rev. I. J. Roberts, one of the missionaries to China. The details of the controversy would be of no importance now, if they were remembered. The Committee examined very carefully the whole matter, and directed Mr. Boyce, one of its members, to draw up an elaborate report. He sat up all night to perform the task. When he came forward the next day with his report, his commanding figure, ringing voice, and look of unpretending genuineness and broad good sense made an impression that has lasted; and the report so marshalled the facts, and explained all the matters involved, as to vindicate the Board, without casting any painful censure upon the zealous missionary. Poindexter remarked afterwards that he had scarcely ever heard a report of a committee that was so ably written and so impressively read. Mr. Boyce was then twenty-eight years old.

It may be well enough to mention that at this meeting of the convention some of us for the first time encountered a new term, and an idea which for the next few years awakened no small controversy. After the organization, some one offered, as usual, a resolution inviting ministers of other denominations to sit with us and participate in our deliberations. This was at once sharply objected to, and there arose a debate which lasted a whole day. Presently the words "Old Landmark" were used; and some of us from distant portions of the South, upon asking what in the world that meant, were told that Rev. J. M. Pendleton, of Kentucky, had published in Nashville a tract entitled, "An Old Landmark Reset." In this he was said to have maintained that it was a former custom of Baptists not to give any invitation or to take any action which might seem to recognize ministers of other persuasions as in a just sense ministers. These were also the views of Rev. J. R. Graves, editor of the "Tennessee Baptist," published at Nashville. These honored brethren, and a number of others from that part of the country, maintained these "Landmark" views with great earnestness and ability. Those who held a different view appeared in many cases to be taken by surprise, through the novelty, as it seemed to them, of the "Old Landmark;" and they did not always agree among themselves, nor maintain any well-considered or very consistent position. After the day's discussion, it was proposed to end the matter by letting the resolution be withdrawn, upon the understanding that those who saw no objection to its passage would concede thus much to the views of their brethren who objected so strongly. Some present thought already that there was no such extreme difference of opinion among us as appeared to exist. The controversy in the next few years rose high, and in some quarters threatened division. But it has now long been felt by most brethren that we could agree to disagree upon the matters involved, and that the great bulk of us were really not very far apart.

CHAPTER VIII.

PROFESSOR OF THEOLOGY IN FURMAN UNIVERSITY.

FURMAN University had grown out of the Furman Academy and Theological Institution, opened at Edgefield Court-House, in January, 1827.[1] The South Carolina Baptists had previously aided many young men in preparing for the ministry, at various private and public institutions. This school of their own was located at Edgefield in the hope that the Georgia Baptists would unite in building up there a theological seminary. Two years later it was removed to the High Hills of Santee, as exclusively a theological school, the name being afterwards changed to the Furman Theological Institution. The professors were Jesse Hartwell and Samuel Furman, the latter being a son of the famous Richard Furman, pastor in Charleston during the Revolutionary days and afterwards, in whose honor the institution was named. Various attempts were made to combine with the theological a classical school, having at one time a Manual Labor feature. The theological professors for some years were Rev. William Hooper, D.D., and Rev. J. L. Reynolds, D.D., who both became eminent men. Professor J. S. Mims was elected in 1842, James C. Furman in 1844, and Peter C. Edwards in 1846. Mims was to teach Systematic Theology, Edwards the Hebrew Language and Biblical Exegesis, and Furman to teach Sacred Rhetoric and Pastoral Duties, and Ecclesiastical History. In 1850 it was decided to remove the institution to the town of Green-

---

[1] See an excellent historical sketch by Professor H. T. Cook in the "Baptist Courier" for July 14, 1892.

ville, as the Theological Department of a new Furman University, which was opened in 1851. The theological instruction was given mainly by Professor Mims, as Professors Furman and Edwards were chiefly occupied with the instruction of the general classes in the University. Professor Mims was a man of high talents and good education, diligent in study, and loved as a teacher. He was a native of North Carolina, interrupted in his youthful studies, and much hindered through life, by rather feeble health. After studying some time at the University of North Carolina and at the Furman Institution, he was graduated at the Newton Theological Institution, near Boston. He strongly opposed the usual Calvinistic view as to the doctrine of Imputation, and defended himself before the Trustees of the Furman Institution in 1848, in a caustic address on "Orthodoxy," which was published as a pamphlet. This probably led to the two long and elaborate series of articles on Imputation which young James Boyce admitted into the "Southern Baptist," while he was editor, in 1849. Professor Mims's health quite gave way during the session of 1854–1855, and he died on June 14, 1855, at the early age of thirty-eight. Some books that came from his collection are found in the library of the S. B. T. Seminary, and there is a certain touch of inspiration, a trace of scholarly enthusiasm and discrimination, even in his brief marginal notes.

When the trustees met, in July, they elected James P. Boyce as successor to Professor Mims. On July 26 he wrote to H. A. Tupper, then in Europe, that he had been appointed professor, and had accepted, on condition that he should have further assistance, and added that on Tupper's return from Europe in the autumn the chair of Biblical Literature and Exegesis would be offered to him. Boyce quite urges his friend to accept the position. He says there are four students in the theological department, and thinks that by February there will be several others, while about twenty are in the collegiate department of the University, preparing for the ministry. Notwithstanding the small number of students, there had been, and was, a high ambition to give them thorough training. Professor Mims had worn himself out with the task. Boyce felt, and judicious friends agreed with him, that alone he could not possibly do the requisite teaching. He declared himself willing to divide the salary with a colleague, or to yield it all, if the colleague should lack other means of support. He wrote again to Tupper, on September 29, after beginning his work: "I cannot teach more than half the classes next term" (when there would be more students and more classes). Mr. Tupper reached Charleston in October, and at Boyce's request met him in Columbia to consult. But he felt obliged to decline, because unwilling (as he wrote to President J. C. Furman) to sever the "sacred and happy relation" that bound him to the church at Washington, Ga., "or to exchange in a measure the office of preaching for that of teaching." Thus Boyce was left to struggle on unaided through his first session. It is stated by students of the time that he actually taught five hours a day, and some days six hours. To prepare all these lessons, with his high standard of thoroughness and kindling ambition, was a severe task, to be sure. Dr. John Mitchell, of North Carolina, who was a tutor in the University that year, says that Boyce "was industrious, laborious, and made a fine impression as a teacher from the first."

Indeed, Furman University was the seat of much thorough study and high teaching. Great advantages are enjoyed by the students and professors of a large and amply endowed institution, and nothing wiser or nobler can be done by generous givers than to build up such endowments. But it must not be forgotten that a very large part of the best educational work that has been done in our new country was performed by small institutions, in which a few struggling professors, ambitious that their students should lack for nothing in the way of instruction, were doing each two men's work on half of one man's salary, and really got closer to the students, got hold of them more strongly and impressively, by reason of not being too far in advance of them, because all were toiling and struggling on together. Every limitation and disadvantage in life has certain compensations where the men concerned possess real talent and kindling aspiration.

President James C. Furman, D.D., son of the Richard Furman after whom the institution was named, had as a young preacher enjoyed very remarkable success in numerous revival meetings at important points in the Carolinas. He was for some years pastor of the singularly interesting community about Society Hill, S. C., in the region lying between Columbia and Wilmington. He greatly longed to be only a preacher and pastor, as was true of some others who have felt compelled to yield their preference, and spend their lives in aiding the preparatory studies of their ministerial brethren. When first elected professor in the Furman Institution, he declined; but he accepted in 1843, and remained in connection with the Institution, and afterwards University, until his death in 1890. Dr. Furman was a man of high and varied talents and accomplishments, a very winning and impressive preacher, and a very lucid and engaging teacher. His singularly mild and gentle tones of voice and his general bearing really harmonized perfectly with his force of character and strong convictions. Had he possessed higher bodily health to endure the immense labor of wide study and varied teaching, and had he been gifted with a more resolute and commanding tone in public speech, he would have been generally recognized as one of the ablest men in the country. Numerous students, through almost fifty years, have felt more and more with the unfolding of their own experience how great a privilege they had enjoyed in his ripe instruction and his charming personal influence and example.

C. H. Judson, the Professor of Mathematics, had been educated at Hamilton and the University of Virginia, and had become professor in Furman University upon its establishment in 1851. The plan of organization of the University, which was adopted the next year, was chiefly prepared by Professor Judson, upon avowed comparison with the documents published by the University of Virginia and by Brown University, which had in 1850 changed its curriculum into a number of separate schools. Professor Judson remarkably combines a special talent for metaphysical thinking, extraordinary gifts as a mathematician, and uncommon energy and skill in practical business affairs. As treasurer, he helped to carry the University through many years of trial, before and after the war. As teacher of mathematics, he has always been remarkable for very clear statement, given in a forcible and cogent way, and with an enthusiasm for the subject which his quiet manner did not prevent from kindling the susceptible student, — a combination making up a great teacher of mathematics. He was also at this time teaching the School of Natural Philosophy and Astronomy, and the School of Chemistry and Natural History.

Professor Peter C. Edwards, born near Society Hill, S. C., had been graduated in South Carolina College and the Newton Theological Institution. He was now a laborious Professor of Ancient Languages in the University, and had little time for the instruction in Biblical Exegesis which he had formerly given in Furman Institution. A man of strong intellect, great powers of imagination, and depth of feeling, he was an enthusiastic student and teacher, but was comparatively deficient in practical knowledge and practical judgment. Upon some thoroughly congenial and in itself kindling theme he would preach a sermon of wonderful charm and power, while most of his discourses failed to interest the average hearer. A question about some favorite theory of Greek syntax would lead him off into endless and impassioned disquisitions, quite unsuspecting that a lad who did not know his lesson had raised that question to stop the recitation. All who knew Professor Edwards well, greatly admired and loved him, and students naturally inclined to the study of language found him a most inspiring teacher.

With the able Professor W. B. Royall as head of the Academic Department, and John Mitchell as tutor, — afterwards Thomas Hall, J. B. Patrick, John F. Lanneau, — the University was prepared to do, and really was doing, much first-rate work in teaching. Our ambitious and laborious young Professor of Theology had come into a busy workshop.

The previous professors — Hooper, Reynolds, and Mims — had taken more interest in the directly Biblical studies than in Systematic Theology. Boyce was most interested and best prepared in Systematic Theology and cognate subjects; and for this reason, as well as the excess of labor, he greatly desired a colleague for the Biblical work; but meantime he went on faithfully teaching all the subjects. Professor Mims's course had been arranged for two years; Boyce proposed to insert a previous "undergraduate year," in which for six months before the Commencement the college students for the ministry would give some attention to Hebrew and Biblical History. Among the little group of students was Rev. John G. Williams, who has long been a popular minister in South Carolina. He writes as follows: —

"Dr. Boyce taught us Systematic Theology (using Dick's Theology as a text-book), Church History, Greek New Testament Exegesis, and Hebrew. It was easy to see then that Theology was his strong point, and had already taken a strong hold on him. I thought his lectures — which he required us to take down — on one of the Gospels were very able, and have always regretted that I lost my notes of them during the late war, with the greater part of my library. Dr. Boyce impressed me as being a very hard student, and one who had found his true calling as a theological professor. It was a calling that stirred his enthusiasm and brought out his real power, thus proving that this was to be his life-work. Dr. Boyce was always interesting, thorough, and patient as a teacher. He took great interest in us, and we felt that he was our friend. We went to his recitation-room, which was in his own house, with the feeling that we were not only going there to be taught, but to have a good time with a warm-hearted, sympathizing friend and brother."

Mr. Williams remembers among his fellow-students at the time A. K. Durham, John Morrall, and J. B. Hartwell. The last was a son of Jesse Hartwell (an early professor in the Furman Institution), and has labored as a missionary in China, and of late to the Chinese in California. During Boyce's second year J. F. B. Mays, of Virginia, was a theological student, and there were some others whose names cannot now be recovered.

When formally inaugurated in July, 1856, he delivered an inaugural address entitled "Three Changes in Theological Institutions," of which we shall have much to say in the next chapter. The young professor, still only twenty-nine years old, and convinced that he was to speak on vital themes at a time of crisis, prepared this address with great care. Three distinct forms of it appear among his manuscripts.

At this meeting of the Board in July, E. T. Winkler was elected to be adjunct professor of theology and of the ancient languages, which would have made him a helper to Professor Edwards also. He declined, and in the following January H. A. Tupper was again elected to the same position, and again declined. We can easily see now that this series of disappointments, fixing the conviction that he could not carry out his cherished plans in a theological department for a single State, was steadily leading Professor Boyce on towards the foundation of a general theological seminary for Southern Baptists, for which the way had been preparing through a dozen years. Four months after this last failure to get a colleague, he was at the educational convention in Louisville, throwing his whole soul into the project of establishing a common theological seminary at Greenville.

Dr. H. A. Tupper would have made an uncommonly accurate and enthusiastic instructor in Hebrew and other Biblical studies. He mentioned in New York to the famous Dr. T. J. Conant, who had been his teacher at Hamilton, that he had been asked to consider a Hebrew professorship, and had declined, because no Hebraist. Dr. Conant gave a noteworthy reply: "You made a mistake. No professor knows much of his chair when he first takes it." Doubtless every professor feels thus, whether he begins teaching in youth or in later years. We may add a companion saying of Dr. Gessner Harrison, of the University of Virginia: "A man ought to stop teaching a subject when he stops learning it."

In February, 1857, Boyce writes to Mr. Tupper that he had been asked to consider an election as President of Mercer University, but did not encourage the idea. He is thinking of a trip to Europe as soon as he is free, " either through resignation or additional help in the theological department, or the establishment of a Central Institution." The Mercer appointment was urged upon him again in May, after the Louisville educational convention, with a salary of $2,500, which for that time and region was remarkable; but he positively declined. In August he was formally and unanimously elected to Mercer, but declined. Brethren were beginning to see clearly that here was a man capable of bringing things to pass, and they wanted him.

Professor Boyce really taught in Furman University only two years. In July, 1857, he tendered his resignation; but the Board requested him to retain the office of professor, and use his time as he should think proper. He spent a considerable part of the next eight months in travelling through the State to raise an endowment for the projected theological seminary. About this period, or somewhat later, he gave gratuitous instruction in several subjects in the Greenville Female College, — for which the trustees voted him their thanks in 1860, — and for one year gratuitously discharged the duties of President of that institution.

Among his sermons we find one on the recent death of A. P. Butler, United States Senator from South Carolina, who died May 25, 1857. The sermon was probably delivered in Greenville, where some relatives of the Senator were personal friends of the preacher. Judge Butler was a man of very high character, greatly honored and beloved, and since the death of Mr. Calhoun he had been very generally looked up to as a great bulwark and defender of the State in the senatorial conflicts. Mr. Boyce was by no means given to high-wrought eulogium, but he speaks in strong terms of the Senator's elevated character, intellectual resources, and patriotic spirit, adding as follows: "Well may the State mourn to-day the loss of such a man. Pure in patriotism, prudent in counsel, pre-eminent above all his contemporaries in that peculiar eloquence which silences and rebukes with withering sarcasm the false charges of unworthy foes, — in these days of misconception, if not of aspersion, of dangers from within and from without, the loss of no man in the national councils could be felt to be more serious. Especially may Carolina mourn the loss of her wise and noble son, of her peerless and invincible champion." A year before his death, Senator Butler had been the subject of a very bitter personal attack in a speech from Senator Charles Sumner. Whether he had provoked this by something of his own "withering sarcasm," we know not. But Mr. Sumner was famous for terrific invective, and it is well remembered that he attacked Mr. Butler in terms so personal and insulting as to be thought

PROFESSOR IN FURMAN UNIVERSITY. 109

by the latter's friends simply intolerable. Butler was sixty years old, and in feeble health. It was these circumstances which led his nephew, Preston S. Brooks, a member of the lower House, to determine that he would avenge the insulting assault upon his uncle by physical chastisement of Mr. Sumner. Weary of waiting for him to come forth, Brooks finally rushed into the Senate chamber, after adjournment, and assailed Senator Sumner with a cane as he sat writing in his seat. This unjustifiable course turned a very general tide of sympathy in favor of Mr. Sumner, and has caused it to be frequently overlooked that the famous Senator sometimes indulged his powers of invective in ways quite overpassing the limits of propriety. How often men forget, in the heated animosities of discussion, that it is a cheap thing to be personally insulting, instead of convincing by earnest argument. If we are to have an end to physical assaults, as is so much to be desired, there ought to be at least some limit to verbal assaults. The hot passions of the period referred to — four years before the war — are revealed by the fact that many men in Carolina and elsewhere not only excused, but unreservedly commended Mr. Brooks's entire course, and many at the North glorified Mr. Sumner as a martyr to free speech, without ever tolerating the suggestion that all the same he had grievously insulted an aged and feeble Senator of the highest character. Even at the present day it is difficult to look back upon that period of varied conflict and judge fairly of one side or the other.

During these years Mr. Boyce also took interest in agriculture, as his home in the edge of Greenville reached out into several fields of arable land. An agricultural monthly of February, 1858, reported that in Greenville District Professor James P. Boyce made on one acre fifty thousand nine hundred and thirty-five pounds of ruta-baga turnips and tops, and the men are named who weighed them. It also states that of wheat he made forty-four bushels and a peck to the acre, — a remarkable yield for the soil of that region, better suited to corn and cotton than to wheat. He also took interest in the introduction of improved stock; yet not as a mere gratification, for everything must pay, so that others might be encouraged to do likewise.

CHAPTER IX.

FOUNDATION OF THE SOUTHERN BAPTIST THEOLOGICAL SEMINARY.[1]

THE idea of a common theological institution for all Southern Baptists is thought by some to have been first suggested by the eminent South Carolina minister, Dr. W. B. Johnson, while others ascribe it to the equally distinguished Dr. R. B. C. Howell, of Tennessee, and Dr. J. B. Jeter, of Virginia. It had doubtless arisen independently in the minds of various brethren in different States; and things were slowly preparing for the movement in many ways.[2]

Nearly every Baptist College at the South had at one time a theological department, like that of Furman University, in which James P. Boyce taught. Indeed, several of them were begun as simply theological institutions, and afterwards grew into colleges (frequently called universities, because it was hoped they would finally reach that character), commonly retaining the theological department, though sometimes dropping it. Thus, when the Baptist

---

[1] Some readers will be likely to exercise, in regard to this and the next chapter, what Sir Walter calls "a faculty of judicious skipping." But persons interested in the Seminary, or in the general matter of theological education, may like to have the historical sketch here given.

[2] A brief historical sketch of these preparatory events was prefixed by Dr. Boyce to the Seminary's first catalogue; and another was published by Dr. Manly in the "Seminary Magazine" for December, 1891. Other materials have been drawn from various sources and from personal recollection.

Seminary at Richmond, Va., was about to be re-organized as Richmond College, a Baptist member of the Legislature earnestly and successfully urged that they should drop the theological department, on the ground that for the Legislature to incorporate a theological institution squinted towards a union of Church and State, — so great was the sensitiveness on that subject which had survived in Virginia from the fierce conflicts of half a century before. The legislator in question insisted that young preachers should study the Bible and theology under the guidance of older pastors, or that seminaries for the purpose could be conducted without incorporation. This sensitiveness passed away, and several theological seminaries of other denominations were afterwards incorporated in Virginia. In most States the theological department was retained, sometimes with two professors, as we have seen Boyce anxious to have it, but oftener with only one. Much earnest and helpful work was done for small classes in these various institutions, yet there were obvious and very serious difficulties, often keenly felt by the struggling professor himself. Several of these professors were among the most earnest advocates of the establishment of a common seminary, though each naturally wished that the institution with which he was connected might become the nucleus for such a new organization.

When Basil Manly, Jr., graduated in 1844 at the University of Alabama (of which his father, Basil Manly, Sr., was president), and determined to devote himself to the ministry, the question how he could be best prepared for the work was earnestly discussed between his father and Dr. John L. Dagg,[1] then Professor of Theology in Mercer University at Penfield, Ga. (since removed to Macon).

[1] Dr. Dagg was a man of great ability and lovable character. His works are worthy of thorough study, especially his small volume, "A Manual of Theology" (Amer. Bap. Pub. Soc.), which is remarkable for clear statement of the profoundest truths, and for devotional sweet-

Dr. Dagg, while residing in Tuscaloosa, Ala., had been associated with young Manly's early religious experience, so that the latter was inclined to study theology at Mercer under his direction. "But he advised," says the narrative above mentioned, "with characteristic earnestness and fidelity, that I should not content myself with that, but should seek at once the best advantages and the fullest course that could be procured. These, it was agreed, could be found then at the Newton Theological Institution, near Boston, Mass. When the disruption of 1845 occurred between Northern and Southern Baptists, in their voluntary missionary organizations, — for the division extended only to these, and never to the actual relations of the churches, — it led to the withdrawal from Newton of the four Southern students who were there, S. C. Clopton, E. T. Winkler, J. W. M. Williams, and myself. The other three went directly into ministerial work,[1] while I determined, as I was younger, to prosecute further preparatory study, and went, under the advice of my father, of Dr. Dagg, of Dr. Francis Wayland, and other friends, to Princeton Theological Seminary. . . . There was not at that period an institution at the South where anything like a full theological course could be enjoyed. It was felt that that state of things ought not to remain so. Articles were written in the leading papers by a number of eminent brethren bearing on the question, and suggesting different plans for relieving the situation."

During the meeting in Augusta, Ga., in 1845, at which it was decided to organize the Southern Baptist Conven-

ness. The writer of this Memoir may be pardoned for bearing witness that after toiling much, in his early years, as a pastor, over Knapp and Turrettin, Dwight and Andrew Fuller, and other elaborate theologians, he found this manual a delight, and has felt through life the pleasing impulse it gave to theological inquiry and reflection. A stepson of Dr. Dagg is the eminent professor of Moral Philosophy in the University of Virginia, Dr. Noah K. Davis.

[1] They had all been at Newton two years, Manly but one.

tion, a conference of brethren from various States was held, to consider the question of establishing a theological seminary of a high order. In 1847, at a meeting of the Indian Mission Association, held at Nashville, Tenn., the subject was again discussed by prominent brethren of Kentucky and Tennessee. When the Southern Baptist Convention was to meet on May 2, 1849,[1] at Nashville, Dr. W. B. Johnson tried to secure a meeting of South Carolina delegates, at Aiken, on their way to Nashville, to consult about this matter, and with a view to put forward the Furman Theological Institution as the nucleus of a common seminary; but this meeting was prevented by the general abandonment of the trip to Nashville. The trustees of Mercer University took action about the same time, favoring the idea of a concentration upon that institution. Some scattered cases of cholera in Nashville excited an alarm in distant States, being magnified into an epidemic, and kept away many of those who would have attended the Southern Baptist Convention at that place. But in the meeting there held, it is stated by Basil Manly, Jr., that "Brethren R. B. C. Howell and J. R. Graves, whom I then met for the first time, were both enthusiastic and zealous for the establishment of the new institution. In fact, they thought the very time had come." Young Manly considered that matters were scarcely ripe for this desirable enterprise, and was challenged by Brother Graves, who was already a skilled and renowned debater, to discuss the matter before the Convention. He declined the discussion, and gives the following reasons: "I did not want to be put into the false position of antagonizing the progressive movement for theological education, which I earnestly favored; and I am not ashamed to say I dreaded

---

[1] Its first regular meeting was held at Richmond in 1846. Being at first triennial, like the old Triennial Convention of Baptists of the whole country, its next meeting fell in 1849. Afterwards it became biennial, and of late years annual.

to cope with so vigorous and able an opponent as Brother Graves in an extempore debate."

The Nashville Convention adjourned to meet in Charleston on May 23. In anticipation of this meeting in Charleston the "Southern Baptist," of which Boyce was just then ceasing to be editor, republished two elaborate articles on this question from the "Monthly Miscellany," edited in Georgia by Joseph S. Baker. The first article was from R. B. C. Howell, D.D., then pastor in Nashville. He recognizes that many men have been, and many will be, very useful in the ministry, without formal education at college or seminary. But he argues that the progress of general knowledge, the necessity of encountering trained ministers of other denominations, the demand of many of our churches for better-prepared pastors, all combine to require a larger proportion of thoroughly educated Baptist ministers. He proposes a union of all existing Baptist theological schools in the Southern States at some central and accessible point; and if this be found impracticable, a new theological institution. This article was replied to in the May number of the "Miscellany" by Robert Ryland, President of Richmond College. He argues that a great central theological school is impracticable, for it would require $100,000, which cannot be had; and as the inevitable failure of the attempt would produce general discouragement, he thinks the scheme had better be abandoned. He also inclines to regard a good college course as the main thing, since a man of trained mind could study theology for himself, as many had been doing with great advantage. He remarks upon the impatience of the young men, as often preventing a sufficiently long attendance upon college, and a great theological school would only increase the difficulty. This last, it may be observed, is really one of the grave difficulties in the way of American theological education, and particularly in the far Southern States, where the young grow up so early, and are so impatient to enter upon the permanent relations of life.

At the Charleston meeting of the Convention, Boyce was one of the delegates, and Basil Manly, Jr., was Assistant Secretary. At a special and separate educational meeting, Dr. W. B. Johnson, President of the S. B. Convention, read an elaborate essay in favor of establishing a central theological institution. Young Manly made an address upon the subject, the notes of which he published in the "Seminary Magazine" (*ut supra*). In this he stated that there were then seven theological professors, in as many Southern Baptist institutions, having in all about thirty students. He argued the great advantage of a single central institution for economy and for efficiency. Some of his points under the latter head ought to be quoted, as showing how thoroughly the subject was understood by the men engaged in promoting the project. "(*a*) A division of labor can be had, so that the professors can give better and more thorough instruction, each taking his special subject. . . . (*c*) A larger number of professors, with their varied characteristics and excellences, would exert a stronger influence, and one not so liable to produce one-sided development, on the students. Strong and good men form their pupils, not only by what they teach, but by what they are; and the more of such men we have together, the larger the benefit. (*d*) The mutual acquaintance of a large body of students, gathered from different parts of our country, would have a strong tendency to promote a general union of Baptists in all good things, and to keep down local or sectional peculiarities and jealousies. (*e*) It would afford greater stimulus to study if the students came into contact with the picked men of a wider area, enjoying, many of them, the advantages of higher culture; and this would be more beneficial to them than if they met simply men from their own State, and brought up under circumstances precisely like their own." He mentions three plans which have been suggested: "(1) Transfer all present theological funds to a new board, to establish one institution at some point to be agreed on. It is doubtful whether this can be legally done. (2) Let the funds remain in the hands of the present local or State boards, but let all agree to use the income for sustaining professors at some common centre. Hard to get all to agree. (3) Establish a new institution, with new board, new funds, possibly using some one of the existing theological departments as a foundation, but giving it into the charge of a board of trustees selected from all States of the Southern Baptist Convention. This last seems most likely to be carried into execution."

After repeated consultation at meetings held during the sessions of the Convention, — for the Southern Baptist Convention itself never at any time took up the question, — a large committee was appointed (A. M. Poindexter, chairman) to correspond with the trustees of existing theological schools, and propose to Conventions or Associations any means "they may believe calculated to secure in the Southern States a thorough and useful training of our young men who are entering the gospel ministry." There was no practical result of all this, but interest in the subject was slowly widening and deepening.

Up to this time James P. Boyce had naturally taken no prominent part in the movement. He was only twenty-two years old, and had not yet begun his theological studies at Princeton. But two or three times, while editing the "Southern Baptist" during the preceding months, he had expressed himself as favorable to the movement. The next action taken, as far as records are accessible, was at the Baptist General Association of Virginia, in June, 1854, proposing a meeting of "the friends of theological education" on May 11, 1855, at Montgomery, Ala., during the session of the Southern Baptist Convention.

We have seen in a previous chapter that Rev. James P. Boyce, who had just resigned his pastorate in South Carolina, was present and active in this Montgomery Convention. At the accompanying educational meetings B. Manly, Jr., was Secretary, and a Committee of Correspondence was appointed, consisting of J. B. Jeter, J. P. Boyce, and others. Resolutions offered by A. M. Poindexter, and unanimously adopted, declared "that in the opinion of this meeting it is demanded by the interests of the cause of truth that the Baptists of the South and Southwest unite in establishing a Theological Institution of high grade," and proposed that a convention be held in regard to this object, at Augusta, Ga., in April of the next year, to be composed of representatives from the various colleges, educational societies, and State conventions.

At this next meeting in Augusta, April, 1856, the attendance was of course chiefly from South Carolina and Georgia; but there were two from Washington city, six from Virginia, one from North Carolina, two from Florida, four from Alabama, one each from Mississippi and Louisiana, and three from Tennessee. A very large proportion of these brethren, who came from a distance for this express purpose, were then, or afterwards became, men of distinction among Southern Baptists.[1] It included two, Boyce and Manly, of the men destined to be the Seminary's first professors; and three had been present at Montgomery. Dr. B. Manly, Sr., was made president, and so in each of the subsequent meetings until the formation of the Seminary. He was then again pastor in Charleston. A large and able committee, headed by the President, reported "that from various causes they find the subject embarrassed by difficulties at every point, which it is useless here to discuss, as it is impossible here

[1] The list is given in the introduction to the Southern Baptist Theological Seminary's first catalogue.

to decide whether they are insuperable." The committee regarded "the attainment of the general object as paramount, but could only recommend that still another convention of properly authenticated delegates, from the Southern colleges and theological schools under the control of Baptists, and from Baptist State Conventions, should be held the following year in Louisville, Ky., during the two days preceding the session of the Southern Baptist Convention. A committee, consisting of B. Manly, Sr., A. M. Poindexter, and J. B. Jeter, was directed to report to the said meeting at Louisville, (1) "what funds exist subject to the control of Baptists for theological instruction in each of the institutions of the South and Southwest; whether the trustees or other parties holding legal control over these funds can and will contribute them in any form — and if any, what — to the uses of a common theological institution, to be located at any other point within or without the limits of their own States severally, should the aforesaid Convention, to assemble at Louisville in 1857, adjudge such different location best for the common good; whether these funds, in case they are limited to a spot, can and will be placed within the control of such a board of trustees as may be appointed by competent authority agreed upon for a common theological institution." The same committee was authorized and requested (2) "to use adequate means for ascertaining what efforts will be made in favor of any location, already occupied or not, by the inhabitants and friends thereof, and what pecuniary subscriptions or pledges will be given as a nucleus, in case such location should be selected for the common institution; the object of all these inquiries being to ascertain, in the fullest manner possible, whether such a demand is felt for a common institution of this kind as may be a basis and encouragement for future united action."

It is clear that this report to the Augusta meeting was written by James P. Boyce, who had been, since the previous autumn, professor in the theological department of Furman University. The long series of apparently fruitless meetings for consultation may now soon lead to some practical result, as pointed to by the close of the report. It soon became evident, as B. Manly, Jr., had held seven years before, that the existing theological departments in several States could not be combined into one institution; and the only hope lay in the establishment of an entirely new theological seminary, or of a seminary incorporating into itself some one of the existing theological departments.

Three months later, the State Convention of the Baptist Denomination in South Carolina met at Greenville, on July 26, 1856. Under the special leadership of Professor Boyce, this Convention proposed to the coming Educational Convention at Louisville to establish at Greenville, S. C., a common theological institution, offering that the funds for theological purposes then held by the Trustees of Furman University (about thirty thousand dollars) should be turned over to the proposed institution, with additional funds to be raised in the State, which should make in all the sum of one hundred thousand dollars; provided that the said institution shall be further endowed with an additional sum of one hundred thousand dollars to be raised in other States. Thus something practical was at last proposed; and the question was whether in the next nine months the sum of seventy thousand dollars could be raised in South Carolina for the requisite endowment.

On July 30 Professor Boyce, now completing his first session as theological professor in Furman University, delivered his inaugural address. This important address was declared by A. M. Poindexter (present as Secretary of the Foreign Mission Board at Richmond) "the ablest thing of the kind he had ever heard," and is certainly a very remarkable production for a young man of twenty-nine. Its ideas entered into the constitution, and chiefly determined the peculiarities, of the Southern Baptist Theological Seminary. It will therefore be proper to give here its chief lines of thought, with a number of extracts.

The address is entitled "Three Changes in Theological Institutions." Summarily stated, the three proposed changes were the following: (1) A Baptist theological school ought not merely to receive college graduates, but men with less of general education, even men having only what is called a common English education, offering to every man such opportunities of theological study as he is prepared for and desires. (2) Besides covering, for those who are prepared, as wide a range of theological study as could be found elsewhere, such an institution ought to offer further and special courses, so that the ablest and most aspiring students might make extraordinary attainments, preparing them for instruction and original authorship, and helping to make our country less dependent upon foreign scholarship. (3) There should be prepared an Abstract of Principles, or careful statement of theological belief, which every professor in such an institution must sign when inaugurated, so as to guard against the rise of erroneous and injurious instruction in such a seat of sacred learning.

He begins by deprecating any hasty conclusion from the sentiments he is about to utter that he is opposed to the thorough training and education of the Christian ministry. We perceive that he foresaw how readily some people would imagine that to unite in the same institution a partial theological education of some and a thorough theological education of others would be to lower the general standard. He wishes it distinctly understood of himself and the University Trustees he is addressing that they —

"hold the education of the ministry a matter of the first importance to the churches of Christ.

"Indeed, did we think otherwise, we could no longer justly

stand forth as exponents in any sense of the opinions upon this subject which prevail in our denomination. The Baptists are unmistakably the friends of education, and the advocates of an educated ministry. Their twenty-four colleges and ten departments or institutions for theological instruction in this country, as well as the extent to which they have assisted in the establishment of general institutions, and of those under the control of other denominations, furnish sufficient testimony to the fact that they feel the value of education, and the importance, under God, of the means it affords for the better performance of the work of the ministry."

Far from wishing to diminish this denominational interest, he says that he —

"would see the means of theological education increased. I would have the facilities for pursuing its studies opened to all who would embrace them; I would lead the strong men of our ministry to feel that no position is equal in responsibility or usefulness to that of one devoted to this cause; and I would spread among our churches such an earnest desire for educated ministers as would make them willing so to increase the support of the ministry as to enable all of those who are now forced, from want of means, to enter without the fullest preparation upon the active duties of the work, so far to anticipate the support they will receive as to feel free to borrow the means by which their education may be completed."

He wishes to propose certain changes which will widen the extent of theological education among us, without at all lowering the standard. The results thus far of establishing theological institutions have been extremely meagre.

"The mind of the whole denomination has been awakened to the want of success under which we have suffered in our past efforts, and the best intellects and hearts in all our Southern bounds are directed to the causes of our failure, and to the means by which success may be attained. . . . The theological seminary has not been a popular institution. But few have sought its advantages; but few have been nurtured by the influences sent forth from it; and while our denomination has continued to increase, and our principles have annually been spreading more widely, it has been sensibly felt that whatever ministerial increase has accompanied has been not only disproportionate to that of our membership, but has owed its origin in no respect to the influence of theological education.

"And this seems to be the general law in the denomination. The complaint is not peculiar to our institution; it seems to exist everywhere, despite all the efforts to counteract it which have been put forth, and not to be confined to Baptists, but to be the lamentation of all. You will see it in the organs of all the prominent denominations, and the cause of it is the subject of earnest inquiry."

There is a greatly increased and ever-increasing demand for more ministers, but no corresponding increase in the number who present themselves.

"Oh, were there ever a time when we should expect that God would answer the prayers of his churches, and overflood the land and the world with a ministry adequate to uphold his cause in every locality, it would seem to be now! — now, when the wealth of the churches is sufficient to send the Gospel to every creature; now, when in the art of printing the Church has again received the gift of tongues; now, when the workings of God himself indicate his readiness to beget a nation in a day; now, when the multiplication a thousand-fold of the laborers will still leave an abundant work for each; but now, alas! now, when our churches at home are not adequately supplied, when dark and destitute places are found in the most favored portions of our own land, when the heathen are at our very doors, and the cry is, 'Help! help!' and there is no help, because there are not laborers enough to meet the wants immediately around us.

"There are serious questions presented to us here: To what are these things due? Have we not disregarded the laws which the providence and word of God have laid down for us? And does he not now chastise us by suffering our schemes to work out their natural results, that we, being left to ourselves, may see our folly, and return to him and to his ways, as the only means of strength?

"In ascribing this evil for the most part to our theological institutions, I would not appear unmindful of the other circumstances upon which an increase of the ministry in our churches depends. Never would I consent to lift my voice upon such a subject as this without a distinct recognition of the sovereignty of God working his own will, and calling forth according to that will the many or the few with whose aid he will secure the blessing. Never could I proceed upon any assumption that would seem to take for granted that there is not the utmost need of more special awakening to devotion and piety in our churches, and a more fervent utterance of prayer for the increase of the laborers. Neither would I have it supposed that all that the theological institution can effect will be fully adequate to our wants, while our pastors neglect to search out and encourage the useful gifts which God has bestowed upon the members of their churches, or the churches themselves neglect the law of God which provides an adequate support for the ministry. But while due prominence is given to all of these circumstances, it yet appears that the chief cause is to be found in our departure from the way which God has marked out for us, and our failure to make provision for the education of such a ministry as he designs to send forth and honor."

He wishes, therefore, as the first and principal change, to offer the opportunity of theological training to all classes of those whom God calls into the ministry, and not simply, as heretofore, to invite into theological schools those who have completed a college course.

"Permit me to ask what has been the prominent idea at the basis of theological education in this country. To arrive at it we have only to notice the requisitions necessary for entrance upon a course of study. Have they not been almost universally that the student should have passed through a regular college course, or made attainments equivalent thereto? And have not even the exceptional cases been rare instances in which the Faculty or Board have, under peculiar circumstances, assumed the responsibility of a deviation from the ordinary course?

"The idea which is prominent as the basis of this action is that the work of the ministry should be intrusted only to those who have been classically educated, — an assumption which, singularly enough, is made for no other profession. It is in vain to say that such is not the theory or the practice of our denomination. It is the theory and the practice of by far the larger portion of those who have controlled our institutions, and have succeeded in engrafting this idea upon them, contrary to the spirit which prevails among the churches. They have done this, without doubt, in the exercise of their best judgment, but have failed because they neglected the better plan pointed out by the providence and word of God.

"The practical operation of this theory has tended in two ways to diminish the ranks of our valuable ministry. It has restrained many from entering upon the work, and has prevented the arrangement of such a course of study as would have enabled those who have entered upon it to fit themselves in a short time for valuable service. The consequences have been that the number of those who have felt themselves called of God to the ministry has been disproportioned to the wants of the churches; and of that number but a very small proportion have entered it with a proper preparation for even common usefulness. And only by energy and zeal, awakened by their devotion to the work, have they been able to succeed in their labors, and to do for themselves the work, the greater part of which the theological school should have accomplished for them.

"In his word and in his providence, God seems to have plainly indicated the principle upon which the instruction of the ministry should be based. It is not that every man should be made a scholar, an adept in philology, an able interpreter of the Bible in its original languages, acquainted with all the sciences upon the various facts and theories of which God's word is attacked and must be defended, and versed in all the systems of true and false philosophy, which some must understand in order to encounter the enemies who attack the very foundations of religion, but that while the privilege of becoming such shall be freely offered to all, and every student shall be encouraged to obtain all the advantages that education can afford, the opportunity should be given to those who cannot or will not make thorough scholastic preparation to obtain that adequate knowledge of the truths of the Scriptures, systematically arranged, and of the laws which govern the interpretation of the text in the English version, which constitutes all that is actually necessary to enable them to preach the Gospel, to build up the churches on their most holy faith, and to instruct them in the practice of the duties incumbent upon them.

"The Scriptural qualifications for the ministry do, indeed, involve the idea of knowledge, but that knowledge is not of the sciences, nor of philosophy, nor of the languages, but of God and of his plan of salvation. He who has not this knowledge, though he be learned in all the learning of the schools, is incapable of preaching the word of God. But he who knows it, not superficially, not merely in those plain and simple declarations known to every believing reader, but in its power, as revealed in its precious and sanctifying doctrines, is fitted to bring forth out of his treasury things new and old, and is a workman that needeth not to be ashamed, although he may speak to his hearers in uncouth words or in manifest ignorance of all the sciences. The one belongs to the class of educated ministers, the other to the ministry of educated men; and the two things are essentially different."

This difference he illustrates by contrasting John Bunyan and Theodore Parker as preachers of the Gospel.

"Who is the minister here, — the man of the schools, or the man of the Scriptures? Who bears the insignia of an ambassador for Christ? Whom does God own? Whom would the Church hear? In whose power would she put forth her strength? And yet these instances, though extreme, will serve to show what may be the ministry of the educated man, and what that of the illiterate man, the educated minister. The perfection of the ministry, it is gladly admitted, would consist in the just combination of the two; but it is not the business of the Church to establish a perfect, but an adequate ministry; and it is only of the latter that we may hope for an abundant supply. The qualification God lays down is the only one he permits us to demand; and the instruction of our theological schools must be based upon such a plan as shall afford this amount of education to those who actually constitute the mass of our ministry, and who cannot obtain more.

"The providential dispensation of God, in the administration of the affairs of his Church, fully illustrates the truth of this principle, so plainly in accordance with his word. That the education of the schools is of great advantage to the minister truly trained in the word of truth, has been illustrated by the labors of Paul, Augustin, Calvin, Beza, Davies, Edwards, and a host of others who have stood forth in their different ages the most prominent of all the ministry of their day, and the most efficient workmen in the cause of Christ; while in the eleven Apostles, in the mass of the ministry of that day, and of all other times and places, God has manifested that he will work out the greater portion of his purposes by men of no previous training, and educated only in the mysteries of that truth which is in Christ Jesus.

"Never has he illustrated that principle more fully than in connection with the progress of the principles of our own denomination. We have had our men of might and power who have shown the advantages of scholastic education as a basis, but we have also seen the great instruments of our progress to have been the labors of a much humbler class. Trace our history back, either through the centuries that have long passed away, or in the workings of God during the last hundred years, and it will be seen that the mass of the vineyard laborers have been from the ranks of fishermen and tax-gatherers, cobblers and tinkers, weavers and ploughmen, to whom God has not disdained to impart gifts, and whom he has qualified as his ambassadors by the presence of that Spirit by which, and not by might, wisdom, or power, is the work of the Lord accomplished.

"The Baptists of America, especially, should be the last to forget this method of working on the part of their Master, and the first to retrace any steps which would seem to indicate such forgetfulness. It has been signally manifested in the establishment of their faith and principles. The names which have been identified with our growth have been those of men of no collegiate education, of no learning or rhetorical eloquence, of no instruction even in schools of theology. Hervey, Gano, Bennet, Semple, Broaddus, Armstrong, Mercer, who were these? Men of education, of collegiate training, of theological schools? Nay, indeed. All praise to those who did possess any of these advantages! They were burning and shining lights. They hid neither talents nor opportunities, but devoted them to the cause they loved, and accomplished much in its behalf. They maintained positions which perhaps none others could have occupied. But their number was not sufficient for the work of the Lord; and he gave a multitude of others, — men who were found in labors oft, in wearisome toils by day and by night, in heat or in cold, facing dangers of every kind, enduring private and public persecution, travelling through swamp and forest to carry the glad tidings of salvation to the lost and perishing of our country. And the Baptists can neither forget them nor the principle taught us in their labors, by the providence of God. Whatever may be the course of those who have the training of their ministry, these ideas have sunk so deeply into the minds of the denomination that they can never be eradicated. And the day will yet come, perhaps has already come, when the churches will rise in their strength and demand that our Theological Institutions make educational provisions for *the mass* of their ministry.

I have spoken of our ministry in the past, as composed of men whose success illustrates the theory of the need only of theological education. And yet it is apparent that they enjoyed none of the advantages for that purpose which are connected with the present arrangements for study. In the absence of these, however, they did attain to the amount of theological education which is essential. This was accomplished through excessive labor, exercised by minds capable of mighty efforts, and drawn forth under circumstances favorable to their development. When we look attentively at the record they have left us, or contemplate those of them whom God's mercy to us permits yet to linger with us, we perceive that they were not the uneducated ministers commonly supposed. It is true, as has been said, that they had not the learning of the schools. A few books of theology — perhaps a single commentary — formed, with their Bibles, their whole apparatus of instruction, and measured the extent of their reading. But of these books they were wont to make themselves masters. By a course of incessant study, accompanied by examinations of the word of God, they were so thoroughly imbued with the processes and results of the best thoughts of their authors that they became, for all practicable purposes, almost the same men. And if, by any course of training, substantially of the same kind, our theological schools can restore to us such a mass ministry as was then enjoyed, the days of our progress and prosperity will be realized to have but just begun; and we shall go forward, by the help of the Lord, to possess the whole land which lieth before us. If by any means to these can be added at least fivefold the number of those now educated in the regular course of theology, I doubt not but it will be felt that the most sanguine hopes they have ever excited will be more than fulfilled."

He now proceeds to inquire whether arrangements can actually be made for offering theological education to that great mass of ministers who have not been to college.

"I believe, gentlemen, that it can be done; and more than this, that in the attempt to do it we shall accomplish an abundantly greater work. Let us abandon the false principle which has so long controlled us, and adopt the one which God points out to us by his word and his providence, and from the very supplies God now gives to us may be wrought out precisely such a ministry. Those who have entered upon the work will be rendered fully capable to perform its duties, and numbers besides will be called forth to it who have heretofore been restrained by insurmountable obstacles."

The suggestions next offered, as to which seminary studies may be pursued by this great mass of students, need not be here introduced, since the more fully developed plans which a year or two later were wrought out, with his assistance, and introduced into the organization of the Southern Baptist Theological Seminary, will be given in our next chapter. He now proceeds to restate the benefits of the change he is advocating: —

"By the means proposed, the theological school will meet the wants of a large class of those who now enter the ministry without the advantages of such instruction, — a class equally with their more learned associates burning with earnest zeal for the glory of God and deep convictions of the value of immortal souls, one possessed of natural gifts capable, even with limited knowledge, of enchaining the attention, affecting the hearts, and enlightening the minds of many who surround them; a class composed, however, of those who, with few exceptions, soon find themselves exhausted of their materials, forced to repeat the same topics in the same way, and finally to aim at nothing but continuous exhortation, bearing constantly upon the same point, or, as is oftentimes the case, destitute of any point at all. In their present condition these ministers are of comparatively little value to the churches, having no capacity to feed them with the word of God, affording no attractions to bring a congregation to the house of God, and no power to set before them when gathered there such an exposition of the word of God as may, through the influences of his Spirit, awaken them to penitence, and lead to faith in the Lord Jesus Christ. What the same men might become, were they better instructed, is apparent from the results attained by men of the same previous education, who, possessed of more leisure, or of a greater natural taste for study, have so improved themselves as to occupy positions of greater respectability and usefulness.

"The class of men whose cause I now plead before you is, of all those which furnish material for our ministry, that which most needs the theological training I would ask for it. Every argument for theological schools bears directly in favor of its interests. Are such schools founded that our ministry may not be ignorant of the truth? Which class of that ministry is more ignorant than this? Is it the object of their endowment that such education may be cheapened? Who are generally in more straitened circumstances? Is it designed to produce an abundant, able, faithful, and practical ministry? Where are the materials more abundant? Whence, for the amount of labor expended, will come more copious harvests? So that it appears that whatever may be our obligations to other classes, or the advantages to be gained in their education, the mere statement of them impresses upon us our duty, and the yet greater advantages to be gained by the education of that class which should comprise two thirds at least of those who receive a theological education.

"The men who go from college walls untaught in theology have yet a training and an amount of knowledge of incalculable benefit. They can do something to make up their deficiencies. But what chance is there for these others? They know not how to begin to study. Let one of them take up the Scriptures, and he finds himself embarrassed in the midst of statements which the Church for centuries after the Apostles had not fully harmonized,— statements which constitute the facts of theology, from which, in like manner with other sciences, by processes of induction and comparison, the absolute truth must be established.

If to escape the difficulty he turns to a text-book of theology, he is puzzled at once by technicalities so easily understood by those better instructed that this technical character is totally unperceived. If he turns in this dilemma to our seminaries, he finds no encouragement to enter. A man of age, perhaps of family, he is called upon to spend years of study in the literary and scientific departments before he is allowed to suppose that he can profitably pursue theology. Straitened, perhaps, in his circumstances, and unwilling to partake of the bounty of others, he is told that he must study during a number of years, his expenses during which would probably exhaust fivefold his little store. With a mind capable of understanding and perceiving the truth, and of expressing judicious opinions upon any subject, the facts of which he comprehends, he is told that he must pass through a course of study, the chief value of which is to train the mind, and which will only benefit him by the amount of knowledge it will incidentally convey. I can readily imagine the despair with which that man would be filled who, impelled by a conviction that it is his duty to preach the Gospel, contemplates under these circumstances the provisions which the friends of an educated ministry have made for him. We know not how many affected by that sentiment are at this moment longing to enter upon preparation for a work which they feel God has intrusted only to those who, because of their knowledge of his word, have an essential element of aptness to teach. Be it yours, gentlemen, to reanimate their drooping hopes by opening up before them the means of attaining this qualification."

But he holds that great benefits will also follow in regard to college-bred men.

"The adoption of the true principle will not only tend, however, to secure for us this education in the masses, which we need, but will also increase fivefold the number of those who will receive a thorough theological education. It will do this by the change of policy to which it will lead in reference to another class of our candidates for the ministry.

"We have among us a number of men who have enjoyed all the advantages of college life, but who have not been able, or willing, to spend the additional years needed for theological study. These are possessed of far greater advantages than those of the other class, — men of polished education, of well-trained minds, capable of extensive usefulness to the cause of Christ; but their deficiencies are plainly apparent, and readily traceable to the lack of a theological education. They are educated men, but not educated ministers; for, while familiar with all the sciences which form parts of the college curriculum, they are ignorant for the most part of that very science which lies at the foundation of all their ministerial labors. The labors of their pastoral charges prevent such study of the word of God, either exegetically or systematically, as will enable them to become masters of its contents. Having entered upon the work of the ministry, however, they are forced to press forward, encountering difficulties at every step, — fearing to touch upon many doctrines of Scripture lest they misstate them, and frequently guilty of such misstatements even in the presentation of the simpler topics they attempt, because they fail to recognize the important connections which exist among all the truths of God. A few, indeed, possessed of giant minds, capable of the most accurate investigations, and filled with indomitable energy in the pursuit of what they feel to be needful, overcome every obstacle, and attain to knowledge often superior to that of others whose training has been more advantageous. But the vast majority find themselves burdened with a weight which they cannot remove, and by which they feel that their energies are almost destroyed. It is needless to say of these that the churches do not grow under their ministry; that, not having partaken of strong meat, they cannot impart it; and that their hearers pass on from Sabbath to Sabbath awakened, indeed, to practical duties, made in many respects efficient in co-operating with Christ's people, but not built up to this condition on their most holy faith, but upon other motives, which, however good, are really insufficient for the best progress, — at least of their own spiritual natures. Such is not the position in the ministry which four-fifths of our educated men should occupy. They will tell you themselves, gentlemen, that this should not be the case. If due to their own precipitancy, they will attach blame to themselves; but if it result from the exclusiveness of theological schools, their declaration is equivalent to testimony in favor of its removal, and of the admission of all who are capable of pursuing the regular course to participate in its advantages. The disturbances felt about unsettled doctrines, the inability experienced to declare the whole counsel of God, the doctrinal mistakes realized as frequently committed, have long since convinced them that all of their other education is of but little value compared with that knowledge of theology which they have lost in its acquisition.

"The theory of the theological school should doubtless be to urge upon every one to take full courses in both departments; but when this is not possible, it should give to those who are forced to select between them, the opportunity of omitting the collegiate, and entering at once upon the theological, course. I see not how any one can rationally question that many, if not all, of those who are fitted for the Sophomore, or even the Freshman, class in college are prepared, so far as knowledge of books or languages is concerned, to enter with very great, though not with the utmost, profit upon the study of theology. The amount of Greek and Latin acquired is ample for this purpose. The study of Hebrew and Chaldee is commenced in the theological course; while that which is really the main object for the younger men in the collegiate course, the training and forming of the mind so far as at all practicable, will for the older students have been already accomplished, or for them and for the younger ones may be compensated in great part by that more thorough training in the studies of the Seminary necessary to all who would acquire such knowledge of theology as will make them fully acquainted with its truths."

The views of the last paragraph and of that which follows would not be acceptable to some college presidents and professors, and are not a necessary part of Dr. Boyce's general scheme. Perhaps the best practical course would be that seminary professors and students should never encourage college men — save in highly exceptional cases — to break off their college course and enter the seminary; and that college professors and students should not treat it as an unpardonable sin if some college men do quit college to enter a theological school at once. After all, the students must be treated as free; and their own instinctive judgments, after proper counsel, will oftener lead them right than wrong.

"Since this is the case, why compel this class to spend their time in studies which, however valuable in themselves, have but a secondary importance, compared with those they are made to supersede? If there be any who will pursue the studies of both departments, their number will never be diminished by the adoption of the plan proposed. If it will, better that this be so than that so many others neglect theology. But we may confidently believe that the results will only be to take from the collegiate course those who would neglect the other, and cause them to spend the same number of years in the study of that which has an immediate bearing upon their work. It is simply a choice as to certain men between a thorough literary and a thorough theological course. The former may make a man more refined and intelligent, better able to sustain a position of influence with the world, and more capable of illustrating, by a wide range of science, the truth he may have arrived at; the latter will improve his Christian graces, will impart to him the whole range of revealed truth, will make him the instructor of his people, truly the man of God prepared in all things to give to each one his portion in due season."

He now concludes his discussion of the first change proposed, by insisting that it will involve no radical alterations in the working of a theological school, and that it will promote just views of ministerial education.

"The same course of Systematic Theology will be sufficient for all classes, the advantages possessed by those more highly educated enabling them simply to add to the text-book or lectures the examination of Turrettin or some other prescribed author. In the study of Scripture Interpretation, it may be necessary to make two divisions, though experience will probably prove the practicability even of uniting these. There will be needed for all classes the same instruction in the Evidences of Christianity, in Pastoral Theology, in the analysis of texts, the construction of skeletons, and the composition of essays and sermons; and in all of these the classes may be united. So that, really, we shall only so far revolutionize the institution as to add numbers to the classes, and permit some of those whom we add to take up those studies only which a plain English education will enable them to pursue profitably. All the inconvenience which may accrue therefrom will be gladly endured by all for the benefit of the masses, and because of the mutual love and esteem which, by their throwing together, will be fostered between the most highly educated and the plainest of our ministry.

"In adopting this change we are so far from saying that education is unnecessary that we proclaim its absolute necessity. We undertake, however, to point out what education it is that is thus essential, and what that which is only valuable; and while we urge upon all to acquire all useful knowledge as an aid to that work, we point out the knowledge of the word of God as that which is first in importance, and we provide the means by which this second class may pursue its appropriate studies, and those by which adequate theological instruction may be given to the four-fifths of our ministry who now enjoy no means of instruction. And we look with confidence for the blessing of God upon this plan, not because we believe that he favors an ignorant ministry, but because, knowing that he requires that his ministry be instructed, and that by his word and his providence he has pointed out the nature of the learning he demands, we believe that the plan proposed is based upon these indications; and that his refusal to send forth laborers has been chastisement inflicted upon us that we may be brought back to his own plans, which we have abandoned for those of men."

The second change which Professor Boyce suggests is that after completing the usual course of theological study, some students should be encouraged to remain for further graduate studies. A proper provision for such graduate studies would tend to promote theological scholarship in our country.

"It has been felt as a sore evil that we have been dependent in great part upon the criticism of Germany for all the more learned investigations in Biblical Criticism and Exegesis, and that in the study of the development of the doctrine of the Church, as well as of its outward progress, we have been compelled to depend upon works in which much of error has been mingled with truth, owing to the defective standpoint occupied by their authors.

"And although the disadvantages of American scholars have

been realized, arising from the want of adequate theological libraries, as well as from the inaccessible nature of much other material, it has been felt that it has been in great part due to the limited extent to which the study of theological science has been pursued among us, that we have been so much dependent upon others, so unable to push forward investigations for ourselves, and even so inadequately acquainted with the valuable results of others who have accomplished the work for us. But a few perhaps have participated in this sentiment, but the evil which awakens it is not, therefore, the less momentous."

In this matter Baptists ought to feel themselves specially concerned.

"It is an evil which may be regarded as pervading the whole field of American religious scholarship, and the remedy should be sought alike by all denominations. It is a matter of the deepest interest to all that we should be placed in a position of independence in this matter, and that our rising ministry should be trained under the scholarship of the Anglo-Saxon mind, which, from its nature, as well as from the circumstances which surround it, is eminently fitted to weigh evidence, and to decide as to its appropriateness and its proper limitations. But the obligation resting on the Baptist denomination is far higher than this. It extends not merely to matters of detail, but to those of vital interest. The history of religious literature and of Christian scholarship has been a history of Baptist wrongs. We have been overlooked, ridiculed, and defamed. Critics have committed the grossest perversions, violated the plainest rules of criticism, and omitted points which could not have been developed without benefit to us. Historians who have professed to write the history of the Church have either utterly ignored the presence of those of our faith, or classed them among fanatics and heretics; or, if forced to acknowledge the prevalence of our principles and practice among the earliest churches, have adopted such false theories as to church power, and the development and growth of the truth and principles of Scripture, that by all, save their most discerning readers, our pretensions to an early origin and a continuous existence have been rejected.

"'The Baptists in the past have been entirely too indifferent to the position they thus occupy. They have depended too much upon the known strength of their principles, and the ease with which from Scripture they could defend them. They have therefore neglected many of those means which extensive learning affords, and which have been used to great advantage in support of other opinions. It is needless to say, gentlemen, that we can no longer consent to occupy this position. We owe a change to ourselves, — as Christians, bound to show an adequate reason for the differences between us and others; as men of even moderate scholarship, that it may appear that we have not made the gross errors in philology and criticism which we must have made if we be not right; as the successors of a glorious spiritual ancestry, illustrated by heroic martyrdom, by the profession of noble principles, by the maintenance of true doctrines; as the Church of Christ, which he has ever preserved as the witness for his truth, by which he has illustrated his wonderful ways, and shown that his promises are sure and steadfast. Nay, we owe it to Christ himself, whose truth we hold so distinctively as to separate us from all others of his believing people; to whom we look confidently to make these principles triumphant; for whose sake, on their account, men have been ever found among us willing to submit to banishment, imprisonment, or martyrdom; and for whose sake, in defence of the same truth, we are willing now to bear the scorn and reproach, not of the world only, but even of those who love our Lord Jesus Christ."

He proceeds to inquire how this object can be accomplished: —

"It is scarcely necessary to remark that any plan which can be devised must be based upon the presence in the institution of a good theological library, — one which shall not only be filled with the gathered lore of the past, but also endowed with the means of annual increase. Without this, no institution can pursue extensive courses of study, or contribute anything directly to the advancement of learning. The professor is cut off from valuable and necessary books, and the student hindered from making even the least important investigations in the course of study he is pursuing.

"The plan I propose to you supposes the possession of such a library; and this, even if it be such, is its only peculiar item of expense. Taking the idea from the provision made in some of our institutions for the degree of Master of Arts, it has occurred to me that an additional course of study might be provided for those who may be graduates of theological institutions. This course might extend over one or two years, according to the amount of study the student may propose to accomplish. In it the study of the Oriental languages might be extended to the Arabic and the Syriac. The writing of exegetical theses would furnish subjects for investigation, and give a more ample acquaintance with the original text and with the laws of its interpretation. The text-books or lectures studied in Systematic and Polemic Theology could be compared with kindred books, the theories of opponents examined in their own writings, and notes taken for future use from rare and costly books. These and similar studies, which should be laid down in a well-digested course, would bestow accurate scholarship, train the student in the methods of original investigation, give him confidence in the results previously attained, and open to him resources from which he might draw extensively in interpreting the Scriptures, and in setting forth the truths they contain. The result would be that a band of scholars would go forth, from almost every one of whom we might expect valuable contributions to our theological literature.

"It is to be expected that but few would take advantage of this course. Such would certainly be the case at first. The only result would be that but little additional provision will be needed. Two additional recitations a week for each of three or four professors would be more than adequate. And though such students should not be more than a twentieth part of those graduated, though not more than one each year, will not their value to the denomination more than counterbalance the little additional attention which will thus be given?"

It is then further shown that these arrangements would help to train missionaries, such as may wish to translate the Scriptures into heathen languages, or to encounter learned and able teachers, heathen or Mohammedan. This would also give special training of various kinds to men suited to become professors in our colleges, seminaries, etc.

The third change, proposed by this address, to be made in theological institutions was that a "declaration of doctrine" should be adopted, which persons assuming professorships should be required to sign, pledging themselves to teach in accordance with, and not contrary to, the doctrines thus laid down. It is urged as very desirable that every particular church among us should have some statement of doctrine in which its members may be instructed. It is shown to be still more important to examine carefully the men about to be ordained as ministers, in order to see whether they are sound in the faith,— a duty generally recognized among us, and more or less faithfully performed by churches and ordaining presbyteries. And then it is argued, *a fortiori*, that above all we ought to ascertain and guard the doctrinal soundness of a theological instructor.

"But the theological professor is to teach ministers, — to place the truth, and all the errors connected with it, in such a manner before his pupils that they shall arrive at the truth without danger of any mixture of error therewith. He cannot do this if he have any erroneous tendencies, and hence his opinions must be expressly affirmed to be, upon every point, in accordance with the truth we believe to be taught in the Scriptures."

This point is strongly set forth and strikingly illustrated, as follows: —

"It is with a single man that error usually commences; and when such a man has influence or position, it is impossible to estimate the evil that will attend it. Ecclesiastical history is full of warning upon this subject. Scarcely a single heresy has ever blighted the Church which has not owed its existence or its development to that one man of power and ability whose name has always been associated with its doctrines. And yet, seldom has an opinion been thus advanced which has not subsequently had its advocate in every age, and which in some ages has not extensively prevailed.

"The history of our own denomination in this country furnishes an illustration. Playing upon the prejudices of the weak and ignorant among our people, decrying creeds as an infringement upon the rights of conscience, making a deep impression by his extensive learning and great abilities, Alexander Campbell threatened at one time the total destruction of our faith. Had he occupied a chair in one of our theological institutions, that destruction might have been completed. There would have been time to disseminate widely and fix deeply his principles, before it became necessary to avow them publicly; and when this necessity arrived, it would have been attended by the support of the vast majority of our best educated ministers. Who can estimate the evil which would then have ensued?

"The danger which threatened in this instance may assail us again. Another such, and yet another, may arise, and, favored by better circumstances, may instil false principles into the minds of his pupils, and, sending them forth to occupy the prominent pulpits of the land, may influence all our churches, and the fair fabric of our faith may be entirely demolished.

"This it is that should make us tremble when we think of our theological institutions. If there be any instrument of our denominational prosperity which we should guard at every point, it is this. The doctrinal sentiments of the Faculty are of far greater importance than the proper investment and expenditure of its funds; and the trusts devolved upon those who watch over its interests should in that respect, if in any, be sacredly guarded."

He thus concludes as to the third proposed change: —

"It is therefore, gentlemen, in perfect consistency with the position of Baptists, as well as of Bible Christians, that the test of doctrine I have suggested to you should be adopted. It is based upon principles and practices sanctioned by the authority of Scripture and by the usage of our people. In so doing, you will be acting simply in accordance with propriety and righteousness. You will infringe the rights of no man, and you will secure the rights of those who have established here an instrumentality for the production of a sound ministry. It is no hardship to those who teach here to be called upon to sign the declaration of their principles; for there are fields of usefulness open elsewhere to every man, and none need accept your call who cannot conscientiously sign your formulary. And while all this is true, you will receive by this an assurance that the trust committed to you by the founders is fulfilling in accordance with their wishes, that the ministry that go forth have here learned to distinguish truth from error, and to embrace the former, and that the same precious truths of the Bible which were so dear to the hearts of its founders, and which I trust are equally dear to yours, will be propagated in our churches, giving to them vigor and strength, and causing them to flourish by the godly sentiments and emotions they will awaken within them. May God impress you deeply with the responsibility under which you must act in reference to it!"

Among the closing paragraphs of the address, the following ought assuredly to be quoted. We have seen that B. Manly, Jr., had made similar suggestions in his address at Charleston; and experience goes to show that the point in question is of very great importance.

"It will be perceived that the great peculiarity of the plans proposed is that they contemplate gathering all our students into a single institution. The courses of study are all to be pursued conjointly. The several classes of young men are to be thrown together in the pursuit of their respective studies. It is for this, as opposed to any other method, that I would strenuously contend. The object is not the centralization of power in a single institution, for I believe the adoption of these changes will make many seminaries necessary. I advocate a single one now, because the demand for more than one does not exist. But it is that our young men may be brought into closer contact with each other. Various prejudices are arising in our denomination among the various classes of the ministry. This would be my scheme to remove them. The young men should be so mingled together as to cause each class to recognize the value of the others, and thus truly to break down entirely any classification. Those who take the plain English course will see the value of learning in the increased facilities for study it affords to their more favored companions. Those who have this learning will see that many of the other class are their superiors in piety, in devotion to God, in readiness to sacrifice for his cause, in willingness to be counted as nothing, so that Christ may be preached. The recognition of such facts will be mutually beneficial. The less-educated ministers will feel that they have the confidence and affection of all their brethren; the better-educated will know the esteem with which they are regarded; and the bonds of mutual love will yearly grow stronger, until we shall see a ministry of different gifts, possessed of extensive attainments, thrown into entirely different positions in the field, yet laboring conjointly, mutually aiding and supporting one another in advancing the kingdom of Christ, in preaching his glorious gospel, in calling forth laborers into his field, and in fostering those influences which shall tend to the education of a sound and practical and able ministry."

This address by Professor Boyce proved to be epoch-making in the history of theological education among Southern Baptists. He was accustomed to say, in conversation on the subject, that his ideas had been partly derived from his revered instructor, President Wayland, of Brown University, to whom we have seen that he always felt himself in many ways very greatly indebted. Besides the general effect of his lectures and conversations upon the quite similarly constituted mind of young Boyce when a student, President Wayland had, three years before the delivery of Boyce's inaugural, given a notable address at the University of Rochester, by request of the New York Baptist Union for Ministerial Education, entitled, "The Apostolic Ministry." In this he had shown that our strong denominational belief in a divine call to the ministry ought to have an important bearing upon our methods of ministerial education.

"If we are willing to follow, and not to lead, the Spirit of God, — that is, if we educate no man for the ministry until we are satisfied, not that he *may be*, but that he *has been*, called of God to the work of preaching the Gospel, — we shall always have among our candidates a large number of those who have passed the period of youth, and for whom the studies of youth would be unsuitable, if not useless. Yet these are the very men to whom appropriate culture would be specially valuable. Others, in various degrees, have been more favored with preparatory education, and the means for more extended discipline. The means and advantages of our candidates must therefore be exceedingly dissimilar. If, then, we would labor to give to the ministry the means of improvement, we must provide those means for them all. A system of ministerial education adapted to the condition of but one in twenty of our candidates, commences with the avowed intention of doing but one-twentieth part of its work, and of helping those only who have the least need of its assistance. We should therefore provide, for all our brethren whom God has called to this service, the best instruction in our power; adapted, as far as possible, not to any theoretical view, but to the actual condition of the mass of our candidates, leaving each individual, in the exercise of a sound and pious discretion, to determine the extent to which he is able to avail himself of our services. While means should be fully provided for pursuing an extended course of education, we must never lose sight of the large number of our brethren to whom an extended course would be impossible."

These views of Dr. Wayland excited at the time considerable newspaper discussion on the part of educators, the discourse being printed in tract form and widely circulated. They probably had some effect upon the existing Baptist Theological Schools, in making them less unwilling to receive students for a partial course. But our Baptist Colleges and Theological Seminaries in America had followed very closely the Congregational and Presbyterian pattern, built upon ideas brought from England and Scotland; and any departure from the curriculum, and introduction of men imperfectly prepared, to pursue an irregular course, was generally regarded with disfavor on the part of presidents and professors. Dr. Wayland had several years earlier made an earnest effort to introduce different ideas and methods, through the re-organization, in 1850, of Brown University. He travelled over the United States, visiting many universities and colleges, and finally succeeded in introducing at Brown a thoroughly elective method, quite similar to that which for twenty-five years had been in successful operation at the University of Virginia.[1] We have seen that he recognized in "The Apostolic Ministry" the propriety of allowing a theological student to exercise some discretion as to the extent of his theological studies. In a famous series of articles published in "The Examiner," and collected into a volume in October, 1856, entitled "Principles and Practices of Baptist Churches," he speaks sarcastically about the existing theological seminaries: —

"If, however, a suggestion in respect to them might be made without presumption, I would ask, could they not be rendered more efficient? By the tables already referred to, they graduate annually about one student and a half to each officer of instruction. Could not this proportion be somewhat exceeded? The labor of teaching such classes cannot be oppressive; might not other courses, adapted to other classes of students, be introduced? So long as our seminaries admit none but those who have pursued a collegiate course or its equivalent, their number of students must be small, and the labor of instructors not burdensome. . . . If it might be done without offence, I would ask, might not more direct effort be exerted to make *preachers*? — I say preachers, in distinction from philologists, translators, professors, teachers, and writers on theology. Other professional schools aim to render men able in the *practice* of their several professions. . . . Why should not the theological school aim more simply at making good and effective preachers? Men need instruction and practice

---

[1] The writer remembers the feeling of denominational pride with which, as a student of the University of Virginia, he was introduced to the famous president and author, and gazed upon his commanding form and noble face while he sat in a lecture-room. Dr. Gessner Harrison and Dr. McGuffey explained to Dr. Wayland, in extended conversations, sought by him, the nature and working of Mr. Jefferson's plans of elective education.

in the every-day duties of the ministry. They should acquire the power — and it is a great power — of unwritten, earnest, effective speech."

He expressed gratification that in Newton particularly arrangements were now made for the especial improvement of theological students who have not passed through a collegiate course.

While Dr. Wayland's ideas were in general rejected, we thus perceive that they had some effect; and through the years that have followed, professors in various Baptist Theological Schools have earnestly striven to do their best for the less-prepared students. They have been embarrassed in this by the fact that all their work rested on the basis of a curriculum; but, whether cheerfully or reluctantly, they have labored in this direction. The recent exclusion from the Rochester Theological Seminary of all who have not been prepared by a college course or its equivalent; the arrangement in the Newton Theological Institution by which less-prepared students are entirely separated from the others, and taught in separate classes; and various other indications, — show that our able and honored Baptist brethren engaged in theological education have deeply felt the difficulty of admitting irregulars upon the basis of a curriculum. And yet the ideas set forth by Dr. Wayland have not ceased to live among thoughtful Baptists of the great North and Northwest. Indeed, he and Professor Boyce were but interpreting the fundamental Baptist ideas of the ministry. And wherever Baptists have striven to *confine* their ministry to men regularly trained in college and seminary, they are still comparatively limited in numbers; while, on the contrary, wherever they have encouraged every man to preach who felt called of God to preach, whom his church indorsed as suitable, and a presbytery as sound, and whom the people were willing to hear, — there the Baptists have grown rapidly, and are a people mighty, at least in numbers, and great in their possible future. No one need be surprised if among our Northern brethren there should come any year a new utterance of ideas like those of Dr. Wayland, and new plans for getting hold in some way of the many ministers who cannot — or (what is for independent Baptists equivalent) will not — go through a regular course at college and seminary.

Some Baptist educators in the Southern States were in like manner wedded to the idea of restricting our exertions to the thorough training of well-prepared men; but in general the history of Baptist progress in the South and Southwest — the vast number of "self-educated" or "uneducated" ministers who had been very useful, together with the spirit of local independence which pervades great agricultural regions, and the disposition of Southern natures to delight much in the oratorical fervor which may be manifested without high mental training — led many thoughtful men among Southern Baptists, in the ministry and out of it, to see the wisdom of Boyce's ideas. Moreover, these ideas were embodied in a representative qualified in an extraordinary manner — by gifts and character, by training and personal influence, by youthful vigor, combined with practical wisdom — to carry these ideas into effect. A long struggle was before him, which if foreseen might well have been deemed hopeless. But we can now perceive that in him, and the older and younger men of whom he would become the leader, and in the situation and aspirations of Southern Baptists, there existed the elements of success.

We return now to the proposition — which, at the suggestion of Professor Boyce, had been made by the South Carolina Baptist State Convention, and directed to be laid before the proposed convention in Louisville in the following May — that the South Carolina Baptists would give one hundred thousand dollars for the endowment of a common theological institution at Greenville (incorporating therein the theological department of Furman University), provided that an additional hundred thousand should be raised elsewhere.

The Educational Convention held in Louisville, May, 1857, in connection with the sessions of the Southern Baptist Convention, included eighty-eight delegates, from Maryland, Virginia, and the Carolinas, from Georgia and Alabama, from Mississippi, Louisiana, and Arkansas, from Tennessee and Kentucky. Much interest was excited by the fact that a definite and generous proposition had been made by the South Carolina brethren, together with the assurances of Professor Boyce and others that the money needed from that State could be raised. A great desire was felt to push the now hopeful movement into practical operation as speedily as possible. After much earnest discussion, it was agreed to propose the establishment of the desired theological institution at Greenville, S. C., in the following year, provided that the sum of one hundred thousand dollars should be raised in that State by May 1, 1858, ready to be placed in the hands of trustees. The interest of this money (seven thousand) was to be used for the support of three professors, for the purchase of books (not exceeding five hundred dollars annually), and for paying a proper agency in the other States to secure the hundred thousand dollars which was to be raised elsewhere; provided, also, that recitation and lecture rooms could be secured in Greenville free of rent for some years. It was further arranged that if the remaining hundred thousand should not be made up within three years, then the endowment furnished from South Carolina should revert to the Furman University, for theological purposes, and the contributions collected elsewhere to their respective donors. These arrangements show Boyce's hand throughout. They were bold and inspiring, and yet carefully guarded. It was then proposed that a special educational convention should be held at Greenville in

May, 1858, to organize the desired institution, provided the South Carolina Baptist Convention should accept these conditions. Committees of five were appointed to prepare a plan of organization, to nominate professors, to secure from the South Carolina Legislature an appropriate charter, to provide for a suitable agency in other States, and to issue an address to Southern Baptists. In announcing the Committee on Plan of Organization, the President, Dr. B. Manly, Sr., said apologetically that he had appointed comparatively young men, because it was proposed to form a new institution suited to the wants of our own ministry, and young men were more likely to be successful in devising new plans. So he announced J. P. Boyce, J. A. Broadus, B. Manly, Jr., E. T. Winkler, William Williams. This is worth mentioning because, as will hereafter appear, these five were destined to be elected as professors in the Seminary, and four of them to serve. Probably the wise old heads of the Convention had their plans already; but certainly one member of the committee had no thought of such a thing.

Dr. Jeter prepared a ringing address to Southern Baptists. He showed that a common institution was demanded, and brethren had for a number of years been earnestly striving to compass its establishment. The scheme now proposed was feasible, having been unanimously approved by a body "which commenced its session with very conflicting views." It was also eminently promising, for Greenville would be a very desirable location, as to accessibility, health, and cheapness of living. He stated that the Seminary was to be organized upon a new plan: —

"Being free from the shackles imposed by the old systems and established precedents, and having all the lights of experience and observation to guide us, we propose to found an institution suited to the genius, wants, and circumstances of our denomination; in which shall be taught with special attention the true principles of expounding the Scriptures and the art of preaching efficiently the Gospel of Christ."

He guarded a point on which some natural apprehension was felt: —

"This scheme will interfere with no existing institution. It does not propose to curtail the labors or influence of any of our State colleges. Some of them will probably continue to give, as they have heretofore done, a limited course of theological instruction, and those who find it desirable will avail themselves of its benefits. But it is proposed in the Greenville institution to furnish a more thorough course of instruction than any as yet adopted in our State seminaries; and also perhaps a more limited course for those students whose age and circumstances will not permit them to pursue an extended course. . . . On the whole, we cannot but think that the divine hand has guided us thus far. Obstacles seemingly insuperable have been removed out of the way, conflicting opinions and interests have been harmonized, and a bright and cheering prospect of success has suddenly opened before us. It only remains that we should trustfully follow the divine guidance."

In July the State Convention of the Baptist denomination in South Carolina adopted the Louisville modification of their proposal, and appointed Rev. J. P. Boyce as agent to collect the needed $70,000. He tendered his resignation as professor in the University, but the Trustees declined to accept, and authorized him to act according to his own judgment in regard to the agency work during the coming year. He probably had very little time for teaching in the course of the next session. We know that in his two-horse buggy, driven by a servant, he travelled far and wide over South Carolina, visiting out-of-the-way churches, and planters on remote plantations, and throwing all the energies and resources of his being into what was then and there a very large and difficult undertaking. It was no doubt often with a sense of heavy sacrifice that the young husband and father left the bright home he loved so well, with the already rich store of choice books in which he so delighted, for these laborious and not always successful journeys. He no doubt cheered himself with the thought that all this would be only for part of one year. If he had foreseen that after a season of great and ruinous calamities he would have to spend a considerable part of every year in like absences for the Seminary's sake, to wear himself out for it, with all manner of heavy sacrifices, one does not know whether even that strong and brave young heart could have faced the life-long task. Our ignorance of the future is often, under the leadings of God's providence, a necessary condition of our worthiest undertakings and largest successes.

In August, 1857, Professor Boyce called a meeting in Richmond, Va., of the committee on the Plan of Organization of the proposed Seminary. He had requested B. Manly, Jr., to draw up an abstract of doctrinal principles, to be signed by each professor; had undertaken himself to devise the legal and practical arrangements in regard to trustees and professors; and had requested J. A. Broadus to prepare the outline of a plan of instruction. The last-mentioned had suggested at Louisville that the "changes" proposed in Boyce's address, especially the apparently difficult matter of uniting all grades of theological students in the same institution, could be effected through a plan adapted from that of the University of Virginia, with which he was familiar. The other two members of the committee did not come. We met in Richmond, at the residence of Manly, who was Principal of the Richmond Female Institute, and discussed together the portions which each had provisionally drawn up. Through their experience as students at Newton and Princeton, Boyce and Manly were able to make valuable emendations of the plan of elective education for a theological school, which after much study of theological catalogues had been drawn in substantial imitation of the method pursued in the great University, — by that time nearing the height of its distinction, having as many students as were then found at Harvard or Yale, and sending its graduates to be professors in colleges and universities all over the South.

It was a great pleasure, during those days of earnest conference, to enter into intimate acquaintance with the young professor, to recognize his energy and wisdom, his courtesy and delicacy, his broad views of every question, his eager desire to make this institution a success beyond all precedent, his true-hearted devotion to the cause of Christ.

The last in this long series of educational conventions for the purpose of establishing a common theological seminary was held in Greenville, S. C., May 1st, 1858. It was a time of general revival throughout the South, and many pastors were on that account kept from carrying out their known purpose of attending the convention. But Dr. G. W. Samson was there from Washington, who had attended two or three previous conventions for this purpose, and had manifested the greatest interest in the enterprise. Drs. Jeter and Poindexter and four others were present from Virginia, with two from North Carolina, one from Louisiana, one from Georgia (Professor William Williams of Mercer University), and thirty-three from different bodies in South Carolina.

The object of this convention was to adopt a plan of organization for the Seminary, to elect professors, and provide for its going into operation the following autumn. The plan of organization proposed by the committee was carefully discussed, at many points, by a committee for the purpose, and by the whole convention. Drs. Poindexter and Samson were particularly earnest, various others also taking part, in discussing the Abstract of Principles; and Dr. Samson remembers the special interest that was taken in the article about the Doctrine of Imputation, which nine years before had been discussed in two long series of articles in the "Southern Baptist," when young Boyce was its editor. Some brethren in the convention had their doubts about the wisdom of arranging no curriculum, but a number of distinct departments, or schools, in each of which a separate diploma or certificate of proficiency should be given. But Boyce had heartily accepted a plan which promised to make it easy for students of every grade of preparation to study together in the same institution, and for the most part in the same classes; and many others cheerfully accepted the scheme. The final vote as to every part of the organization is believed to have been unanimous; but the discussions had been so free and full as to occupy five days.

Instead of three professors, as had been suggested at Louisville, Boyce boldly proposed the appointment of four professors. He had obtained nearly all of the requisite $70,000, and was sure of the rest in a few weeks. Part had been paid in cash, and the remainder was held in bonds bearing seven per cent interest. He felt confident that special contributions for income could be had, if necessary; and his boldness in planning was upheld by the fact — one not very common in the case of young ministers founding institutions — that he had a large private income. He had made arrangements for securing, without rent, the recently vacated house of worship of the Greenville Baptist Church, which was just then entering its new and beautiful building. This small but well-built house could be adapted with little cost to use for lecture-rooms and library. He stated it as his opinion that the Seminary ought to abstain from spending money upon buildings until it should first have secured an ample endowment for support of the instruction. In hearty approval of this idea, an expression was thrown out by one of the speakers, which was repeated years afterwards in

New York, and has spread all over the country. Rev. Thomas Curtis, D.D., a member of the convention, and Principal of the Limestone (S. C.) Female Institute, was an Englishman, a man of commanding appearance and abilities. He said, with sonorous English tones and rolling *r*'s, "The requisites for an institution of learning are three *b*'s, — bricks, books, brains. Our brethren usually begin at the wrong end of the three *b*'s; they spend all their money for bricks, have nothing to buy books, and must take such brains as they can pick up. But our brethren ought to begin at the other end of the three *b*'s."

Seven years later, when the question was of undertaking to carry on the Seminary after the war, with the endowment lost, and in a land swept as by a cyclone, it was remembered with special gratitude that Boyce's plan had been adopted in regard to buildings; for even a few thousand dollars of debt would then have sunk the enterprise beyond redemption.

Hon. A. B. Woodruff remembers that during the discussions Boyce once spoke, according to his plans and hopes, of "the great Southern Baptist Theological Seminary." Dr. Basil Manly, Sr., who was presiding, checked him, — "Don't say *great* until you succeed in your work of endowment. When you have your Seminary safely endowed, I don't care if you write 'great' with a pencil as long as a streak of lightning; but don't say it yet."

Upon nomination by a committee of leading men, the convention unanimously elected four professors, — J. P. Boyce, J. A. Broadus, B. Manly, Jr., E. T. Winkler. It has been often said that but for the presence of William Williams upon the nominating committee (he being the only delegate present from Georgia), he would have been nominated and elected. However that may be, Winkler would have filled with great ability the chair of Church History, and of Church Government and Pastoral Duties, as Williams afterwards did.

But Winkler promptly declined the election. Another one of those elected carried the matter home as a great burden, because Poindexter and others were pressing it upon him, and, after weeks of anxious consideration, felt bound to decline also. As only Boyce and Manly had accepted, it was thought best to delay for another year the opening of the Seminary. The income could thus be used for more extensive and efficient agency in collecting the hundred thousand dollars from other States. The Board of Trustees, which the Convention had appointed, was to hold its first meeting in connection with the Southern Baptist Convention at Richmond, in May, 1859, and could then fill the vacant chairs. Boyce had placed it among the fundamental and unalterable regulations of the Seminary that a professor should not be elected except at a regular annual meeting of the Board. So it was hoped that by a year's delay the Seminary might open in a satisfactory condition. When the Board met at Richmond they re-elected Broadus and Winkler; as the latter again declined, they elected William Williams. Few, if any, theological seminaries in the United States had at that time more than four professors. Boyce reported the finances as in a very hopeful condition; and the Seminary seemed likely to open, the following autumn, with good prospects.

CHAPTER X.

THE SEMINARY'S PLAN OF INSTRUCTION

WE have seen that the Southern Baptist Theological Seminary was organized with the avowed view of giving theological instruction to young ministers in every grade of general education. Men thoroughly prepared by college studies or their equivalent were to have as extensive and thorough a theological course as could be found elsewhere. Men who were entering the ministry with only a partial college training, or without having attended college at all, were to have an opportunity of carefully studying the English Scriptures, and all the other branches of theology for which they were prepared. Men who could attend the Seminary only a single year must be welcomed to such theological studies as would give them the best practical training for their work. It was thought to be highly important that all these grades of students should live together in the same institution, and, so far as possible, study together in the same classes, seeing that this would tend to prevent invidious distinctions in the ministry, would promote mutual appreciation, and prepare for an intelligent and cordial co-operation. But the question was, how could all this be effected? To establish a curriculum suited to college graduates, and then to carry along in the same institution a number of men who knew no Greek or Latin, probably no psychology or logic, some of them having only the plainest English education, would obviously be a surpassingly difficult task; and the experiments which had been tried in one or two Baptist theological schools were understood to be hardly encouraging. Thoughtful men who had read President Wayland's address on "The Apostolic Ministry," and who now found Professor Boyce's address on "Three Changes in Theological Institutions," setting forth more fully and forcibly the need of some such arrangement, and earnestly asserting that surely the thing could somehow be managed, were asking each other the question, in correspondence and conversation, how can it be done? How can we prevent the less thoroughly prepared students, and the men designing only a single session's work, from feeling themselves to be placed in an inferior position, from being discouraged rather than stimulated, by their proximity to the regular students in the regular course? How save the men pursuing their curriculum from being hindered and embarrassed by the presence of these others, especially if reciting in the same classes?

The attempt was made to solve all these real difficulties by a thoroughly elective system, patterned after that which had for thirty years been in highly successful operation at the University of Virginia. The term "elective" has of late years become common in many universities and colleges, and some theological schools, to denote studies, not all required as part of the curriculum, but a certain number of which may be chosen by each student, in addition to those required, so as to make out his complete course. But something very different is meant when we say that all the studies of this Theological Seminary were to be elective. One who really cares to understand the plan upon which this institution was organized, and upon which it has ever since been consistently carried on, must lay aside all other conceptions of elective studies, and look a moment at the elective method here in question.

It was arranged that the Seminary should comprise eight distinct, and in a sense independent, departments of instruction, or schools, namely: —

THE SEMINARY'S PLAN OF INSTRUCTION. 157

I. Biblical Introduction. In this school would be taught the Canon of Scripture and Inspiration, with Biblical Geography and Antiquities, etc.

II. Interpretation of the Old Testament. Here there would be two classes, — (1) The Interpretation of the Old Testament in English ; (2) Hebrew and Chaldee, and Hebrew Exegesis. It was added that other Oriental languages, as Arabic, Syriac, etc., might also be taught.

III. Interpretation of the New Testament. (1) Interpretation of the New Testament in English. (2) New Testament Greek, and Greek Exegesis.

IV. Systematic Theology. (1) A general course, in which the instruction should not presuppose any acquaintance with the learned languages. (2) A special and more erudite course, in which there might be read theological works in the Latin, etc.

V. Polemic Theology and Apologetics.

VI. Homiletics, or Preparation and Delivery of Sermons.

VII. Church History.

VIII. Church Government and Pastoral Duties.

"In each of these schools a separate diploma shall be given to those students who exhibit, upon due examination, a satisfactory acquaintance with the studies of that school. In those schools which comprise two classes, a general and a special course, the diploma shall require a competent knowledge of both; while to those whose attainments extend only to a general or English course, there shall be awarded a Certificate of Proficiency."

From this it will appear that the English classes, in the Bible and in Systematic Theology, were not at all designed as a makeshift for persons who could not pursue a more thorough course. The diploma in any such school must cover both the general and the special course. The study of the Hebrew and Greek Scriptures would not constitute the regular and sufficient course, for which some study of the English Scriptures might be substituted by men having no acquaintance with Hebrew or Greek; but the study of the English Scriptures was recommended to all students, and required of those who pursued Hebrew and

Greek Exegesis also, if they desired the Diploma in Old Testament or in New Testament, or the General Diploma of the Seminary, which was to be given to those who had obtained diplomas in all the separate schools.

It was left entirely free for any student, if he chose, to study in only the Hebrew or the Greek class, omitting the English; though in that case no diploma would be given. In point of fact, not one student in a hundred of those entering the Seminary through its whole history has failed to enter the classes for study of the English Bible; and no one has ever thought of studying the more erudite course in Systematic Theology, without also taking the general or English course. The Seminary's classes in the English Bible have proved to be one of its most marked features. The course runs over the entire Old Testament or New Testament history, locating the Prophets, etc., and the Epistles, where they most probably belong in chronological relation to the history, dividing the history into periods, analyzing each book into its natural divisions, studying a book as a whole, and a group of books in their relation to each other, and taking in general such broad views of Scripture as are not possible for those who have in hand only the partially known Hebrew or Greek. At the same time as much exercise as possible is given in the careful exegesis of particular passages and of entire books. As the students in the Hebrew and Greek classes in this way have gained, or are at the same time gaining, so much general knowledge of the Bible in English, they can afford to bestow more attention upon the Hebrew and Greek languages themselves, than if they must hurry on to exegesis. While having abundant specimens of exegetical study of the originals, they can be especially trained to make exegesis for themselves, by thorough and prolonged study of the language in hand. It was soon found that a good many college graduates, from all parts of the country, possessed a quite inadequate acquaintance with Greek. So,

THE SEMINARY'S PLAN OF INSTRUCTION. 159

after a few years the original plan of having the course in every school completed in one session was abandoned so far as concerned Greek and Hebrew, each of these being divided into a Junior and a Senior class. Yet one who brings a really good knowledge of Greek can of course enter the Senior class at once; and in a few rare cases this has been done by students of Hebrew.

It was confidently hoped at the outset that by this completely elective plan the thoroughly prepared students would be able to pursue their separate special studies in the Bible and Systematic Theology, without being at all hindered by the presence of so many other students in other classes. Indeed, the plan seems at once to insure such a result. But it was soon found, as the years went on, that more than this was gained by the arrangement. As the whole course could be studied, except the special classes in Hebrew and Greek and in "Latin Theology," by intelligent men having only an "English education," men were not pressed into studying the original languages without some real talent for acquiring a knowledge of language, and some strong personal desire to know Hebrew and Greek. Even the Junior classes in those languages thus included only persons impelled to enter them by personal aspiration. Added to this natural selection was the further selection of those who advanced from the Junior to the Senior classes in Greek and Hebrew. Consequently, these Senior classes can be carried over a much wider and more thorough range of learned study than would be possible if the class comprised also a number of men who were members of it only as a thing necessary to obtaining a diploma, or to taking a respectable position before their fellow-students and the country. It has thus been found that the system of free choice has greatly promoted true scholarship, while lessening the number of nominal scholars. Persons who give a moment's careless observation or reflection to this Seminary, which admits so large a number of mere English scholars, have often taken it for granted that the whole thing must be of comparatively low grade. The reason is that the idea of a curriculum underlies all their thinking on the subject; and so they take for granted that a course which begins so low will of necessity be prevented from reaching very high. Yet the completely and consistently elective system is found to work exactly otherwise; and those who are willing to give the matter some attention must sooner or later find that such is the case.

In all the other schools of this Seminary — *i. e.*, except Old Testament, New Testament, and Systematic Theology — it was arranged that there should be only one class for all grades of students, as indeed all study together also in the general or English classes of the three schools just excepted. Critics having little or no experience in the matter often take for granted that men of such various qualifications cannot without great difficulty hear the same lectures and take part in the same recitations and examinations. The real difficulties are found to be very slight, compared with the great advantages of throwing all the students together in these various departments. The less erudite men soon find that work will tell, and that they can often share very comfortably in a recitation with some college graduate. At the same time, they have occasion to observe the advantage possessed by fellow-students, or the professor, from an acquaintance with the learned languages; and every year there are some men, endowed with a natural talent for language, who quit after one session, and go off to college for a thorough course, or who go to work, by private instruction or resolute unaided study, to master Greek, some of them with real success. Others who come as college graduates, soon find, and show, that they have really little talent for language, and when disposed to leave the Hebrew and Greek, and confine themselves to the English course, they are not dissuaded. Thus

THE SEMINARY'S PLAN OF INSTRUCTION. 161

the elements move freely up and down. Men do that for which they have preparation, turn of mind, and time or patience; and get credit for exactly what they do. Every year some men come for a single session, and are led to complete an English or a full course. Every year some enter for a full course, and leave at the end, or before the end, of the first session. Here, as in the New Testament form of Church Government, the benefits of freedom far outweigh its inconveniencies. The free choice of studies, provided for by James P. Boyce and his associates, has shown itself thoroughly adequate to furnish theological education for students of very diverse grades as to preparation, all in the same institution and for the most part in the same classes.

But thoroughly elective education necessarily requires that the graduation be made difficult. Without this, the more aspiring men will be tempted to undertake too much, — which is one of the chief snares of an elective system. As to the bulk of students, they will lack the impulse given by a curriculum which bears the whole mass along together, and so they must have a more powerful individual stimulus in the difficulty of graduation. Such has always been the experience of the University of Virginia, and so likewise in this Seminary. A man must pass independently in each of the schools before he can receive a general diploma. No allowance can be made in one subject for his having done well in others. Accordingly, in the Seminary as in the University, it is the rule to have in every school, or class of a school, an intermediate and a final written examination, lasting nine or ten hours, with a brief oral examination in addition upon certain subjects. These written examinations are a severe test of a man's acquaintance with the whole course of study in that school or class, and his power of satisfactorily stating what he knows. A man who has in the course of three or four years reached the degree of Full Graduate in the Seminary has passed more than twenty of these all-day written examinations. Every question is separately valued, on a scale of one hundred for the whole; and his paper must be worth at least seventy-five per cent on the whole in order to pass. Many fail to pass who have yet studied with great profit. The result of all this is that the number of general graduates will seem small in proportion to the whole number of students, when looked at by persons familiar only with a curriculum. Some students remain only one or two sessions; some pass in various subjects, but fail in others. As a whole, the students are powerfully stimulated by the high standard of graduation. Those who obtain a diploma know that it means something. Those who fail to obtain it often feel, and sometimes voluntarily say, that they would rather fail with a high standard than succeed with a low one.

At first it was arranged to have only one general diploma, with the title of Full Graduate, to be given to those who had obtained separate diplomas in all the separate schools. In the year 1876 it was provided that the degree of English Graduate should be given to students who have been graduated in all the schools except the classes of Hebrew and Greek and the class called "Latin Theology." This has perhaps prevented a few students from studying the original languages, since they could obtain a general degree without it; but it has certainly led a good many to remain two or three years, and complete all the schools required for "English Graduate," who would otherwise have left sooner or omitted some subjects. In the year 1890 a further provision was made for the degree of Eclectic Graduate. This is given to those who have been separately graduated in the Junior classes of Hebrew and Greek, in Systematic Theology (the general or English class), Church History, and Homiletics, and in *any four* of the remaining nine schools or classes. The degree can be taken in two years by a well-prepared student,

THE SEMINARY'S PLAN OF INSTRUCTION. 163

otherwise in three years. It gives as much knowledge of Hebrew and New Testament Greek as is gained in the majority of theological institutions, and prepares the student to use the elaborate learned commentaries, and, if he will keep up these studies, to use the original in examining his texts; while yet he is not required to work through the extensive and difficult course of the Senior classes in Hebrew and Greek. Some excellent students, who are pressed by lack of time or means, can thus in two years obtain a highly valuable degree. Some content themselves with this who might perhaps otherwise have remained and toiled through the entire eight schools (thirteen classes); but others are encouraged, by finding that they can take this degree, to remain and complete the whole range of study for the degree of Full Graduate. All works freely, with the occasional disadvantages of freedom, but with its constant and high advantages.

Besides these eight schools (thirteen classes), which constitute the range of study required for the degree of Full Graduate, there have been established numerous special departments, such as of late years have been introduced in various other theological seminaries. In this Seminary there are now thirteen of these special studies, including the Arabic, Aramaic, Assyrian, Coptic, and Modern Greek languages, Patristic Greek and Patristic Latin, Old Testament Prophecy, Textual Criticism of the New Testament, Foreign Hymnology (Latin and Greek Hymns, German and French Hymns), History of Doctrines, Historical Seminary (original researches and essays in Church History), and Theological German (two classes for reading German works in Exegesis, Systematic or Practical Theology, Church History, etc.). In each of these special departments the Faculty has authority to give a separate diploma; and so in other departments, which may be organized as needed. But these special diplomas cannot be substituted for any part of the range of study required in order to the degree of Full Graduate.

In May, 1892, the Board of Trustees established a new system of titles. The degree of English Graduate is to carry the title of Th. G., or Graduate in Theology; the degree of Eclectic Graduate, that of Th. B., or Bachelor in Theology; the degree of Full Graduate, that of Th. M., or Master in Theology,— corresponding very much to the famous old degree of Master of Arts in the University of Virginia, and to the similar M. A. in several Southern colleges. And any one who, after taking the Master's degree, remains as a close student in the Seminary for at least one whole session of eight months, and has been graduated in at least five of the special departments above mentioned (the choice to be approved by the Faculty), and who, furthermore and especially, has prepared a satisfactory thesis, presenting the results of original research or original thought in some subject connected with theological studies, shall receive the degree of Th. D., or Doctor in Theology.

As originally organized, the Seminary had no president, but Professor Boyce was made Chairman of the Faculty. In May, 1888, the title was changed to that of President, but with the express provision that the government should remain in the hands of the Faculty. Several colleges have in like manner imitated the University of Virginia by having only a Chairman of the Faculty. This was Mr. Jefferson's democratic reaction against the autocratic power exercised by some presidents of universities or colleges, not only as to discipline, but as to the appointment and removal of professors. In theological schools, where there are usually but few professors, and very little has to be done in the way of discipline, it is best that the faculty should govern the institution, whatever title may be given to the presiding officer. But in a university or college there is much reason for thinking it desirable to have a real president, who shall give unity to the general work, and shall be the recognized representative of the institution, busily canvassing for students, and striving, through personal acquaintance and influence, to obtain additional gifts for endowment and support.

CHAPTER XI.

THE SEMINARY'S THREE FIRST SESSIONS, 1859–1862.

THE new Seminary opened at Greenville with many encouragements. The long series of efforts to secure a common institution awakened greater interest than if it had been easily and promptly established. The leading pastors, educators, and private brethren who had taken part in the successive conventions now gave the institution a cordial support. The fact that its plan of instruction had been specially arranged to meet the wants of Baptist ministers in all grades of general education, and seemed well adapted to that desirable end, awakened high hopes of something more widely useful than had previously existed. The South Carolina contribution of $100,000 for the endowment had all been provided, in cash or in the seven-per-cent bonds of planters, — a first-class security. Considerable progress had been made in several other States towards raising the remaining $100,000, and there was no fear of failure.

Greenville was found to be a pretty town of some three thousand inhabitants, spreading out, in Southern fashion, over several pleasing hills. Through the midst flowed a bright stream, called the Reedy River, a branch of the Saluda. Within the limits of the town it formed a considerable waterfall, supplying mills of different kinds. From the hills there is a fine view of the Blue Ridge, some thirty miles away, whose beautiful proportions and charming color are a perpetual delight. The mountains are there about as high as in Central Virginia, the loftiest portions lying between, in North Carolina. Some five miles northwest of the town is Paris Mountain,—a short out-lying range of the Blue Ridge, particularly well adapted to the growth of peaches and other fruits of the vicinage. Among other persons living upon this mountain was General Waddy Thompson, who had been a member of Congress and minister to Mexico, and who liked to be told by the guests who enjoyed his cordial hospitalities that his mountain abode reminded them of Monticello, the home of Thomas Jefferson. General Thompson's former residence in the edge of Greenville had been purchased some years before by Professor Boyce, the large and airy wooden house, with its broad gardens and spacious lawn and grand forest trees, making a beautiful Southern abode. There were many other admirable residences in the town, most of them furnished with ample encompassing space, in which from early spring were bright flowers and luxuriant shrubbery. The buildings recently erected for Furman University had an admirable site south of the river, and their architectural symmetry and general effect were uncommonly pleasing. The proximity to the mountains gives a considerable elevation to the locality, the hills and ravines make a perfect drainage, the sandy streets and grounds quickly absorb falling rain, and the place is healthy in a very high degree. A railroad had been completed some two or three years before, which connected the town with Columbia and Charleston, and so by a circuitous route with the North and the South and West. The people of Greenville presented an uncommonly large proportion of intelligent and refined families. The place was in all respects well suited to be the seat of educational institutions, and besides the University and the Theological Seminary there was a prosperous Female College, with a good building.

The old Baptist house of worship had been divided by partitions into two lecture-rooms and a library. The theological portion of the library of Furman University had been turned over, amounting to some two thousand volumes, and the following summer, at the suggestion of Dr. G. W. Samson, the Columbian College of Washington City presented nearly two hundred volumes, including several sets of complete works of the highest value. The now large private library of Dr. Boyce was a treasure to his colleagues in pursuing the studies connected with their several schools. The four professors were all young, and full of enthusiasm for their new undertaking, while none of them was without considerable experience in preaching and instruction. The Baptist Colleges of the South had amiably recognized their destitution of all titles of dignity, and at the Commencements of May and June had made each of them a D.D. Surely all was now ready.

The preparation of James P. Boyce for this position appears from all that we have seen of his history and character. Recall his thorough general education at the College of Charleston and at Brown University, his useful experience as editor in Charleston and full theological course at Princeton, his four years as pastor in Columbia, and now four years as theological professor in Furman University, two of them spent in laborious teaching there, and two in agency work for the proposed institution. He presented a remarkable combination of business talent, with thorough education and wide reading, and with experience as a preacher and professor, and was singularly adapted to be at once the Chairman of the Faculty and Treasurer of the Seminary, and its Professor of Systematic and of Polemic Theology.

We have seen that Basil Manly, Jr., now thirty-three years old, had been graduated at the State University of Alabama, and had taken a full theological course at Newton and Princeton. After a rich pastoral experience, including four years in the famous First Baptist Church of Richmond, Va., he had now been for five years the principal of the Richmond Female Institute, taking a large part in the

THE SEMINARY'S THREE FIRST SESSIONS. 169

higher instruction. He was already well known to be a man of great versatility and varied attainments, as strong in will as he was gentle in spirit, and sure to be warmly loved by his associates and pupils.

William Williams was now thirty-eight years old, a native of Georgia, and a graduate of the University of Georgia. He practised several years as a lawyer, having been graduated in the Law School of Harvard University. From 1851 he was a pastor in Alabama and Georgia, and since 1856 had been Professor of Theology in Mercer University, then located at Penfield, Ga. His legal studies and practice had disciplined his great mental acuteness. He had extraordinary power in the clear and terse statement of truth, and when kindled in preaching or lecturing he spoke with such intensity as is rarely equalled. He was also a man of great purity of character, certain to command the profoundest respect.

John A. Broadus was thirty-two years old, being a few days younger than Boyce. A native of Virginia, and from early youth a school-teacher by inheritance, he had been graduated in 1850 as M. A. of the University of Virginia. After another year of teaching he was pastor of the Baptist Church at Charlottesville, the seat of the University, from 1851 to 1859. During the first two years of this period he was also assistant-instructor in Latin and Greek, under the revered guidance of the famous Dr. Gessner Harrison. For the two years from 1855 to 1857 he again resided in the University as chaplain, his place in the Charlottesville church being filled by Rev. A. E. Dickinson. Then two remaining years in Charlottesville, and he went to the Seminary.

The number of students for the first session was twenty-six, which Dr. Boyce found, upon examination, to be a much larger number than had attended the first session of any other theological school in America. Ten of these were from Virginia, three from North Carolina, nine from South

Carolina, one from Florida, two from Alabama, and one from Missouri.

True to the design of the Seminary, there were among these students men of the most varied general preparation. W. L. Ballard, of South Carolina, whose name comes first on the list, was a plain country pastor, perhaps forty-five years old, a deeply pious man and a deeply earnest student, who remained one session; and in the country churches accustomed to hear him it was freely said the next year that his preaching was most wonderfully improved. Let him stand as a representative case of one thing which the Seminary set itself to do, of a class of students for whom the professors have through all the years often thanked God. Several were men of whom the faculty afterwards knew little; but most of them doubtless filled places of usefulness in their several States, and could not fail to have been somewhat benefited. A considerable proportion remained only the one session. R. B. Boatwright has been just such a lovable and useful pastor in Virginia as he promised to be, and has cause to rejoice in a brilliant son, who is professor in Richmond College. J. A. Chambliss, of Alabama, remained two years, and was the Seminary's first Full Graduate, being a man of fine powers, and well prepared. The course was afterwards so extended in several departments that no other student has ever become Full Graduate in two years, except two men who brought a good knowledge of Hebrew. Dr. Chambliss has filled a number of important pastorates in different Southern States, including four years in Richmond and ten years in Charleston, and he is now pastor at East Orange, N. J. W. L. Curry had been a student at Princeton, and remained two years at the Seminary, being graduated in a number of schools. He has been useful as a pastor of various country and village churches, chiefly in Georgia. Rufus Figh, of Alabama, came from Howard College, and remained two sessions, and was a much beloved and very useful pastor in Georgia, Alabama, and Texas, down to his death in 1889. G. W. Hyde, of Missouri, remained three sessions, and was the second Full Graduate; he was a chaplain in the Confederate Army in Virginia during the last three years of the war, and has since been greatly beloved in Missouri as pastor of various churches, and as General Agent for State Missions or Home Missions. Hilary E. Hatcher, of Virginia, came as a graduate of Richmond College, and remained at the Seminary two sessions, being graduated in most of the principal schools; he was then a chaplain in General Lee's army, and after the war preached to churches in Orange County, Va., till his death, in 1892. J. Wm. Jones, of Virginia, had been for some years a student at the University of Virginia, and remained one year in the Seminary, being graduated in a number of schools; he was chaplain in Lee's army throughout the war, then pastor at Lexington, Va., for several years, and afterwards at other points, and is now the widely known Assistant-Secretary of the Home Mission Board of the Southern Baptist Convention at Atlanta, and author of several highly popular and useful books; Dr. Jones has the distinction of being the first alumnus to send a son to the Seminary, and of having had up to the present time four sons in all who attended it as students. Robert H. Marsh, of North Carolina, came from the University of that State, and remained in the Seminary two sessions, being graduated in several schools; he was chaplain in the Confederate army two years, and then pastor of various important churches in his State; Dr. Marsh has also been an honored instructor in several institutions. C. H. Ryland, of Virginia, came from Richmond College, and remained in the Seminary two years, being graduated in a number of schools; he labored diligently as army colporteur during the war, and, after useful service as pastor at Alexandria and other points, has since 1874 been financial secretary of Richmond College, and at the same time pastor of churches within reach. Dr. Ryland is a man warmly loved and very influential. T. B. Shepherd, of Virginia, came from Columbian College (now Columbian University), and remained in the Seminary one year, being graduated in all the schools he attended; he has been a useful pastor at various points in the State. W. J. Shipman, of Virginia, who came from Richmond College, and remained one year, being graduated in several schools, has also been a very faithful and useful man, including important pastorates in Richmond and at Halifax Court-House; he was the second alumnus who sent a son to the Seminary. C. H. Toy, of Virginia, was a Master of Arts of the University of that State, and took in one session some three fourths of the Seminary's course, being easily graduated in every school he attended; he was ordained the following summer, with the expectation of becoming a missionary to Japan; this being prevented by the war, he served as chaplain to the close of the war. Some years later, as we shall see, he became professor in the Seminary, and is now professor in Harvard University.[1]

During the three or four central months of this first session the Professor of the New Testament and Homiletics was so enfeebled by illness as to be entirely cut off from teaching. The classes were taken in hand by his colleagues, — a hard task, when all were toiling through a first session. But Boyce and Williams had enjoyed the experience of teaching a variety of theological subjects, and Manly was, by his versatile constitution and varied training, able to teach almost anything. They did the work, of course; but they did it so ably, and with such

[1] It has seemed appropriate to give some brief account of several students of the first session or two, though of course this cannot be continued for every subsequent year. Others not here mentioned have doubtless been very useful ; but the writer has, unfortunately, not had opportunity to know so well concerning them and their work.

cheerful kindness, such unfailing and delicate efforts to prevent their colleague from being pained by the situation, that, now when they have all passed away, the matter is remembered with unspeakable gratitude and affection. As a part of his ample home establishment, Dr. Boyce had several ponies, trained for the saddle, on which his wife and her sister were accustomed to ride, accompanied by a groom. One of these ponies was promptly placed at the disposal of his colleague, who soon sought permission to take the groom's place in the long rides through that beautiful neighborhood, and thus early formed an intimate acquaintance, which he has ever since most highly valued.

Dr. Boyce's own health was at that time superb. and his power of endurance seemed to be almost unlimited. In January he took his family for a few days to Charleston, in order to visit his relatives and look after the many business interests of his father's estate. He invited his invalid colleague to accompany him on what would be a first visit to the beautiful city by the sea. The journey had to begin at 4 A. M., and continue till towards midnight; but he wrapped his friend in a wonderful overcoat, — a miracle of softness and warmth, — and when we reached Charleston carried him in his own arms from the carriage into his room at the hotel. He seemed strong like a giant, and he was tender as a woman. He shrank from equestrianism, but loved to drive about Greenville and vicinity a fine pair of horses, with which he also went once a month to a country church twenty-five miles away, of which he was pastor. On one of these journeys he took the same colleague with him. We spent the night in a large double cabin built of logs, whose owner was poor and far from cultivated, but had a heart as big as all out-doors, and a joyous delight in everything religious. It was beautiful to see how completely at home Dr. Boyce appeared, and how completely at ease he made everybody around him.

The story was afterwards told by some one else that when the rich preacher from Greenville made his first visit to this church as pastor, having been called upon the recommendation of his predecessor, when the people saw the fine horses and stylish negro driver of the buggy, there was quite a sensation. The church included persons of intelligence, dwelling in comfortable homes, who afterwards came to love him warmly. But on that occasion, when the church-meeting which followed the sermon had ended, there arose a new and lively discussion as to who should take the pastor home with him. Various brethren suggested to various others, "Can't you take our pastor to-night?" But each one found it impossible to do so. At length the hero of the double cabin spoke out warmly, and said, "Well, brethren, I don't mind it, I'll take him." Let it not be imagined that there was about him any particle of display. He took two excellent horses in order to shorten the trip and save time, and he took a servant to drive, in order that he might be able to think of his sermon. Some years later, the writer himself became pastor of the same church, and had ample occasion to learn how highly Dr. Boyce was appreciated and loved by all the people.

Dr. J. Wm. Jones has written with great earnestness as to Dr. Boyce's cordial kindness to the students during this first session. He invited them in groups to dinner or tea, and urged them to visit him informally. He privately offered financial aid to such as needed it, seeing that the Seminary had not yet any fund for this purpose. Learning that Toy and Jones were walking three miles out to a mission Sunday-school, he insisted on their driving his ponies. When the prayer-meetings conducted by students in private houses overflowed, he suggested building a mission chapel, promising to pay whatever they could not collect; but the war troubles broke up the plan. In general, he delighted in all religious work done by the students, in the town and its vicinity, and especially when he heard of conversions in their meetings. He longed to have it understood that the Seminary wished to train zealous preachers and working pastors.

About the end of the session Dr. Boyce preached at the dedication of the new Baptist Church at Columbia. He had, of course, fulfilled his generous offer of ten thousand dollars towards its erection, but had made the payments only in proportion as other contributions were paid. All his giving was managed with the greatest care, so as to bring from it good results in every direction. The sermon refers feelingly to the "eight years of sacrifice and toil and pain" through which the Church has pressed on to the erection of this building. He distinguishes between "sacramental" and "sacrilegious" theories as to the character of a house of worship, urging that its sacred design and associations shall not be violated by employing it for mere secular gatherings and addresses.

At the Commencement for this first session, near the end of May, 1860, a missionary sermon was preached by President G. W. Samson, D.D., of Washington City, and an address was made by the venerable Dr. B. Manly, Sr., both of whom had taken a great interest in the various conventions leading to the formation of the Seminary. By request of Dr. Boyce, Professor B. Manly, Jr., wrote a Commencement hymn, beginning, "Soldiers of Christ, in truth arrayed," which has been sung at every subsequent Commencement, and it is hoped will be sung for ages to come. As a whole, the opening session was thought to have been highly successful and encouraging. But the summer and autumn of that year were marked by the political canvass which led to the election of Abraham Lincoln. There was immense popular excitement, which the men of to-day may be glad that they can scarcely imagine. It was very generally believed that the election of Mr. Lincoln would lead to great political changes, and not a few thought the result would be war. At such times young men find it hard to settle down for a course of quiet study.

Yet the second session showed a gratifying increase of attendance, namely, from twenty-six to thirty-six. Of these Virginia sent ten, North Carolina four, South Carolina nine, Georgia one, Alabama five, Mississippi five, Missouri one, Massachusetts one. Eleven students of the first session returned, and some others were doubtless prevented only by the political excitement. The large attendance from Alabama and Mississippi showed that the interest in the Seminary was widening. Among the new students, at least a few ought to be mentioned. F. M. Daniel, of Alabama, came from Howard College, and remained two sessions. He has long been a highly useful pastor at various places in Georgia. Joseph F. Deans, of Virginia, was a graduate of Columbian College, and came now for one session, returning after the war for two sessions more. He was a chaplain in the Confederate Army, and has been a laborious and useful pastor and teacher in Virginia. C. E. W. Dobbs, of Virginia, who came one session, has been widely known as pastor in Kentucky and Indiana, in Mississippi and Georgia, and as a writer for the religious press. P. C. Dozier, of South Carolina, attended two sessions, and has long lived in California, of late as professor at Los Angeles. J. L. Pettigrew came from Mississippi College and attended one session, and has been a vigorous pastor and teacher in Mississippi. James B. Taylor, Jr., of Virginia, educated at Richmond College and the University of Virginia, attended the Seminary one session, and has been an honored and useful pastor in North Carolina and Virginia. His father was the revered Secretary of the Foreign Mission Board; his brothers are Dr. George B. Taylor, missionary to Italy, and President Charles E. Taylor, of Wake Forest. John W. Taylor, of Alabama, remained one session, — a man of rare gifts and

THE SEMINARY'S THREE FIRST SESSIONS. 177

lovely character, whose class-work is vividly remembered across all the years, but whose rich promise was blighted by an early death. George F. Williams, of Massachusetts, had a sister who was the wife of Thomas P. Miller, a prominent Baptist merchant of Mobile. He had been graduated at Rochester University, and remained at the Seminary two sessions. He was missionary in the Confederate Army for three years, and has shown a remarkable talent for pastoral and city mission work, in which he is now engaged in Richmond, Va.

It was a difficult thing during that second session for professors and students to go quietly on. The presidential election occurred when the session was but a month old. Then promptly arose the great Secession excitement in South Carolina, and we went about our daily tasks beneath dark and stormy skies. A State Convention was speedily called by the Legislature, to meet in December. Dr. Boyce felt constrained to become a candidate in opposition to Secession; yet, though Greenville District had long been a Union stronghold, he was overwhelmingly beaten. His political history during the period of the war will be given in the next chapter.

The students almost all remained throughout the session, and they and their instructors strove to study faithfully. But you could hear nothing on the streets, or in the homes where the students boarded, save excited political discussion. Well might it be so, for the times were big with destiny. The students themselves were greatly divided in opinion about the course which ought to be pursued by South Carolina and the other States, as were their professors. Mr. G. F. Williams, who was known to some as a Northern man, in returning from lecture one day made some sharp remark on the street in opposition to secession, and several rough youngsters threatened to mob him. A good-natured livery-stable keeper quieted them with a phrase that was remembered: "Let him alone, fellows;

don't you know a man can't study geography before he's born?"

The secession of South Carolina was promptly followed by that of several other States, and in February a Provisional Congress met in Montgomery, and elected Jefferson Davis as President of the Confederate States. Still we went on trying to teach and learn, hoping and fearing and wondering what manner of life was before us, when the capture of Fort Sumter, April 12, ended all prospect of peaceful settlement, and threw the whole South and the whole country into the fiercest excitement.

The second Commencement of the Seminary was held on May 27, 1861, and the anniversary address, given by Dr. E. T. Winkler, of Charleston, was published. There is not a word in it about the political situation. The Southern feeling was strong that ministers must not preach on political questions, and we were all diligently endeavoring to concentrate attention upon our own business. Dr. Winkler spoke in characteristically graceful and very hearty commendation of the Seminary's wise plans, and its gratifying successes and prospects; and then set himself to exalt the great work which ministers have to do in the world.

Three weeks before the close of the session, Dr. Boyce and the writer went to Savannah to attend a meeting of the Southern Baptist Convention. At Charleston we took a sail-boat, in company with Boyce's early friend, William G. Whilden, and visited Fort Sumter, to see the effect of the bombardment which had caused its surrender by the United States troops. We lunched on Morris Island, which afterwards became famous in connection with the blockade and siege. In returning, we encountered a very high wind, which made the voyage of the little sail-boat increasingly difficult, and at last dangerous. Whenever we tacked, in beating up against the wind, the waves burst over us, wetting the whole person and deluging the boat. We learned afterwards that many boats were upset

THE SEMINARY'S THREE FIRST SESSIONS. 179

in the Bay, and some lives were lost. At length we gave up the attempt, and went before the wind to Point Pleasant, returning to the city at night when the storm was over. Boyce was a good swimmer, having had much boyish practice in those very waters, and was characteristically cheerful, and even hilarious when the waves would break over us. It is still remembered in what a comical quandary his colleague was, who could not swim, as to the proper generosity in his assurances that the negro boatman should be rewarded if the boat capsized and his life was saved. Enough must be promised, and yet not too much, or the boat might be helped in going over. The Convention at Savannah passed resolutions showing sympathy with the cause of the Confederacy. Dr. Boyce discouraged anything of the kind, and through life he always strongly opposed the interference of religious bodies, as such, with political affairs.

A good many of our students went at once into the army, some as chaplains, others as soldiers. The first battle of Manassas was fought on July 21st. The following Sunday was the time of meeting of the Baptist State Convention of South Carolina in Spartanburg. There was naturally much exultation. A thanksgiving service was appointed for Sunday morning. The preacher urged our entire dependence on Providence, and the great importance of not taking everything for granted from a single success. The tone of his sermon was commended by some leading brethren, but others evidently felt that he was not quite up to the requirements of the occasion. Our Southern cause was right. The right must succeed. Yes, the right had succeeded, and this must continue. Such was the feeling of many good men, while of course others, such as Dr. Boyce, were more thoughtful, and better acquainted with the illustrations given by history to the true and Scriptural doctrine of providence.

In the autumn we could see clearly that the number of students for a third session must be greatly reduced. In fact, it fell off to twenty, of whom eight had been students of the previous session. Of these twenty, Virginia sent seven, North Carolina two, South Carolina seven, Alabama one, Mississippi one, Missouri one, Massachusetts one. Several of these have been mentioned in connection with the preceding sessions. William H. Williams, of Virginia, returned in 1866 for two sessions more, became a full graduate, was pastor in Charleston and in Virginia, and is now editor of the "Central Baptist." W. E. Phillips, of South Carolina, a promising student, was killed in battle the following year. A. B. Woodfin, of Virginia, is the well-known pastor in Alabama and Virginia. Several others are known to have made very useful men. Every now and then some one of these twenty would find himself unable to continue studying, and go off to volunteer with his friends. We studied on as best we could. In the autumn or winter a new volunteer regiment was gathered in Greenville District, and Dr. Boyce accepted the place of Chaplain of this regiment. It was evidently useless to attempt to hold another session of the Seminary while the war continued. The Confederate Congress was already providing for a general conscription. Ministers were of course to be excepted, but we were unwilling to ask any special exemption for ministerial students, which would have placed all concerned under a shadow of reproach. We attempted no formal Commencement at the close, as very few students were present, and Boyce had already left, with his regiment. The Seminary had opened, as we have seen, with prospects bright almost beyond parallel in the country. The second $100,000 of endowment had by this time been nearly all subscribed in the other States. But now — the war!

Dr. Boyce made what he thought the wisest arrangements for the future of the institution. He requested the professors to retain their connection with the Seminary, so as to begin again whenever practicable, and paid their salaries regularly in the Confederate currency, which was already beginning to depreciate. Drs. Williams and Manly, who had each a number of servants, rented plantations in Abbeville District, a hundred miles down the railroad, and did much good as pastors of interesting country churches in that region, while striving to continue their studies. Dr. Broadus remained in Greenville, and began likewise to preach to churches within reach. It was probably in the autumn of that year, 1862, that Boyce gave a curious proof of his far-sighted wisdom. One day when at home he said to his colleague: "I am satisfied the war will last several years longer. The Federal Government will blockade our ports, and everything imported will grow very scarce and high. So I recommend that you let me purchase for you a large supply of groceries, enough to last you several years. Some day you may find it very convenient to trade them off for other things." His friend hesitated, as he shared the general opinion that the war could not last very long, and as he had no money to advance for such a purchase. But Boyce insisted, offering to lend him the money. And when the Confederate currency had become sorely depreciated, and the necessaries of life were sadly hard to procure in cities and towns; when at one time, before the manufacture of salt began in the Confederacy, thirty two-horse loads of oakwood were cheerfully bartered by a farmer, upon his own proposition, for thirty teacupfuls [1] of Turk's Island salt,— often and often in those years of strange experiences there was much gratitude in the family for his wisdom and kindness. It was learned afterwards that a celebrated Baptist in Richmond, Va., James Thomas, Jr., a man of extraordinary business talent, made a similar forecast. As soon as he heard that the Confederates had captured Fort Sumter, he began to arrange all his business relations with different parts of the world, and laid in groceries for his large family,

[1] It is fair to add that the lady of the house voluntarily chose her largest teacup, and heaped it every time.

enough for five years. When asked why he was buying so much, he said there would be a long and terrible war, lasting several years, and all such things would become very scarce. Yet Mr. Seward was not probably saying, "The war will end in ninety days," merely for effect, but honestly believed it; and many able men at the South felt a similar confidence.

In the summer of 1862, and afterwards, many subscribers for the Seminary's endowment began to offer payment in Confederate currency. Boyce was never very sanguine as to Confederate success, but he took the money offered, and invested it in Confederate bonds. He would say, "If the South succeeds, these bonds will have value; if it fails, the private bonds and subscriptions we hold will be worthless, because property and business will go to pieces, and we could never collect." But he repeatedly remarked that he would not think of converting *ante-bellum* investments into Confederate securities.

Amid all the distractions and anxieties of these first years of the Seminary, Dr. Boyce was an eager and diligent student. Being very zealous as to his special class for the study of theology in Turrettin and other Latin text-books, and not satisfied with his own knowledge of the Latin language, he made an engagement for a regular series of recitations in the language to one of his friends, who was known to have made Latin a specialty. It was simply wonderful to see how regularly he attended, with so many labors and responsibilities, and how carefully he prepared. Throughout his life, being well known as a great business man, many people took for granted that he could hardly be much of a scholar. But his attainments were very extensive, his appetencies for high scholarship were insatiable, and the great financial sacrifices he made in later years in order to build up the Seminary were in his estimation of little moment compared with the sad and sore hindrance to his plans of study.

CHAPTER XII.

DR. BOYCE'S PART IN THE WAR.

JAMES P. BOYCE had grown up an opponent of Secession, as his father was, and his namesake, Mr. Petigru, and a good many other prominent men in South Carolina. He held that the State had no constitutional right of Secession, and that if a secession were made by any State, it would be simply a revolutionary act, and could be defended only on the ground by which other revolutions are justified.[1] When Mr. Lincoln was elected, on the platform of refusing slavery any admission into the Territories of the United States, and thus restricting it absolutely to the States in which it already existed, it was considered evident that the triumphant party would ultimately go farther still, and begin to interfere, in one way or another, with the existing Slave States. This was regarded as a menace, not only to the institution of slavery, but to State rights and the fundamental principles of American liberty. Dr. Boyce believed that the Southern States ought to seek from the party coming into power some reliable guarantees of non-interference with the existing Slave States. When the Legislature of South Carolina summoned a Convention, in which Secession was well understood to be the issue, he came out as an Anti-Secession candidate for the Convention, in connection with Major B. F. Perry, a man of commanding

[1] The Right of Secession is discussed with great force — for and against — and great beauty of style in Jefferson Davis's "Rise and Fall of the Confederate Government," and James G. Blaine's "Twenty Years of Congress."

character, and long a leader among the Union men, who had hitherto constituted a majority in the up-country districts. But it speedily became manifest that in the low country and the middle country the tide was all in favor of Secession. The South Carolinians were not at all, as was imagined in many parts of the country, a restless and hot-headed folk, inclined to change, *novis rebus studentes*. On the contrary, they were the most conservative community in the whole country, — even retaining many old institutions and customs that were no longer useful, simply through their aversion to change. But the Secession leaders now persuaded the people in general that the only way to conserve their State independence, their property, and their characteristic civilization was to quit the Union and seek to establish a Confederation of the Southern States. These views rapidly spread into the upper districts also; and even in Greenville District, which had always been a stronghold of Union sentiment, Perry and Boyce and their ticket received only a few hundred votes. The Secession ticket of the district included Rev. James C. Furman, D. D., President of Furman University, who had long been a pronounced advocate of Secession. The Convention met in December, and promptly passed an Ordinance of Secession, without a dissenting vote.

Two days before this Secession Convention met, Dr. Boyce wrote to H. A. Tupper: —

"I have been all along in favor of resistance, by demanding first new guarantees, and if these were not granted, then forming a Southern Confederacy. If you Georgia people come in, we are safe enough; though we shall yet suffer, because the plan of co-operation has not *preceded* Secession. We are going to have the Confederacy of New England, the Free City of New York, the Confederacy of the Middle States, and that of the West, — or the two united, — and that cutting through our Southern territory to the Gulf, the Confederacy of the Border States, that of the

Cotton States, — Texas standing alone, — and the Confederacy of the Pacific. Alas, my country! . . . I know I am cautious about taking any step without arranging for the consequences. I have always had such a desire for justice, even to my foes, that I wish to leave no one any ground to charge me even with failure in form. I do wish to see the North put entirely in the wrong, by making them dissolve the Union, if it must be, through refusing to grant what we ask. And again, I have always been old fogy enough to love the past, with all its glorious associations. Moreover, I believe I see in all this the end of slavery. I believe we are cutting its throat, curtailing its domain. And I have been, and am, an ultra pro-slavery man. Yet I bow to what God will do. I feel that our sins as to this institution have cursed us, — that the negroes have not been cared for in their marital and religious relations as they should be; and I fear God is going to sweep it away, after having left it thus long to show us how great we might be, were we to act as we ought in this matter."

Again, on Jan. 10, 1861, he writes to his sister, —

"I am proud to say I love my State, and my whole country, too well to support the present movement. It is to me one of the proudest recollections of my father that he helped so manfully in 1852 to stay this folly; and were he only here in 1860 and '61, I feel well assured where he would stand. The country *his* father bled for, and for which he himself gave his strength and means in 1852, is still dear to me. Nor do I yet despair; I believe that ere many months have gone by we shall all be safe again under the folds of the glorious Stars and Stripes of our own United States. I believe that the Southern States will yet present their ultimatum to the North, and when they do, that it will be accepted. If not, then I am ready to leave them; though I believe in so doing we have nothing before us but constant civil discord, until slavery will be entirely abolished. It is as a pro-slavery man that I would preserve the Union. God deliver us from the follies to which, out of it, the fire-eaters will try to carry us, and the civil discord that will thus come on us! And all this if we are left to ourselves, which I do not expect. As sure as we do not arrange some propositions for the North, we shall have to go through a long and bloody war."

There were many thoughtful men all over the South who fully shared this conviction that the Secession movement would lead to endless discord within the Southern States, and to the ultimate destruction of slavery, even if the United States Government should not attempt coercion of the seceded States, or in attempting should fail. Some few of these — in South Carolina a very few — refused to give the least moral support to the State or the Confederacy in the war that followed. Except in some parts of the Border States, it was folly for them to resist the local authorities, and they could only remain quiet. These were usually old men; and where their character commanded respect they were not molested, and sometimes were even treated with high personal consideration. Thus, at this very time Mr. James L. Petigru was appointed by the Secession Legislature of South Carolina to codify the laws of the State, though his Union sentiments were perfectly well understood, and in fact openly avowed in conversation. But the great mass of those who opposed the Secession movement, and foresaw many of its disastrous consequences, still decided to go with the State. An eminent Union leader in the up-country was reported to have said, "South Carolina is going to the devil, and I'm going with her." Reared as nearly all of us had been, to regard the State as primary, and the United States government as the creature of the States, — or, at any rate, to feel that somehow we owed principal allegiance to the State, — we could not do otherwise. People who care enough for historical truth and personal justice to take any pains towards understanding our position must recognize this fact. The time had come when we were compelled to choose between going with the State and supporting the Union, and we felt bound to go with the State. Robert E. Lee, who is reported to have said about this time that if he owned all the slaves in the country he would gladly give them up to save the Union, to whom

General Scott virtually offered the position of Commander-in-Chief of the United States army, yet quietly resigned his colonel's commission, and went home to his native State of Virginia, when she had seceded, to offer her his services. Even those who most strongly condemn the views entertained, surely cannot fail to respect the sacrifices quietly made by many men throughout the South from a sentiment of duty.

The outbreak of the war brought to Dr. Boyce the prospect of heavy financial losses in New York city. The great dry-goods jobbing-house in which his father had been the principal partner had been continued by a new company, comprising two of Dr. Boyce's brothers-in-law, with himself and his brother, Kerr Boyce. Some time before the war, James Boyce formally withdrew from the company, but left them his share of the capital as a loan. Their trade was chiefly at the South, and he thought they were expanding it too rapidly; and he stipulated that in case of approaching failure they should first amply secure him for the loan by the transfer of Southern debts. In the summer of 1861 the house was compelled to suspend, and did transfer to him a seemingly ample amount of Southern notes and accounts. But it rapidly grew impossible to collect these, and the large amount involved was mainly a loss, while the matter was destined to come up in a still more formidable shape after the war.

In the autumn of 1861 a new regiment of volunteers was recruited in Greenville District by C. J. Elford, a famous Greenville lawyer, with a wide reputation as Sunday-school superintendent in the Baptist Church. He and Boyce were ardent friends; and the latter yielded to the suggestion of Elford and others, and consented to become chaplain to the regiment. His brother-in-law, H. A. Tupper, had for some time been acting as chaplain to the Ninth Georgia. To him Boyce wrote in November that the new regiment was expected to be wanted only for special service, local in South Carolina, and during the winter months. There will be another minister in the regiment, who can give some aid when he is compelled to be absent. If he should be unable to get a furlough in April, when the affairs of the estate will require his special attention, he will resign. He explains the arrangements that he has made as to the estate in general, and his private affairs, in case anything should happen to him. He then goes on: —

"My greatest anxiety is for the Seminary, as its funds are not yet all raised. But I think it is safely fixed; and if my past policy prevails, and no buildings are commenced until the means are on hand, I have no fear of its final success. My wife and children ought to have an ample support from my estate. You may think that I am writing gloomily, but not so; I am stating to you, lest you feel troubled on my account, how truly safe all things are. My times are in the hands of God. If he has other use for me here, he will keep me, at home or in the field as well. Thank you for your good wishes for my work; I fully reciprocate them. The Lord be with us both, and make us useful."

In the early part of 1862 Dr. Boyce left the Seminary, with its small and diminishing number of students, in the care of his colleagues, and went down to the coast with his regiment.[1] In regard to his brief term of service in that capacity we have the following from James McCullough, who succeeded Elford as colonel of the regiment: —

"Dr. Boyce served with us as chaplain while in this State, on the coast, in the winter of 1861-1862, at Charleston, Adams Run, Johns Island, and elsewhere. He was always found at his post of duty, and was highly esteemed and much loved by the entire regiment. They all had absolute confidence in his Christian integrity and manhood. He used to preach us some very

[1] In all his absences during the war, his wife took care of the home, the farm, the servants, with great skill and devotion, as did many another noble Southern lady in those trying years.

able and feeling sermons. My mind recurs to one especially, where he had almost the entire regiment in tears. . . . I loved Dr. Boyce very much, and so did my men; and I believe the influence of his godly life was felt by more than one."[1]

Not only at that time, but throughout the war, he was very zealous in visiting the military hospitals, and personally striving to promote the bodily and spiritual welfare of the sufferers.

The manuscripts contain but little trace of his preaching as chaplain. He doubtless found that to read a sermon, which had been his favorite method, would seldom answer in camp; and there can be no doubt that his preaching gained in directness of aim, in personal point, by this experience. There are not a few who remember this preaching to the soldiers in camp as the most thoroughly delightful of all their ministerial experiences. There was none of the dull decorum and dead-sea formality which often embarrass the preacher's efforts in church, no thousand miles of cold air between the preacher and the nearest hearer, — nothing but live men, who came because they pleased, and listened because they liked; among whom you could stand, and lay your hand on a man's head if you chose, and look right into his eyes, and talk, man to man, about the highest things in time and eternity.

Dr. Boyce enjoyed his work, but felt compelled to leave it, as he had feared might prove necessary, through the pressing claims of business in connection with his father's estate, its wide and complicated affairs being necessarily thrown into great confusion because of the war. So he resigned the chaplaincy in May, 1862. Returning home, he was elected in October as a representative of Greenville District in the South Carolina Legislature. Two years later he was re-elected to this office, and served to the close

---

[1] This excellent gentleman, Colonel McCullough, lived until September, 1892.

of the war, — say April, 1865. He was remarkably well suited for public life. His keen practical insight and sound practical judgment had long been exercised with the liveliest interest upon public affairs. His extensive business relations gave him an extraordinary intelligence as to the business interests of the State. He was a born financier; and, while keenly alive to all that the State Legislature could do in any respect, he was from the beginning specially interested in the Confederate finances. As early as the summer of 1861, when General McClellan was reported to have said, while organizing the great army in Washington, that artillery was going to decide the war, Boyce remarked to a friend, "Pshaw! The war will be decided by money; the side that manages its finances best will succeed." By the end of 1862 everybody could see that the financial situation of the Federal Government was difficult, and that of the Confederate Government was perilous. In the beginning of December, 1862, shortly after the Legislature assembled, he introduced a resolution to the effect that South Carolina would endorse her proportion of two hundred millions of Confederate bonds. When this came back from committee he made an elaborate speech, beginning as follows: —

"Mr. Speaker: At the time I introduced the resolution which has secured this favorable report from the Committee of Ways and Means, I was not aware that any suggestions of the kind had been made. I confess that during several months the plan had appeared to my mind so advantageous that I was surprised that it had not been proposed. Before the committee, however, had acted upon the matter the honorable chairman of the Committee of Privileges and Elections Mr. Trenholm] showed me a letter from one of the most distinguished financiers of this country, suggesting the importance of such a scheme, and urging him to bring it to the attention of this Legislature. The morning after this report and bill was presented to this House, the resolutions of the State of Alabama (to which I shall hereafter refer) appeared in the 'Guardian' of this city; and a paragraph in the Charleston 'Courier' of yesterday, copied from the Richmond 'Whig,' informs us that at as early a period as the 16th of May last, the subject of a guarantee of the Confederate debt by the different States was suggested to Congress by the State of Virginia, accompanied by the request that it be brought before the attention of the other States. The facts thus referred to, joined with the unanimous approval of a committee of the House, have emboldened me to task your attention for a short time, that I may urge upon this House a measure which I deem of the most vital interest to the whole government and people.

"The superficial observer looks upon our present national struggle simply in the light of its military achievement. The abilities of our generals, the bravery of our troops, the successful issue of our battles, — these are to such an one the great objects of interest, and by them he measures the fate of the Republic. That these do enter, and that largely, into the issue, none can question; without the men whom God has given as leaders, and without the troops, such as have never been excelled for bravery or daring, more than all, without that military success which, under the blessing of God, we have achieved, we might well despair, nay, we had been already ruined.

"But there is another power, which, though almost unperceived, affects more deeply the issues of the contest, — the power of the purse: a power in modern times that far exceeds that of the sword, and in fact controls the world. It has long been recognized in Europe, the crowned heads of which are completely dependent upon it. At its beck war is made, and peace is declared. In this hemisphere, in the present war, its gigantic influence has been felt. Were it not for the aid obtained from Wall Street and the other financial circles of the United States, the President of that government could not continue a single day this unnatural warfare; on the other hand, had not the action of the banks of this Confederacy been as patriotic and self-sacrificing as it has, we were already ruined, — flying before our ruthless foe, unable to sustain ourselves at all against the vast hosts which have been raised up against us. They who wield the finances in each section have, in truth, in their grasp the welfare of both, and we have reason not only to be proud of, but to be grateful to, the banks of this country for the unlimited confidence which they have manifested towards our government, and the determination they have shown to sustain it at all hazards, even at the risk of their own financial destruction.

"It is because the welfare of the country is thus so indissolubly united with its financial prosperity that I regard the measure before us as one of the greatest importance. It is in vain to attempt to raise armies if, when called into the field, they can neither be paid, supported, clothed, fed, nor armed. To do these things requires immense resources. With prosperous finances, we can fight on amid the heaviest losses and reverses. With our finances in ruin, our armies become demoralized, our sources of supply are cut off, and the advancing tread of the invader is triumphant. How important, then, that they be looked after, and if evils arise, that the cause of those evils and their proper remedy be sought.

"The time has come, Mr. Speaker, when it behooves us to look well to this matter. The present condition of our finances is fearful, and were it not for the remedy which we have, would be actually appalling. The amount of our expenditures has already reached five hundred millions of dollars. Do gentlemen realize this? Do they know what it means? Have we ever attempted to get any other conception of it than that it is a vast sum of money, beyond the ordinary measure of calculation? Let us try to realize what it is. According to the late War Tax returns, the whole value of South Carolina — lands, negroes, money at interest, and the various other items included under that scheme — was a little less than four hundred millions of dollars. And the Confederacy has spent five hundred millions of dollars in the prosecution of the war thus far. It is as though the whole State of South Carolina had been blotted from the resources of this Confederacy. Nor can we fully estimate what the war has actually cost our people until an accurate account be taken as well of the vast amount of voluntary contributions for hospital purposes, raised by the energies mostly of the noble women of the land, as of the munificent expenditures of individual citizens and corporations in raising and equipping regiments for the field."

Mr. Boyce then went on to show, with great practical point and clearness, and the most comprehensive view of all the conditions involved, the advantages of such an arrangement. The result was that the bill passed both Houses, and became a law. A proposition had been made in Alabama that the State should endorse *all* of the Confederate debt, without limitation. Mr. Boyce showed the great advantage of his plan, since the endorsed bonds would at once command a premium, and enable the Confederate Government to bring its finances into a more healthy situation. On December 30th he wrote an elaborate letter to the Richmond "Enquirer" upon this point, showing beyond question the great superiority of a limited endorsement. The Confederate Government took hold of this movement with heartiness. The Secretary of the Treasury appointed Mr. Boyce as its "agent or commissioner to the Legislatures of various States, to endeavor to secure the passage of Acts for State endorsement of Confederate bonds, similar to that which he carried through the Legislature of South Carolina." We have a report of an address which he made in this capacity before the Georgia Legislature on April 1st, 1863, in which the objections to the proposed plan are carefully stated, and answered with great terseness and force. One expression was definitely prophetic of what occurred within two years. "But let our finances be ruined, let food and clothing continue to advance until our soldiers find their families are starving and naked, they will return to attend to that first of all duties, — to provide for their own households." It was precisely this that reduced General Lee's army, during the winter of 1864-1865, to such small numbers that he was compelled to evacuate the Petersburg defences, and presently to surrender at Appomattox. When the soldier's monthly pay would buy scarcely half a bushel of corn, when word came from many a home that they were already suffering for lack of food, and hopeless as to raising a crop for the coming year, then many a husband and father did that which nothing else on earth could have induced him to do, — left his place in the ranks, and went home. As Boyce had said four years before, it was money that decided the war.

We have no definite information as to the reason why Dr. Boyce's project was not carried through. But we know that three months after his speech before the Georgia Legislature, General Lee was defeated at Gettysburg, and hope of European intervention, or of European demand for Confederate securities, was nearly lost, while at the same time General Grant captured Vicksburg, and pressed into the interior of Mississippi; and these facts would appear sufficiently to explain why the plan in question was tacitly abandoned.

Still, the Confederates had no thought of anything else than perseverance in the struggle. In August, 1863, Dr. Boyce became a candidate for the Confederate Congress, in opposition to Colonel James Farrow, of Spartanburg. He stumped the district for a number of weeks in August, September, and October. At many points he was met by Colonel Farrow, in the old-fashioned joint debate. Rev. Edward C. Logan, an Episcopal clergyman, of South Carolina, who had been Boyce's fellow-student at the Charleston College, was refugeeing at Reidville, in Spartanburg District, and went to hear Boyce at a place not far distant. "He greeted me very cordially, and seemed gratified at having an old class-mate and fellow-Charlestonian to hear him. He spoke well. His first speech (leading off in the debate) was in manuscript, and he read it tolerably closely; but in replying to Colonel Farrow he spoke of course without notes, and spoke well. He lost the election; but that is not much to be wondered at when we consider that he was pitted against a gentleman who had won, I am told, in thirty popular elections."

Besides the remarkable popularity of his antagonist, Boyce's defeat was partly due to the fact that a good many Baptists, who were numerous in that Congressional District, were really opposed to having a Baptist minister go to Congress. It is possible that if he had been elected, his service in the Confederate Congress would have produced such a *penchant* for political debate and public life that he might not have resisted the earnest efforts of some friends after the war to bring him out as candidate for the Congress of the United States. His experience in stump-speaking, as well as in the Legislature, distinctly improved his methods of preaching, as he himself was aware in later years. Mr. Logan heard him at an early period in his round of the Congressional District, and the manuscript is believed to have been pretty soon abandoned. He continued through life to prefer reading a sermon; but he was much at his best in a practical address before some religious convention or association, when saturated with his subject, and speaking with perfect freedom.

In a letter of Sept. 23, 1864, to his sister, Mrs. Tupper (whose husband was in the army as chaplain), he tells her that kid gloves are not to be had, and lisle-thread gloves cost fifteen dollars. He had some time before seen single-width merino dress-goods in Augusta at fifty dollars a yard, and hears it is now a hundred, but thinks he can still get it for her at fifty. Many queer stories might be gathered about prices during the last twelve months of the war, that would be a warning now to the "plenty of money" people, if anything could warn them.

From November, 1864, to the end of the war, Mr. Boyce was aide-de-camp to Governor A. G. Magrath, with the rank of lieutenant-colonel, and was a member of the Council of State, repeatedly consulted by the governor in those troublous times. As aide-de-camp, Colonel Boyce was acting Provost-Marshal of Columbia at the time of its capture by General Sherman. The general states in his Memoirs — of course upon information given him — that the burning of Columbia was due to a quantity of cotton piled in one of the streets, and fired by some of

Hampton's cavalry in retiring at his approach. But Boyce always declared that so far as he could ascertain, then or afterwards, he was himself the very last Confederate that rode out of Columbia, as the invaders came up the street, and the cotton had not then been fired at all. He retreated with the governor to Charlotte in North Carolina, and thence made his way across a hundred miles, a good part of the distance on foot, to his home at Greenville.

A few weeks later, a small brigade of Union cavalry came across the Blue Ridge, with a view to intercept the retreat of Jefferson Davis and his party through Central South Carolina into Georgia. The troops encamped at Greenville, and under pretext of searching for firearms, they searched many houses for jewelry and other valuables. Dr. Boyce's house stood in the edge of the town, and the large building and spacious lawn would soon attract their attention, besides the fact that from some source they were informed that the family possessed a large amount of plate and jewelry, including some diamonds. So, after seizing the horses, they proceeded to plunder the entire house, bursting open closets and wardrobes and trunks, and flinging everything about, in the wild search for precious things. Then they held pistols to Dr. Boyce's head, and demanded to know what had become of his wife's diamonds and the other jewelry. He told them quietly that, learning of their approach the day before, he had intrusted all his plate and other valuables to his brother, who had taken them in a wagon and driven away. They asked furiously where his brother had gone; and he answered that he did not know at all, that he had asked his brother not to tell him. They stormed, and threatened to burn and kill; but his calm replies at length convinced them, and they left, carrying away, among many other articles of clothing and what not, the wonderful warm overcoat in which Boyce had so carefully wrapped his invalid friend five years before,—

which must have been small comfort to them on that summer expedition, but was doubtless worth carrying back to the climate they came from. Many other dwellings in Greenville were plundered in like manner; though the higher officers, when they could be got at, would usually send a subaltern with us to the house indicated, and order the men away. A party of them learned by inquiry where the bank was ; and entering the building, they went promptly to the cellar, tapped the wall till the sound changed, then tore out the bricks, and appropriated a good many thousands in specie which the careful bank president had very secretly walled in, some months before. Ah, they were old hands. Walt Whitman ought to have written a so-called poem in their praise.

CHAPTER XIII.

FIRST SIX YEARS AT GREENVILLE AFTER THE WAR.
1865-1871.

EARLY in the summer of 1865 Dr. Boyce called the four professors together at Greenville to consult as to the possibility of keeping the Seminary alive, and beginning operations in October.

The prospect was sufficiently discouraging. The Seminary had practically nothing. A large part of the subscriptions for endowment had, as we have seen, been paid in Confederate money and invested in Confederate bonds, and so had become an utter loss. Fortunately there was no debt. In fact, like many other things that we call "fortunate," this was the result of wise arrangements from the beginning. Had Boyce undertaken at the outset to erect buildings, as most institutions do, we should have had an unfinished building and a debt. But subscriptions remaining unpaid were now practically worthless. The whole land had been swept as by a cyclone. Several thousand millions of property in the Southern States had perished, including the value of the slaves, the Confederate debt, and outstanding currency, the war debt of several States (which they were required to repudiate in order to reconstruction), and the greatly diminished value of land. Almost all those who had been wealthy before the war were now really poor, many of them burdened with old debts which had formerly seemed a trifle, but now, with accumulated interest, were a millstone around the neck of the impoverished planter or merchant. The whole labor system was broken into fragments as by an earthquake, and no man could calculate on the business future. There was no currency in circulation until the cotton which planters had kept on hand could perchance be sold. Numerous families, formerly prosperous, or at least comfortable, had not a dollar of money for many months after the close of the war. How could it be deemed possible, in such a situation, and amid all the social and political uncertainty, that people would contribute thousands of dollars during the next twelve months to support an institution of higher education? There were the churches to be sustained; the schools of every grade must be revived, if possible; the colleges had lost much or all of their endowment; and the State universities were likely to be helpless, when it could hardly be said that the States any longer existed.

On the other hand, the logic of human nature proved that people would do something. By a remarkable special providence, the war had ended at such a time that if the Confederate soldiers hurried home, and went to work immediately on arriving, they might hope to raise crops of corn and cotton. So, far and wide over the land the planters were at work. Moreover, the colored people were in general well disposed towards their former owners, because in general they had been kindly treated, and thus most of them were working too, with such temporary and indefinite plans as could be arranged between them and the owners of land. We knew also that the Southern whites were upon the whole a high-toned people. They had submitted to the arbitrament of war, and would keep their word; but they had not lost all self-respect and self-reliance. They had nothing to be ashamed of in the way they had struggled against overwhelming superiority of resources. The returned soldiers could talk without fear about the battles they had fought. There was pluck in the people. Most of all, we felt a submissive trust in Providence. Through all the dark years our people had been trying to do their duty according to their light, and multitudes only wanted to know what was their duty now.

Dr. Boyce stated that he held five thousand dollars of Georgia Railroad bonds,[1] which in all probability could be sold before long, not for par, but for a considerable sum. While quite unable to tell as yet whether much would be left of his own estate, he offered to make a personal contribution of one thousand dollars for the coming session; and he believed that when the cotton on hand in various parts of the country should be sold, and the new crop should come in, it would be possible to find friends here and there who would make larger or smaller gifts. It was an uncertain future, but everything around us was uncertain. He pointed out that our Seminary, which after years of effort made so hopeful a beginning, had no small hold on the confidence and affection of the Baptist people in several States, and so might possibly keep alive; while if it were abandoned, a whole generation or more must elapse, and we be all in our graves, before brethren would have the heart to attempt again the establishment of a Common Theological School. We had prayed over the question, again and again. Presently some one said, "Suppose we quietly agree that the Seminary may die, but we'll die first." All heads were silently bowed, and the matter was decided.

We had small means of advertising the intention to re-open the institution. The religious newspapers had nearly all stopped, and were able to resume only in the autumn or

---

[1] These had come from H. A. Tupper, in payment of his original subscription for the Seminary, and they probably saved its life at this crisis. The sale was postponed till November, 1866, when they brought 3,878 dollars. Boyce's own subscription of like amount was paid before the war in land in the edge of Greenville well worth that amount. After the war this was unsalable, but before we removed from Greenville it was sold at a very handsome advance upon the original subscription.

winter. It was some time before the United States mail could be re-established, especially as many railroads were destroyed. We could not hope to have many students, but we could begin, and hope for a future. So the session opened October 1st, and the whole number of students that came during the session was seven, — from Virginia one, North Carolina one, South Carolina four, Alabama one. It is remembered that the Professor of Homiletics had but one student in the class, and that a blind man. But we were determined to keep up the instruction in every department; and as the student could not read text-books, the professor tried to lay out a somewhat complete course, and give it to him in lectures, to which the brother listened with unfailing manifestations of kindly interest. A work which appeared five years later, entitled, "Preparation and Delivery of Sermons," and which a good many persons have found useful, quite possibly owed its origin to that year's lessons with the blind student. We often find that by "doing the thing that is next" to us, even though it be "the day of small things," we find the way opening for undertakings which otherwise might never have been planned. It would be pleasant to speak of several men among the seven students, two or three of them now quite well known; but such mention cannot be kept up throughout the coming history, and is better abandoned at once.

Let us look now at Dr. Boyce's personal history just after the war. In August, 1865, President Andrew Johnson, through the military governor, called a "Constitutional Convention of the State of South Carolina," and of this Convention James P. Boyce was elected a member. Among the members were Ex-Governor Pickens, Colonel Orr, Chancellor Lesesne, General McGowan, and others of the most distinguished men of the State. The important point was to get for the new constitution a proper statement as to slavery, which had been actually abolished as a military act, but must now be forbidden by the State itself. It is stated by Mr. W. G. Whilden that after numerous forms had been proposed by eminent members, with much discussion, the article finally adopted for the constitution was that suggested by Dr. Boyce. In October we find, from a letter to Mr. Tupper, that friends were earnestly urging Boyce to become a candidate for the United States Congress; but he meant to keep out of it if possible. During that month he was in New York city, and bought a variety of articles of clothing for the Tupper family, and doubtless also for his own. The long years of war had left us all in a queer fix as to decent clothing, and the want had to be supplied by most of us very slowly; for, besides the difficulty of securing money, everything was at fully double price, owing to the inflation of the United States currency and the general feeling of uncertainty as to finance.

The war caused Dr. Boyce heavy losses in many directions. After the Confederate bonds became of doubtful value he invested largely in some new bonds issued by the State of Alabama; but President Johnson required these to be repudiated as a condition of reconstruction. We have seen that he lost nearly all of the large sum lent to the New York house conducted by his brothers-in-law and brother, in consequence of their failure at the outset of the war, and the difficulty of collecting the Southern debts turned over to him. But this was not the worst. The New York creditors tried to hold him responsible for all the debts of the establishment, which would have swept away every cent he had. Their lawyers detected some technical defect in the articles of agreement by which he had withdrawn from the house, and had simply lent to the new company what had formerly been his share in the capital. Their course was flagrantly unjust, for the design of the agreement was obvious; but most men insist upon all that the law will give them. It was a mere question of legal quibble and conflict. For some time he could not enter the city of New York, at least openly, for fear of being arrested by these men. On one occasion he sent Dr. Manly to look into the matter. At another time he stayed a good while in Newark, N. J. Mr. Whilden was then with him, and speaks of the cheerfulness which Boyce maintained under all this pressure of obvious wrong and possible ruin. He often entertained his friend for hours by reading aloud, — a pastime to which his rich, sonorous voice and his sympathetic nature always gave a special charm. Whilden still remembers various passages of Scripture as he read them.

At length Dr. Boyce himself, more keen-sighted than his lawyers, detected a legal flaw in the procedure of his adversaries. The law required (if the matter is correctly remembered) that notice of any business claim which was interrupted by war should be sent within six months after the cessation of hostilities. The notice received by Boyce was dated much more than six months after the end of the war, and it made no allusion to any previous notice to the same effect. This is a good example of proving a negative in a way sufficient for practical conviction, though not theoretically complete. With one technicality arrayed against another, the result was a compromise; and the considerable sum which he agreed to pay occupied much of his attention for several years, and drew heavily upon what remained of his estate. Furthermore, he had been one of the committee for erecting the Female College building in Greenville, and in like manner of the committee for building the Baptist church. A large debt remained in each case, now greatly increased by interest at seven per cent per annum. In both committees Dr. Boyce was about the only man who had any available property left, and with him all was uncertain, because of the New York affair and other matters. These debts also he finally compromised at about one third of principal and interest, the church aiding a good deal in the payment of the debt for its house of worship.

This rate for settlement of *ante-bellum* debt rapidly became common in upper South Carolina, at the suggestion of the celebrated James L. Orr, who had become judge of the Circuit Court. In opening court at Greenville, Judge Orr reviewed the financial situation, and dwelt especially upon these old debts. He pointed out that if the debts had been paid before the war, and invested, as was common, in land and negroes, the owners would not now be possessing more than one third of the original value, as the slave property was gone, and the land depreciated. He said the Legislature could do nothing to give relief in such cases; for if it should pass any law "impairing the obligation of contract," the courts must necessarily declare it in violation of the United States Constitution, and therefore of no effect. But he said that a petty jury is a very remarkable institution. When a debt has been proven, the jury can give judgment for such amount as it may think right and proper; and if, in case of these debts from before the war, the juries should, as a rule (making exception of peculiar cases), give judgment for about one third of principal and interest, he did not see how the court would have any cause to object, and it was quite likely that the public welfare would be greatly promoted. Upon this hint several juries quietly acted, until creditors began to apprehend the situation, and would agree to settle at this rate, without the expense and delay of a lawsuit. The idea spread rapidly in that region, being quite generally approved by the judgment of thoughtful men. Pity something equivalent was not done in many other Southern States, where the old debts occasioned grievous distress for years and years.

The above details of Dr. Boyce's private affairs have been given in order to show how difficult and trying was the situation in which he undertook to hold up the Seminary. A good many of its friends were prompt to think that he would sustain the institution from his private means, and the idea spread widely that he was actually doing so. He could not afford to let his real business situation become known to the public, because that would have brought demands from every side, and cut him off from the possibility of working matters through. What he did was to borrow money in bank, as a personal debt, secured by his own collateral, and use this to meet the salaries of the professors, which were small enough, and really worth only one half, in consequence of the high prices. In April, 1866, he gave such a note in bank for seven thousand dollars, in order to settle for the year, having already advanced the money from time to time. This state of things continued for years and years, with sums varying according to the contributions received. In April, 1868, his notes in bank for the purpose rose to eleven thousand dollars, eighteen months later were reduced to half that amount, and afterwards increased again. To keep up these loans was often a sore burden. He needed his collateral for other purposes. He saw opportunities for profitable investment, but could not use them. Of course the Seminary paid the interest on loans thus effected for its benefit.

In the summer of 1866 he made desperate exertions to collect for the Seminary's support. In May, when the Southern Baptist Convention met, at Russellville, Ky., for the first time after the war, he received in cash $1203.50. In June he got in Baltimore $367, and in Richmond $359. In July he made collections in Missouri and Kentucky to the amount of $654. Some few persons made partial payments on old bonds. It cost heavily to send out agents in different directions, and to pay the travelling expenses of various professors sent to different points, in addition to his own journeys.

So the matter went on year after year, with earnest appeals at every promising point that could be reached. On July 1, 1867, he sent far and wide a lithographed letter, explaining the work of the Seminary, and setting forth its pressing needs. This states that during the year preceding he had obtained some $50,000 in bonds for five annual payments;[1] but on most of these the first payment was not yet due, and money was sorely needed. Through the unsettled state of business in every respect, a considerable portion of these annual bonds was in fact never paid, and the amount had to be supplemented in every possible way. Some years later, a similar effort was made to obtain five-year bonds.

[1] Rev. Cleon Keyes, a gifted and now venerable minister in northern Kentucky, relates that Dr. Boyce came in 1866 to the Bracken Association, in the region adjacent to Cincinnati. He wanted to meet the popular objections to ministerial, especially to theological, education, and it was privately arranged that Keyes should speak in opposition to the resolution introduced. He brought out strongly the familiar objections, and felt persuaded in concluding that Boyce would have difficulty in answering; he even feared that harm might be done. But his narrative proceeds: "The Doctor arose, perfectly calm and self-possessed, to make his address. He was then in his prime, — a magnificent specimen of well-developed manhood; his voice was clear and strong, and his words as they fell from his lips seemed as if coined for the occasion. He at first, in the most courteous manner, completely demolished the objections raised in my speech, and then proceeded to deliver one of the ablest addresses on theological education I have ever heard from any one. When he closed, he had captured the whole Association. Everybody seemed ready to give a bond, running five years, to keep the Seminary alive until a permanent endowment could be secured. Many thought strange that his opponent in the discussion was the first to offer a bond, and some said afterwards, to the great amusement of Dr. Boyce, that it was the quickest conversion they had ever witnessed." The two men became warm friends, and in later years, when Boyce removed to Kentucky, and sought to provide for removing the Seminary, Mr. Keyes was an ever-ready helper, even travelling with him for two weeks through the churches of the Bracken. Mr. Keyes speaks very warmly of some sermons Boyce preached during these journeys, and adds: "Had he devoted himself to the pulpit, he would, I doubt not, have taken rank with the ablest preachers of the American pulpit. . . . As an agent he was a prince among men, commanding the confidence and love of all."

It is hardly best to go through the details of these varied and often desperate exertions, year after year. At one time he concluded that it would be best to cease borrowing money for paying the salaries, and let it be understood that they were far in arrears. So pretty soon the professors had received no salary for twelve months, and could not be sure they ever would receive it; and under these circumstances they had to buy the necessaries of life from Greenville dealers on twelve months credit, with corresponding addition to the price as a matter of course. Pathetic details might be given of the real distress and humiliation under which the professors worked on through those years of trial. But let all that pass. There were not a few other professors, in various Southern colleges, who suffered equally, in some cases perhaps more. To do the work of two or three men on half the salary of one man, with that salary in arrears and no certainty of ever receiving it, was a common experience. Some of these men were repeatedly invited to comparatively large salaries in more favored institutions or more prosperous parts of the country, but they stood by the work which Providence had appointed them. And above all the heroic sacrifices which professors made in those days, above even the unconquerable and really splendid exertions of Dr. Boyce to obtain the necessary funds, rose the zealous devotion of many contributors. Struggling business men who needed every dollar they could command, pastors and other men living on uncertain salary, who knew not whether they could make ends meet with the ending year, often gave gifts very large for their circumstances, and accompanied by words of utmost kindness and cheer. It was simply magnificent, the way in which our Southern people during the years that followed the war, just struggling to get on their feet financially, amid all the humiliations and solicitudes of the Reconstruction period, yet resolutely held up their churches and their colleges, and whatever belonged to their higher civilization. These and their homes often seemed all that was left to them. These must not, should not, perish. An inferior people would have let the higher education go. But Southerners had always valued *higher* education, however deficient their provision for instructing poor children. And they not simply did themselves honor, they revealed their real character, by holding up those institutions through all the years of Reconstruction, which in some States were far more trying than the years of war.

It would be a pleasure to mention some notably generous givers whose names appear in the treasurer's books for this period. But one would not know where to cease. And small sums were often given with quite as much of sacrifice and loving devotion as the largest gifts. The record is tempting, for it contains names of Baptist men and women greatly honored among us, and greatly deserving to be honored. It must be mentioned that in 1868 the Board requested Professor Manly "to solicit funds, especially at the North," for the personal expenses of needy students. In Philadelphia and New York he obtained contributions for this purpose that were not only liberal, but given with marked cordiality; and this was continued in response to like application in several following years. At a later period also the Seminary will be found to have received very generous aid from honored brethren at the North.

In 1868, amid all his wearisome journeying, and often poorly successful appeals, and struggling efforts of every kind to sustain the Seminary, and his personal losses and anxieties, Dr. Boyce was privately offered, and urged to accept, the office of President of the South Carolina Railroad Company, with a salary of $10,000 per annum. To Mr. Whilden, who had been asked to communicate the offer, he replied, "Thank the gentlemen for me, but tell them I must decline, as I have decided to devote my life, if need be, to building up the Southern Baptist Theological Seminary." There were like offers in later years. It was not simply a personal sacrifice to turn away from such opportunities, for besides the fact that by living in Charleston or in New York city he might have regained his own estate, he felt an intense desire to help his brothers and sisters in regard to their property, so much of which had been lost in consequence of the war. He was also sadly hindered in his work as professor by this frequent journeying and almost perpetual anxiety in regard to the Seminary's finances. How often he must have looked sadly around upon his noble library when setting out for some new begging expedition, and felt the pang of parting from the books he loved so well! He was also ambitious as to his special studies. His colleagues in their departments, and professors elsewhere in his department, could be pushing their studies, mastering their subjects; but he — he must go off again and beg. True, there was some compensation. He liked to travel. It gave him needed exercise, which at home he was apt to neglect. He could sleep well on the train, even when sitting in the ordinary car. He read a great deal on such journeys, chiefly poetry, of which he was very fond, or romances and other light works, including many French books in the original, but sometimes a history, occasionally a work of profound thought, according to his mood and his health. It is a man's duty to make the best of everything, and he had a cheerful spirit, which would usually rise triumphant over all sacrifice and trial.

In October, 1869, he wrote from Charleston to a young relative who was a pupil in Professor John Hart's famous school for girls at Charlottesville, Va., and we make an extract : —

"While you are in Virginia you will hear a great deal about the war, and see many men who have been in battle. Suppose you keep a little book, and whenever you hear any matter of interest write it down in your book, being particular to keep the dates and names of persons perfectly correct, and to state the events as fully as you can recollect them. Always be accurate, only putting down what you know was said, and also the name of the narrator. You will hear a great deal as interesting as 'Surrey of Eagle's Nest,' or as many other books you have read of adventure and heroism. Whatever else may be the verdict of history, — let its writers be so befogged as to believe that the North fought to free the slaves, and not for its own selfish interests of gain, and that the South fought to defend slavery, and not the constitutional rights of the States, — one thing is sure, that history must accord to the Confederate army in Virginia, under Generals Lee, Jackson, and others, the exhibition of fortitude, bravery, chivalric courtesy, and knightly courage never surpassed in any nation or period of time. Try then to hear of these things, and remember."

The internal history of the Seminary during these years showed steady progress. We have seen that in the first session after the war there were but seven students. In the second there were fifteen, and in the third thirty-one. In these two sessions (1866–1868) Virginia still kept the lead, and South Carolina had very few, — probably on account of the Reconstruction troubles, which in that State were felt so keenly. In the next session (1868–1869) Virginia fell off to five, and South Carolina rose to fourteen, and always afterwards kept the lead while the Seminary remained in that State. The whole number that fourth year was forty-six, and for the next year it rose to sixty-one, with a marked increase from Georgia, Alabama, and Mississippi, with two from Texas, five from Kentucky, and four from Missouri. The following year (1870-1871) the number fell back to fifty-three; but afterwards steadily grew again, till for the four last sessions at Greenville there were from sixty-six to sixty-eight students.

In 1869 the finances were in a more hopeful condition, and the Board of Trustees approved Boyce's purchase (on credit) of the Goodlet House, — a hotel which had been occupied by the United States garrison after the war, and which, as now thoroughly repaired, furnished dormitories and dining-room for the students, where they could live

AT GREENVILLE AFTER THE WAR. 211

much more cheaply than in boarding-houses or private families. It was otherwise also a good investment, for the building was sold, when the Seminary moved away, for much more than it had cost.

The same year the Board appointed, at the faculty's request, a fifth professor, Rev. Crawford H. Toy. It has been heretofore mentioned that Professor Toy was a student of the Seminary during its first year. Since the war he had spent two years in Europe, devoting himself chiefly to the Arabic and Sanscrit languages. He had now been for a year the Professor of Greek in Furman University, and was already a man of great attainments, not only in language, but in physical science and in general literature. In the Seminary he was made Professor of the Old Testament and Oriental Languages.[1] The special desire in adding a fifth professor was to relieve Dr. Boyce of teaching Polemics, and Dr. Broadus of Homiletics, as the latter's health

---

[1] Professor Toy's inaugural lecture was published as a pamphlet, and discussed "The Claims of Biblical Interpretation on Baptists." He shows that "on Baptists there rests a special obligation in regard to the Scriptures," because of "our complete dependence on the Bible." We profess to make it, and it alone, our religion. We accept all that it teaches, and nothing else. . . . If we could lean on the decisions of Councils, Convocations, or Assemblies, . . . royal or episcopal decrees, array of patristic, scholastic, and other lore, . . . it might not be so needful for us to cling close to the word of God as our sole guide; but now we have no other resource. It is our pole-star. Without it we are on a boundless ocean, wrapped in darkness." He urges that for right interpretation of the Bible we need, on the one hand, "learning and thought," and, on the other hand, "the inspiration and guidance of the Holy Spirit." After discussing at length the history of interpretation in all ages, he points out as the result that we must in any passage consider, (1) the meaning of the words; (2) the context; (3) the relations of this passage to the whole of the divine revelation of truth; (4) the Christian consciousness, with solemn invocation of the presence of the Holy Spirit. He says: "A fundamental principle of our Hermeneutics must be that the Bible, its real assertions being known, is in every iota of its substance absolutely and infallibly true."

was impaired, and Homiletics, in addition to New Testament, was proving too much for him, and as Dr. Boyce was so much hindered by business cares and journeyings. Dr. Manly, who was highly versatile, and quite varied in his attainments, consented to take Polemics and Homiletics in connection with Biblical Introduction, which he retained. These arrangements gave needed relief and promised excellent results, and the large increase in the number of students the following session was very encouraging.

Still, the financial needs would grow pressing, and Boyce must journey in this direction or that, and repeat his vehement pleadings. His sister relates that he once made an appeal, in the Citadel Square Church of Charleston, until she sat and wept to hear him beg so hard. In addressing the Southern Baptist Convention he once said, "I have begged for this Seminary as I would not beg for myself if I were starving;" and his proud face proved it true. Judge Pressley relates that in January, 1870, he went with Dr. Boyce from Charleston to Chattanooga as attorney for the Boyce estate, to supervise the sale of certain property. Unexpected legal complications were contrived by the purchasers, which would long delay payment. At one o'clock at night Pressley awoke in their chamber, and found that Boyce, in the other bed, was not asleep. So he said, "I think all this will come out straight!" Boyce replied, "What I am troubled about is the Seminary. I have been advancing funds, and more money is pressingly needed now. I expected to get the money here; how can I keep the Seminary going?" Pressley suggested that the institution might be suspended; but Boyce answered, "That would kill it; and I'll spend every cent I have rather than suspend." Soon after this he began a new effort to obtain five-year bonds, and the responses were so encouraging that he grew more hopeful.

In May, 1870, Dr. Boyce gave a signal proof of his personal generosity, in suggesting to the Board of Trustees that his colleague, Professor Broadus, should be sent to Europe for his health, on leave of absence for a year, with salary and provision for expenses. Boyce had long keenly desired to go to Europe himself. He spoke of it in his letters when a student at Princeton, when pastor at Columbia, when professor in Furman University. But he saw that the Seminary could not go forward without his presence and exertions to care for the finances. So, without a word about himself, postponing still his cherished wish, he cared for his suffering colleague. The latter's health had been sorely strained in the years following the war, by teaching all the week and then preaching every Sunday, till in 1868 the Board had requested him "to dissolve his pastoral relations, in view of the state of his health." This request was designed, and employed, to satisfy esteemed friends in the churches served, that a resignation was necessary. Now that Professor Toy was present, and could help carry the burdens of instruction, and the finances were more hopeful, Boyce proposed the journey mentioned; and thus prolonged a life which otherwise could not have lasted many years, or could have lasted only with frail health and little power for work. He overcame by cordial assurances the natural reluctance to impose such expense upon the Seminary, and exerted himself in various ways to remove every sting from the journey and add to it every element of enjoyment and profit. He also taught the New Testament English class during the professor's absence, while Professor Toy took the Greek.

Dr. Boyce was elected President of an important Baptist Educational Convention at Marion, Ala., in 1870, and of another at Richmond, Va., in 1871. In November of that year he was elected President of the South Carolina Baptist State Convention, and would no doubt have been often re-elected, but for his removal to Kentucky. The degree of LL.D. was conferred on him in 1872 by Union University, Murfreesboro, Tenn.

In the summer of 1871 Dr. Basil Manly, Jr., accepted an invitation to become President of Georgetown College, Kentucky. One inducement was the opportunity it would give for educating his growing sons under his own eye, and partly by his own instruction, as his honored father had educated him. Another reason was that, somewhat to the surprise of his colleagues, he took no fancy to teaching Homiletics. We all thought him eminently adapted to the interesting and helpful correction of written sermons and other exercises; but he disliked the drudgery of the task, and the dislike grew upon him. There was also a better salary at Georgetown, which, with his large and growing family, was a thing proper to be regarded. And he thought the Seminary could do without him now, as there were four other professors. His colleagues vehemently opposed his leaving, feeling assured that the loss of so gifted an instructor, with a personal influence so winning and wholesome, would be irreparable.

Dr. Boyce's published writings up to this time were not extensive. His "Three Changes in Theological Institutions," and his published sermon at the dedication of the church in Columbia, have been heretofore mentioned, as also his speeches and articles about the financial question he brought before the South Carolina Legislature. At the funeral of the venerated Dr. Basil Manly, Sr., which occurred at Greenville, Dec. 22, 1868, the Funeral Discourse was given by Dr. Boyce, and was afterwards published under the title, "Life and Death the Christian's Portion." Half of the discourse gives a singularly strong and helpful discussion of the two great thoughts that Life belongs to the Christian, and Death belongs to the Christian, from the text, 1 Cor. iii. 21, 22: "For all things are yours; whether Paul, or Apollos, or Cephas, or the world, or life, or death, or things present, or things to come; all are yours." The other half gives a very interesting outline of Dr. Manly's life, a portion of which we have heretofore quoted, as containing Boyce's early recollections of the beloved pastor in Charleston. We cannot refrain from here further extracting the very striking and suggestive comparison of Dr. Manly with two other celebrated educators: —

"He now entered upon an untried sphere, — the Presidency of the University of Alabama, located at Tuscaloosa in that State; but he went only to gather fresh laurels, and to become additionally useful to his country and to the cause of Christ. It was indeed to secular education only that he was giving himself; but he knew how the influence obtained in thus educating the youth of a State could be made available to the cause of the Redeemer. And of all men there was none who could so use it more effectively.

"As a College President, Dr. Manly was undoubtedly one of the most successful. In this respect he will bear full comparison with his beloved friend, the lamented Wayland. Differing in many particulars, both intellectually and physically, located under different influences, entirely unlike in the character of their pulpit efforts, they were remarkably similar in their administrative capacity, and in the impress they left upon the educational interests in their respective sections. They were both in the fullest sense the presidents, the controlling spirits, of their respective universities. The students, the faculty, the very Board of Trustees, looked up to them as to the heads, by which all was to be governed. Neither of them could have brooked any other position. The responsibility of their office was felt, and in bearing its responsibility they felt that they must exercise its authority.

"In the impress made upon their respective students, however, there were contrasts, which marked the differences of the men. Dr. Wayland stamped his mind more upon his students; Dr. Manly, his heart. The influence of the latter was more over the spiritual, that of the former more over the intellectual, nature. Yet we are not here to find evidence of superior intellect in the one, any more than of superior spiritual life in the other. The truth is, to compare them in either respect is difficult. In some intellectual points, Dr. Wayland was the superior of Dr. Manly; but in others, decidedly the inferior. The judgment of Dr. Manly was far better, much more accurate, much more certain to be correct. This was true even upon subjects which Dr. Wayland had more thoroughly studied. Especially was it true upon the intricate questions of moral and intellectual philosophy. In Dr. Manly there was much less tendency to push theories to extremes, or to overlook the modifications in a theory, suggested by other facts and theories. Dr. Wayland's vision was telescopic, reaching a long distance, and bringing objects near which to other men were distant; but when thus near, he could still view them only in the isolation in which a telescopic object is presented, and his observations were left unmodified by the information given by other objects or through the senses. Dr. Manly saw not so piercingly; but in seeing, he looked not at the object alone, but all its surroundings, and received the instruction given by his other powers, equally exercised for the attainment of knowledge. The truth is, that in that very analytical power by which Dr. Wayland would disintegrate a subject and isolate its parts, — a power, I believe, more remarkable in him than in any man America has ever produced, — in that very power, which thus constituted the strength of Dr. Wayland, and the source of his reputation, lurked a weakness which led him to conclusions containing erroneous elements which men of less acute analysis, but of better judgment, could better perceive. It is on this account that, while indicating my conviction of the similarity between them as Presidents of Colleges, I yet recognize such great differences that it seems unfit to compare them intellectually or spiritually with each other. Those with whom they came in contact were often led to overlook the deep spiritual nature of Dr. Wayland, while recognizing his powers of intellect, and to fail to perceive the great mental powers of Dr. Manly while under the spell of his deeply spiritual and emotional nature. Under the powerful frame and massive intellectuality and commanding, oftentimes stern, aspect of Wayland, there was the most childlike spirit that I ever knew in man, the most sympathizing heart, the most fatherly affection. Under the gentle and quiet and unobtrusive nature of Manly there was a mind of wonderful powers, of accurate and acute thought, capable of the exactest statement, attended by a logical enforcement that carried conviction at once to his hearers; yet, withal, this was so gently done that the effect alone was apt to be felt, — the efficient causes were usually overlooked.

"In these respects he very strongly resembled the late Dr. Archibald Alexander, of Princeton. This will at once be admitted by all who knew them both. Their bodily forms were not unlike, their habits of life very similar. Their mode of intercourse with others was marked by the same gentleness and kindness. Their methods of preaching were quite similar. The reputation in this respect of each had been achieved in early manhood, and that of the one was remarkably like that of the other. Each of them was more loved than feared, though both were deeply reverenced. The judgment of each was submitted to as to an oracle. But similar as they were in these and many other respects, it was not until their mental characteristics had been compared — their ways of thinking, the simplicity and accuracy of their statements, and the just views to which their correct judgment commonly led — that there was seen that remarkable resemblance which must have struck every observer well acquainted with them both."

In the "Baptist Quarterly" for October, 1870, Dr. Boyce published an elaborate and quite valuable article on "The Suffering Christ," the substance of which was afterwards given in his "Abstract of Theology."

CHAPTER XIV.

SERIES OF EFFORTS TO REMOVE THE SEMINARY.

DURING the first years after the war, the idea necessarily occurred to various persons that it would be better to remove the Seminary to some other State. The State feeling has always been so strong at the South that no general institution could expect to obtain adequate endowment unless a large portion came from the State in which it was located. Accordingly, at the original establishment of the Seminary, as we have seen, the South Carolina Baptists agreed to give one half of the then proposed endowment. This $100,000 had been fully subscribed when the Seminary went into operation. But much of it was paid in Confederate money, and invested in Confederate bonds or other securities that perished with the war. The Theological department of Furman University was to turn over nearly $30,000 of the amount. The larger part of this was paid in Confederate money, and the noble University was, after the war, struggling for its existence, and quite unable to pay over the remainder. The private bonds of planters and others which remained unpaid were for the most part worthless. And when we looked to the future, it was simply out of the question to hope that South Carolina could furnish half of the larger endowment that would now be necessary, through the greatly increased cost of living, and the necessity of having additional professors. The wealthy Baptists of South Carolina had been nearly all planters, who were now almost uniformly impoverished. The generous and noble men and women of the State contributed "to their power, yea, and beyond

EFFORTS TO REMOVE THE SEMINARY.

their power," for the annual support of the Seminary; but large endowments have to come chiefly from wealthy people, and of these there were then practically none. (Of course the situation has considerably improved since that time.) Moreover, Furman University must soon have endowment, or perish; and any general effort to obtain South Carolina endowment for the Seminary would be damaging, if not fatal, to the University.

Yet during the first years the idea of removal was never mentioned without prompt rejection. No one concerned wished to leave South Carolina or Greenville, which, both as to climate and community, had proven itself a delightful place of residence, even beyond the opening promise. And the people of South Carolina in general, though often curiously misunderstood at a distance, could never be thoroughly known by any person of elevated principles and tastes without being held in high admiration and esteem. So we struggled on, hoping that perhaps sufficient endowment might come from other States, though we knew not how. Dr. Boyce, though a large-hearted man, deeply interested in the whole South and the whole country, was yet warmly attached to his native State and to the many friends of his early years, and surpassingly reluctant to take away from Carolina the institution to which he had devoted his life.

The first known attempt to effect a removal of the Seminary came in April, 1869, four years after the war. The Trustees of Union University, at Murfreesboro, Tenn., invited a removal of the Seminary to that place, and proffered $50,000 towards its establishment there. The Trustees of the Seminary, at Macon, in May, respectfully declined the invitation. They said that funds contributed in South Carolina might be jeoparded by any removal, in consequence of the original agreement that in case of removal from the State all such funds should revert to Furman University. They state also that "larger sums have been offered for the location of the Seminary in other places." They explain that the only serious difficulty as to continuing the Seminary at Greenville was the comparative difficulty of access, as it could be reached only by a single railroad from Columbia; and that this difficulty was about to be removed, as a railway was in construction which would connect Greenville directly with Atlanta on one side, and on the other with Central North Carolina and Virginia. Dr. Jeter, President of the Board, was requested to publish an article in the "Religious Herald," setting forth reasons for not removing the Seminary. The report thus adopted by the Board of Trustees is in Dr. Boyce's handwriting, and the fact is mentioned to show that he was zealous to prevent removal.

Next year, May, 1870, when the Trustees met in connection with the Southern Baptist Convention at Louisville, a committee was appointed, with A. M. Poindexter as chairman, to devise some plan for raising a permanent endowment, and recommended that agents be appointed to attempt raising from $150,000 to $200,000, including $50 each from a thousand ladies. The existence of several notable Baptist ladies in Louisville, able and accustomed to give generously, must have suggested this last rather fanciful proposition. No definite action was taken, but all concerned were evidently anxious to maintain the institution at Greenville if possible.

In February, 1871, Dr. Boyce wrote to H. A. Tupper that he was sending out another circular, adding, "I *must* have this money." In the circular he appeals to *pastors* to take up a special collection, and says: "I am filled with anxiety that the Seminary should obtain immediate relief. . . . As to the final success of the Seminary, I have no fears; but I am anxious to see it carried through these years of trial and poverty at the South without being too much crippled." He was perhaps more depressed and anxious because about that time he began to have occasional attacks of rheumatic gout, inherited from his father, compelling him to support his heavy frame on crutches.

In April of this year some friends in Kentucky requested Dr. Boyce to engage in a public debate at Lexington against a Campbellite. He wrote to Rev. George Hunt: "What could all of you mean? Why, there are twenty men in Kentucky who could outstrip me in such work as you propose. You yourself would do tenfold better. We folks here [in South Carolina] are too little troubled with Campbellism to be as familiar with it as a debater should be. And then I am slow of speech. No, no, I must beg off. Kentucky Baptists must not send to South Carolina to get a champion, and then find him whipped."

Some time in 1871 or the early part of 1872 influential Trustees of Brown University asked Dr. Boyce's permission to nominate him for President of the University. The idea must have been very attractive to him, and he would have filled the position with distinguished ability. But he did not feel at liberty to leave the South and the Seminary.

In May, 1871, the Board met again with the Convention at St. Louis. Notice was received of action taken the previous summer by the Trustees of Furman University, and by the State Convention of the Baptist denomination in South Carolina, proposing on their part to release the Seminary from all claims that contributions to it shall revert to Furman University in case of the Seminary's removal from the State, on condition that the Seminary upon its part will release Furman University and the State Convention from all claims for amounts due on account of the Theological department, etc. This was accompanied by a note from President James C. Furman that the Trustees of Furman University would deplore the removal of the Seminary to another site, and only desired to relieve the University from liabilities. The Trustees of the Seminary acceded to the proposed agreement, and further resolved that the Seminary shall be removed, if thereby "endowment can be obtained of sufficient amount to secure the permanency of the institution." The Executive Committee was directed to make public this willingness to remove, and invite proposals; but they must state that the Board will not be governed *solely* by the amount pledged from one or another locality.

In March, 1872, Dr. Boyce personally visited Chattanooga and Memphis, inquiring as to the possibility of removal to one of those places. At Chattanooga his father's estate, still in his hands as executor, had large and promising investments. He himself confidently believed that sooner or later Chattanooga would become a great city, as now seems increasingly probable. It was also quite central for the Southern States. He would have been personally much gratified to see the Seminary removed to that place, and wrote to persuade his father's heirs that it would be wise for the estate to subscribe handsomely towards the endowment, in case of removal, since he could then give constant personal attention to the development of their property. Yet he was not the man to be affected by personal interest, if something better could be done elsewhere for the general good. He had suffered a very heavy loss early in 1871 by the failure of a business house in Charleston in which he was a partner, but he went straight on with his Seminary work.

In 1872 the Trustees met with the Southern Baptist Convention at Raleigh, N. C. It appeared that propositions for removal had been made by friends of the Seminary in various cities. The eloquent Dr. T. G. Jones spoke strongly for Nashville. President N. K. Davis brought a carefully elaborated and very generous proposition for removal to Russellville, Ky., and incorporation with Bethel College, of that place, into "The Southern Baptist University." Informal but earnest propositions were brought for removal to Chattanooga, to Memphis, to Atlanta, to

Louisville. The Board resolved that it was expedient to remove, but that it was proper to avoid all complications with existing or proposed institutions of learning, and that this would restrict them (among the places to which the Seminary had been invited) to Louisville, Nashville, Chattanooga, or Atlanta. They further resolved that at least three hundred thousand dollars ought to be secured in the city and State where the Seminary should be placed, with the expectation that two hundred thousand more would be raised elsewhere. They appointed a committee of seven to visit proposed places, examine proposed sites, etc., and inquire into the amount and validity of the subscriptions. Whenever these matters should be satisfactorily arranged by the Committee of Visitation, and the necessary legal measures should have been adopted, the Executive Committee was authorized to effect a removal. This important removal committee consisted of J. B. Jeter, T. H. Pritchard, S. L. Helm, T. P. Smith, S. Henderson, M. Hillsman, Joseph E. Brown; and Dr. Boyce was requested by the Board to accompany the committee in visiting various cities.

Nearly all of this committee, with Dr. Boyce, shortly after visited the several cities suggested, and reached the conclusion that it was best to remove to Louisville, so soon as the requisite amount for endowment should be subscribed in the city and the State. Louisville was much the largest of the cities proposed, and while by no means geographically central to the Southern States, it was already evident that railroads would ultimately make it easily accessible from all parts of the South. There were several strong Baptist churches in the city, and wealthy Baptist members; and it was believed that when there should be opportunity for full explanation of what the Seminary could do, not only for the cause at large, but for the city of its location in particular, these intelligent and generous Baptists would quite generally become its friends, as some of them were from the beginning. It was supposed that not more than a year or two would be required to obtain the proposed subscription in Louisville and Kentucky, no one foreseeing the great financial crisis of the following year.

Meantime important changes had to be made in the faculty. When Professor Manly left, in 1871, it was too late for any appointment to be made by the Board. Professor Toy could take Biblical Introduction. Dr. Boyce readily resumed Polemics, which he had previously taught. He urged Dr. Williams to take the School of Homiletics, promising that if it should prove agreeable to him, a new professor should be found the next year for Church History, — a subject which Williams had never particularly liked, though he did all his work faithfully and ably. Dr. Boyce was persuaded, and the other professors, that Dr. Williams would teach Homiletics with signal ability, as he was a very able preacher, whose sermons were always carefully constructed, his style a model of terseness and lucidity, and his delivery forcible, and often intensely earnest. Dr. Williams protested — and the matter is recorded simply because of a valuable distinction — that whatever he might be able to do as a preacher, he was wholly unsuited for teaching other men how to preach. He said: "If a man brings me a bad sermon, I can sit down and write him a better one; but I can't tell him how to make his sermon better. I can't make my mind work in other men's lines." He said he was quite willing to do anything he could do, but would utterly refuse to attempt what he knew he could not do. Boyce urged his plan with growing vehemence, until Williams rejected it with decided heat; "and the contention was sharp between them." This was the only time in all the Seminary's history that there ever arose the slightest unpleasantness between professors; and this was gone next day. Dr. Boyce quietly said that he would take the School of Homiletics himself. The professor who had been relieved of it two years before was ready to undertake the subject again, but Boyce earnestly objected. He said he had good health, and although he had neither taste nor training for correcting exercises, he would do his best, and would not allow one whose health was still uncertain to resume the burden. So Dr. Boyce himself taught Homiletics that session, as he had taught New Testament the previous session.

The next year, May, 1872, Rev. William Heth Whitsitt was elected Professor of Biblical Introduction and Polemic Theology, and Assistant-Professor of New Testament Greek, this aid rendering it possible for Professor Broadus to resume the School of Homiletics. Professor Whitsitt was a native of Tennessee, and a graduate of Union University. He served in the army all through the war, first as a private, but presently as chaplain, in Forrest's celebrated cavalry command. After the war he spent a year at the University of Virginia, and from 1867 two years in our Seminary, after which he devoted more than two years (1869–1871) to study in Leipsic and Berlin. After a pastorate of some months in Albany, Ga., he accepted the post of Professor in the Seminary. His inaugural address, Sept. 2, 1872, discussed the "Position of the Baptists in the History of American Culture." This address was published in the "Baptist Quarterly" and in pamphlet form, and a second edition of it in 1874. He states with great force the ideas and practices upon which Baptists have laid special emphasis, thereby contributing no little to whatever is best in American thought and life. He glories in the fact "that although the Baptists are one of the foremost denominations in the United States, their direct and palpable influence upon our political destinies — in controlling public elections, exciting agitation, or manipulating the legislative, judicial, or executive authorities — is quite inappreciable and insignificant. There is nothing that furnishes to our own people, and to all the friends of religion, a juster ground of pride and thankfulness." His concluding exhortation is very wholesome: —

"The people with whom your lot is cast, my brethren, have emancipated the intellect, and have opened the Bible to all. You will be called to move among men of active, independent minds. Your principal claim to their respect, and, as a consequence, your best prospects for usefulness, will depend upon your intellectual and moral endowments and culture. They recognize the validity of no sacramental theories: you will therefore be surrounded by no halo of priestly sanctity. Hence it is imperatively necessary that you should employ diligence in arming yourself thoroughly for the duties before you. Remember, too, that the pulpits of a people professing these levelling, humanitarian principles, these earnest Gospel truths, are no fit theatre for over-cultivated, weak-thoughted, intellectual exquisites, doling out diluted and harmless treatises on philosophy or æsthetics. Men of robust spirit are in demand, who, like our blessed Master, keep in sympathy with the common people, and are gladly heard by them; who in connection with apostolic ruggedness and vigor cultivate also apostolic gentleness and simplicity."

That same year, 1872, Dr. Boyce made a remarkable sacrifice for the benefit of the Seminary. A good deal of objection had been made in some quarters to certain teachings of Dr. Williams in the class of Church Government, particularly to his teaching that persons who have been immersed by Pedobaptists or Campbellites may be properly received into a Baptist church without being baptized by a Baptist minister. Some newspaper articles had severely assailed Dr. Williams for those views, and the Seminary on that account. Dr. Boyce greatly desired that the Seminary should attract to its privileges all sorts of Baptists, from every part of the Southern country, and should not be looked upon as representing one party among us in opposition to some other party. He knew that his own views of Church Government would be less objectionable than those of Dr. Williams in the quarters indicated. He also knew that Williams would always have preferred to teach Systematic Theology rather than Church History, as the former greatly better suited his mental constitution and general culture. It would be a great sacrifice for Boyce to cease teaching Theology, in which he had always delighted, and had now enjoyed a dozen years of experience, and to turn his attention to Church History, — a subject so vast, and demanding boundless reading. And warnings had begun that his health was no longer perfect. But he thought the matter over, and decided to offer Williams an exchange of subjects, with the understanding that while Boyce should have to be absent on agency work in gathering the endowment and effecting the proposed removal, Williams would also continue to teach his former subject. This seemed a very wise arrangement to make Dr. Boyce foot-loose for the present, and have the work in both departments ably done. Dr. Williams entered with great delight upon his favorite subject, to which he had given his chief attention when professor in the Theological Department of Mercer University. He had extraordinary power of terse, comprehensive, and clear statement of truth. After two or three years of experience, his lectures in Systematic Theology must have been of an excellence rarely equalled, for their exact definitions, their closely concatenated arguments, and their profound spiritual sympathy; they were highly valued by the students. But the unanticipated delay which kept Dr. Boyce away for several years after, caused Dr. Williams to wear himself out, as we shall sadly see, under the burden of two great departments of teaching. None the less was Dr. Boyce making at the time a great personal sacrifice, in relinquishing the subject which he greatly preferred and in which he had already a rich experience, and promising to turn, when he could resume teaching, to entirely new work, all for the Seminary's sake. Only a teacher, and one who has reached the age of forty-five, as Dr. Boyce had now done, can fully understand what a sacrifice was here made.

At this meeting of the Southern Baptist Convention, May, 1872, Dr. Boyce was elected President of that body. He was re-elected annually till 1879, and again in 1888. His predecessor, Dr. P. H. Mell, of Georgia, was universally considered an unrivalled presiding officer. People soon began to say that Dr. Boyce presided better than any one they had ever seen, except Dr. Mell, and some went further still. To preside well over a big Baptist Convention is no ordinary task; the Speaker in the National House of Representatives, or the president of a National Nominating Convention, has scarcely greater difficulties to overcome. Every Baptist of them all feels himself perfectly free, and wishes to be personally uncontrolled, and yet all desire that the president shall maintain perfect order. In appointing committees, due regard must be paid to the different sides of a question, and to the States from which men come. In deciding points of order, the president must be prompt and positive. Dr. Mell used to say that it is better for a presiding officer to err sometimes than ever to hesitate. Dr. Kerfoot has quaintly put this by reversing a celebrated phrase: "It is better to be president than to be right." Dr. Boyce seemed never wanting in mastery of the whole situation, nor in perfect courtesy and fairness to all, while it would be hard to find his equal in the glowing cordiality and vivid sympathy with which every speaker was recognized. It must have often caused the man to feel more hopeful of making a good speech.[1] Some years later, when Dr. Boyce began to teach Church

---

[1] Dr. Folk, of the "Baptist Reflector," stated, after Boyce's death, that during the Convention at Nashville in 1878 a distinguished gentleman, already familiar with deliberative bodies, and afterwards a United States Senator, was very much struck with the ability of Dr. Boyce as a presiding officer, and expressed his admiration openly, though not a Baptist, nor personally acquainted.

Government and Pastoral Duties, he accepted the suggestion that it was desirable to give regular lessons in Parliamentary proceedings, as time is often lost in churches, associations and conventions from lack of thorough acquaintance with this matter. He introduced Dr. Mell's "Parliamentary Practice" as a text-book, and made the course of instruction quite a feature of the Seminary's work, which is kept up with marked ability by his successor, Dr. Kerfoot.

In the latter part of May, 1872, Dr. Boyce had a notable experience in attending a meeting of the American Baptist Educational Commission at Philadelphia. In the course of an earnest discussion as to the propriety of continuing the meetings of the convention of educators thus designated, a vigorous and distinguished brother from New York made some sort of personal issue against Dr. Boyce, the precise nature of which is not remembered. In reply, Boyce stated his position, and then said he appealed to the audience as to whether he had not stated it fairly. The response was in overwhelming applause, amounting to quite a discomfiture for the assailant. At a public breakfast given the next morning at Fairmount by Philadelphia brethren, Dr. Boyce was asked to speak, and in the course of his remarks came round to the subject of Christian friendship and brotherly regard. He presently said that sometimes in the heat of discussion one may seem to bear hard on a brother, but that a Christian man will be sure to regret this, and wish to restore cordial relations. Then, advancing towards the brother encountered the day before, and dropping the crutches which through an attack of gout he was carrying, Boyce threw his arms around him, with a look full of warm-hearted sincerity, and altogether in a manner that called forth the greatest applause, and made a lasting impression.

When it had been decided that summer, as above narrated, that the Seminary would be removed to Louisville so soon as the necessary subscription for endowment should be secured in the city and State, Dr. Boyce concluded to take up his own abode in Louisville and devote himself to that task. In October, 1872, he wrote to his sister, Mrs. Burckmyer, that he and his family had just reached Louisville, and adds: "There is a great deal of opposition, from lack of acquaintance with the matter; but this will all be overcome as I am able to set forth the merits of the case." A month later, he writes to Dr. Heman Lincoln: "I have too hard a work here to be sanguine of success. I have had some large subscriptions, — one of twenty thousand dollars; but all this will not suffice unless many others help." After spending nearly twelve months at the Louisville Hotel, Dr. Boyce lived several years at 117 West Broadway, afterwards at 742 Fourth Avenue, and finally at 102 West Chesnut.

It was of course a deeply painful thing to leave his native State. His feelings are expressed in a letter of October 22 to Rev. J. O. B. Dargan, D. D., of Darlington, S. C., father of the present professor in the Seminary.

"Your very kind letter of October 17 has just been received. I thank you for its expressions of fraternal love, which are ardently reciprocated. I wish I could be at the convention at Darlington, but duty forbids me. I must work hard here to accomplish my task. One of my colleagues has promised to attend the convention and represent the Seminary. In coming here I am not separated from my native State, I come here to do her work, as well as that of the others. I could not be otherwise than still fond of her, and still anxious for all her interests. My heart will go back constantly, especially to the dear brethren with whom I have labored and toiled and sacrificed and consulted. Noble band of brothers, when shall I find their like? I say nothing in disparagement of the brethren here when I say that my heart can find no such sympathy or resting-place as I have found in my dear Carolina. It has been no ordinary struggle to leave the State and my mountain home, especially when I leave her in so sorrowful a plight. No temptation heretofore, in several brilliant offers I have had, has sufficed. But the Seminary is my child. I prize it perhaps too highly; yet have I ever striven to hold it in due proportion to other causes of the kingdom of Christ. For it I am now undergoing more than I can tell, and as yet my future is uncertain. My dear brother, pray for me, and for the Seminary's success, that it may prove a blessing, and for the poor sinner whom God permits, though so unworthy, to labor with him. God bless you and all yours."

On Jan. 4, 1873, he wrote from Louisville to a gifted friend in South Carolina, Hon. William Henry Trescot, who has long held important positions in the State Department at Washington and in the public service abroad, and who had frequently been Boyce's guest at Greenville. The letter abounds in expressions of cordial regard for him and other friends in South Carolina. Mr. Trescot was at the time seeking some office to which the Legislature must elect, and Boyce refers to the matter in terms that are suggestive: —

"If I can further your election in any way, write. But as I have no former servant in the Legislature, no influence with the whites, and feel in conscience bound not to bribe, even if I had the money, you must point out the way of successful operation."

On the same day he wrote a letter to a venerable and honored lady who had long been his near neighbor and friend in Greenville. Mrs. Butler was the sister of Commodore Oliver Hazard Perry; her husband, Dr. Butler, deceased some years before, was the brother of Senator A. P. Butler, upon whose death Dr. Boyce preached a sermon, as heretofore mentioned; her son is General M. C. Butler, of Confederate cavalry fame, and who has long been United States Senator from South Carolina. She was a notable figure in Greenville society, held in great respect by everybody, and, as the letter shows, in high esteem by those who knew her well. She had recently gone to visit her son the General at Columbia, and had written to the

Boyces, complaining that she had not heard from them. After referring to these circumstances, Dr. Boyce's letter proceeds: —

"Forget you! — I never could do that; how could I? I have never had a better friend, nor any outside of my relatives who seemed to care as much for me as you, and I assure you I have appreciated it. For such small favors as I have been able to show you, — after all, mere neighborly acts, — you have seemed more grateful than I felt was due; so much so as to lead me often to feel ashamed that I could do and had done so little. Nor can I ever forget the great kindness you have always shown to my family. Yet, after all, let me tell you what, amid the excellences of a character which has been the wonder and admiration of your many friends, has always been to me your most beautiful trait. Not that maternal devotion which you have exemplified to all, but the depths of which in my private talks with you I have had the privilege to know as few but your children know it; not that wonderful force of character which has carried you, with God's help, through so much tribulation and strugglings with the world, and which perhaps is the trait most appreciated by your friends in general, — but that self-sacrificing spirit which has never sent the poor away unaided, even from an empty larder and a stock of clothing really needed for yourself. I have seen this in so many ways displayed, putting the blush upon myself and all those around you, that I have learned to love you even more for what you are not to me than for what you are.

"You will laugh, and say I am flattering you. Well, I might feel like flattering if I were not talking about serious things, and might claim my right as a man to do so with a woman. But it is not so now. I am telling you, however, truths upon paper which I could not tell you to your face. I am not very demonstrative, although by no means cold or altogether lacking; still, I hide much of my feeling of affection within myself. Why should I not, however, say these things to one who cannot be injured by them, and who will appreciate, I know, even the love which in her modesty she disclaims, and denies the truthfulness of the character I have drawn?

"In your letter to my wife you say that you are seventy years old. God has truly blessed you with a long life: may he add to it still many other years! Yet, after all, our living here is not the best. It is the life to come to which it is our privilege to look, and for which God helps us to long. I trust that he has put this spirit in your heart. In our weariness and distress, it is easy to say, 'O that I had wings like a dove; then would I fly away and be at rest.' But it is our privilege to feel the same even in our joys. If God's presence be sweet to us, and we enjoy the blessing of constant communion with him, then are our hearts gladdened with the hope of his appearing. Even amid our joys we can say, 'Lord Jesus, come quickly.' God has deeply afflicted you, and I know your heart has been often uttering this prayer, — I trust not only in the hour of sadness, but in the quiet moment of contemplation. That God should be *our* God is a great and glorious truth. How fearful the description of the unbelieving, 'having no hope, and without God in the world'! How delightful is that twenty-third Psalm, read especially in connection with the passages in the New Testament where Christ speaks of himself as the Shepherd. How especially comforting in our depressions of spirit, and when we feel that God has deserted us or forsaken us, to look at David in the case as recorded in the 23d and 24th chapters of I. Samuel, and then turn to the 142d Psalm, — which David calls Maschil, a mystery, — and read his experience. Especially look at the third verse, 'When my spirit was overwhelmed within me, then *thou* knewest my path.' And then our hearts may say as he does at the close, 'Bring my soul out of prison, that I may praise thy name.'

"Have you yet been able to say heartily, 'Thy will be done,' in all your afflictions? I know that you have prayed this, and kept on uttering the prayer, and I have prayed God to help you to continue to do so, hard as it was to persevere in the darkness that surrounded you. And I have felt sure that if you continued, your God would give strength, and enable you to feel that he is right in all things; and not only right, but merciful and wise.

"How many evils have taken place in our State, and especially in Greenville, since I left! . . . I do not know whether I should tell you that I hope to be in South Carolina some time about February 1st, and may have a chance of seeing you. I shall do so if I can, even if I have to stop especially for that purpose."

After a brief visit to South Carolina, as indicated, he was hastily summoned to Washington, Ga., by the death of his wife's honored mother. Returning to Louisville, his energies were again earnestly devoted to the sufficiently difficult task before him. Some of the leading Baptists of Louisville took hold at once of his enterprise, giving generous subscriptions and all their moral influence. But several eminent and honored men decidedly opposed the movement, believing that it was not best for the Baptist cause in Louisville and Kentucky. Some said that while a university would be of great service to the city, in educating its young men, a theological school would do no local service, as its students would almost all come from a distance and return. Some contended that it was not best for the general usefulness of the Southern Seminary to place it on the border of the Southern country. But the main objection was from the idea that it would turn away denominational attention and support from the two Kentucky Baptist Colleges,— Georgetown College, and Bethel College at Russellville. Each of these had a theological department, which would probably be practically abandoned if a theological seminary were established in the State. Brethren who had never seen a Baptist college working without a theological department, supposed that to give up this theological instruction would be to turn away from the college pretty much all the students who were preparing for the ministry. That would greatly weaken the interest of the churches in the college, and would take away from the other students the moral influence of those who were preparing for the ministry. With such views and expectations, they very naturally objected. Others, not entering so far into probable results, simply thought that to interest the denomination of the State in a new institution at Louisville would prevent their contributing to the colleges, both of which needed increased endowment. There were also in Louisville a few honored brethren who had their doubts about the propriety of putting young men through a theological course. They believed in sending them to college, but held that then, with their minds well trained, they could best learn theology from the Bible and through talking with the old ministers while engaged in actual preaching. Such opposition from a number of leading brethren, honored for their intelligence and liberality in other things, was of course sufficient to prevent a great many from contributing. It is comparatively easy to hinder giving; a mere pebble may stop a wheel that is going up hill. Even outside of Louisville, certain prominent friends of the two colleges, at their respective locations or elsewhere, wrote letters or made visits to Louisville, decidedly opposing the project. Some of these were men of high character and intelligence, acting upon convictions which only a wider experience than they had enjoyed of such matters could correct. Dr. Boyce very soon began to perceive, as extracts from the letters above given show, that his task was hard.

After some weeks, in consultation with friends, he got up a public meeting of citizens of Louisville, at the lecture hall of the Public Library, now the Polytechnic Society. It was pretty well attended. The president was the venerable Judge Bullock, a devout Episcopalian. One of the addresses was by Rev. E. P. Humphrey, D. D., an eminent and justly beloved Presbyterian pastor, who had formerly been professor at Centre College, Danville, Ky. Dr. Humphrey spoke, with characteristic superiority to all denominational narrowness, in favor of bringing to Louisville an institution that would greatly promote the cause of religion in the city; and he ended by giving a generous contribution himself. In regard to this occasion Mr. Theodore Harris, the celebrated Louisville banker, who became a very intimate friend of Dr. Boyce, and who is a man of fine literary taste, as his own writings show, has said that Dr. Boyce's address struck him very much, not only by its practical wisdom and strength, but by the elevation and finish of the style, — quite superior to his sermons. Mr. Harris thought the address must have been very carefully composed and committed to memory, and was surprised to learn some time afterwards that it was entirely unwritten. The fact is, that only in such a situation was Dr. Boyce at his best. When his magnificent practical faculties were thoroughly aroused by some great undertaking, and his soul was kindled with strong desire to carry his point, and the growing sympathy of the audience wrought him up more and more, then the imaginative and æsthetical side of his nature came into full play. *This* was the man that so much delighted in pictures and in poetry. *Now* the practical side of him and the æsthetical side of him were lifted into vivid and harmonious action. But in writing most of his sermons, though interested in the train of thought, and anxious to do good, there was no such exaltation of imagination, passion, and taste. Only when treating a theme of uncommon practical importance, and at the same time congenial to his deepest feelings, does one of his written sermons rise to this level. If he could have worked on to middle age as exclusively a pastor, his powers as a preacher would have been much more frequently exercised in such symmetrical and exalted action.

Dr. Peter remembers a like remarkable exhibition of power at a meeting in Walnut Street Baptist Church, when President Noah K. Davis, of Bethel College, spoke with his signal ability against the removal of the Seminary to Louisville. Dr. Boyce's reply is said to have been able and impressive in the extreme.

It may be well to mention a matter incidentally connected with the distinguished brother just referred to, which ought to be a warning to men who can see so much deeper into a millstone than there is a hole in it. The

EFFORTS TO REMOVE THE SEMINARY. 237

following June, President Davis was elected Professor of Moral Philosophy in the University of Virginia, where, as teacher and author, he has ever since been amply fulfilling the high hopes of his friends. Several Kentucky Associations of the summer were visited by a brother from another State, who meant no unkindness whatever, but thought he perceived a piece of superb management, and took interest in pointing it out. "Did you ever see," he would say, "such a manager as this man Boyce? He knew that the colleges would be in the way of his scheme; and, do you observe, he sent one of his colleagues beforehand to be President of Georgetown College, and now he has worked to get the President of Bethel College moved away to another State. Isn't that splendid?" When Dr. Boyce heard of this commendation, he said quietly that all he had to do with Manly's going to Georgetown was to oppose it with all his might to the very last; and all he had to do with Professor Davis's going to Virginia was that he received a letter from a friend asking him to recommend Professor Davis, and he was of course glad to recommend a very able man for a very desirable position, if he cared to have it. Thus the splendid piece of management was wholly imaginary; as the Germans say, it was "grasped out of pure air."

In May, 1873, the Southern Baptist Convention met at Mobile, and with it, as usual, the Trustees of the Seminary; and there Dr. Boyce made what some of us regard as the most notable speech of his life. An esteemed brother from North Carolina, in attending the Commencement of the Seminary at Greenville just before, had become fully persuaded that it was quite improper to remove the institution from Greenville. On the way to Mobile he communicated this view to delegates from the Carolinas and Georgia, and a strong feeling arose to that effect. Whenever any one of them sat down by a professor on the way to talk about the matter, his simple answer was, "Wait till you hear Boyce; he knows all about it."

The Trustees having requested the Convention to approve the removal on which they had decided, the Convention went into Committee of the Whole. Putting another brother, of course, into the chair, Dr. Boyce took the floor at a time he had not expected, and spoke a whole hour. He reviewed the history of the Seminary, the terrible losses by the war, the noble generosity of the brethren in South Carolina and elsewhere in gifts for current support; he then showed the necessity of permanent endowment, and the impossibility of obtaining this save in a State where the Baptists had much greater financial strength than was then true of the State he himself loved so well. But this statement, or any statement, must be unjust to an address full of fact and argument and passionate appeal. It was a lifetime concentrating itself upon one point; a great mind and a great heart surcharged with thought and feeling; a man of noble nature appealing to all that was noblest in his hearers; a Christian speaking in Christ's name to his brethren. Drs. J. C. Furman and J. O. B. Dargan, of South Carolina, then spoke in a spirit worthy of themselves and of their State. When the matter came to a vote, the Convention gave a most animated and cordial vote of approval; and the resolute and consistent brother from North Carolina, with his solitary "Nay," helped the matter by showing that it was in no sense a vote *nem. con.*

In the summer of that year there came a great financial crisis,— one of those penalties of inflation which every now and then prostrate the business affairs of the country, and bring to a standstill all large projects for the future. Of course men in Louisville could not then be expected to make any considerable engagements for the Seminary's endowment. Yet Boyce could not give up his work, or it would have been regarded in subsequent years as simply one of the projects that had perished with the crisis. It appears that as nothing could then be done in the city, he struck out into the country churches and associations, where the financial troubles would not be so promptly felt, and where time would be well spent in extending his personal acquaintance. This interruption of his plans must have been a great trial to all the strong elements of his character. Dr. M. Cary Peter, of Louisville, whose father, Dr. Arthur Peter, had pledged the first large contribution, remembers that during that first winter he was himself in poor health and laid aside from business, and that at his noble mother's suggestion he went about the city with Dr. Boyce, introducing him. He says few things in all his life have so much impressed him as the unconquerable fortitude, the patient gentleness and never-failing courtesy with which Dr. Boyce endured many successive failures, sometimes attended by unkind words. Such a winter of struggling effort, and then such a summer of sad interruption,— these are the times that try men's souls! and here was a soul born to conquer. This was a proud man, who keenly felt the personal humiliation of being refused like a beggar. But he steadfastly endured it all, because fully persuaded that he was working for the real good of mankind and for the glory of Christ the Lord, and hopeful, amid all delays and difficulties, that he would not prove to be working in vain.

Late in the year he went to Richmond, Va., seeking a special contribution to pay notes due for salaries. Ten years later he wrote to Dr. A. E. Dickinson, volunteering a contribution for Richmond College, out of gratitude for the cheerful and generous help which the Richmond brethren and sisters had given him in that season of financial panic.

In April, 1874, Boyce wrote to Joshua Levering, of Baltimore, who is now a leading Trustee of the Seminary, and Vice-President of the Board. Mr. Levering's lamented father, Eugene Levering, had left a generous bequest to the Seminary, which Boyce thought it would be better not to pay over immediately, lest it should be consumed in annual expenses, when it ought to be kept for endowment. He refers to an appeal he has recently made, now the third time, for five-year bonds for annual support. The movement to endow and remove the Seminary has been so delayed, and is likely to be so protracted, that he feels it necessary to provide for current support during several years to come. These bonds to give so much a year for five years had been sent by mail in a gratifying manner. "We have up to this time about $26,000, and are getting about $1,000 a day. I hope this will increase. I think it very doubtful if we shall secure $40,000 before the Convention meets, and if not, I fear we had better give up the sessions for a year or two, until we get our permanent endowment." The Southern Baptist Convention met a few weeks later, at Jefferson, Tex., and the amount of bonds received by mail or handed him by the delegates came up to $40,000, showing that the enterprise had a strong hold upon the brotherhood. Yet $30,000 more would be necessary, and was it possible to obtain this at the Convention? The brethren from other States had been contributing again and again for nine years. The chief hope must be in Texas, where the denomination was beginning to grow conscious of strength; but the Seminary was very little known. At the request of the Trustees a suitable time was granted by the Convention, and Boyce explained the history and design of the institution, and its present hopes and needs. The noble brethren, though just rallying from the financial collapse of the year before, gave him the pledges he asked for $30,000.

This $14,000 a year would support the professors and necessary agents, if all paid. But experience had shown that deaths, failures in business, and other changes would prevent full payment, and a margin was needed to make the operation safe. When the Convention adjourned, most of the brethren from other States went off upon excursions

EFFORTS TO REMOVE THE SEMINARY. 241

which the Texas friends had kindly provided. But Boyce and a colleague returned together in anxious consultation about the necessary margin of five-year bonds. We seemed to have exhausted every resource. What could be done? To go on without additional bonds would be to accumulate debt, year after year. What could be done? A week or two later, the colleague had to speak in Washington city at the Baptist Anniversaries, including a Jubilee of the American Baptist Publication Society. During the anniversaries he was approached by Dr. S. S. Cutting and Samuel Colgate, Esq., chief promoters of the American Baptist Educational Commission, who said they had seen something in the papers about an effort to secure current support for the Southern Seminary, and wanted to know how it stood. The result was that they begged half an hour from the American Baptist Home Mission Society one evening, and invited a five minutes' statement of the Seminary's condition and wants. Then the brethren began to make pledges of cash, or so much a year for five years, and presently Dr. Richard Fuller took the meeting in charge for a good quarter of an hour, in his large-hearted way; the great assembly grew more and more interested, the half hour was somewhat overrun by common consent, and the noble Northern brethren had pledged over $10,000. They paid it too, scarcely a dollar ever failing,— it is a way they have, to pay the pledges they make in public meetings.

For that summer of 1874 Dr. Boyce arranged a tour of central Kentucky, accompanied by one of his colleagues, with appointments published in advance, and running through near forty days. Twice on Sunday, and every evening in the week but Saturday, there was a sermon, after which he made his plea for the Seminary, asked for contributions, then begged those who had promised them to remain after the dismission and sign his bonds. Beginning late on the summer evenings, and with all this to go through, it was usually near midnight before we could retire, and we must take an early train in the morning for the next place. One of the party suffered much from the loss of sleep, and sometimes strove to make it up in the afternoons. But Boyce seemed never to need more than five or six hours of sleep, and was in fine health all the time. Every week, sometimes oftener than once a week, one or the other would begin to get low-spirited, through some case of poor success; but the moment either would show any despondency, the other began to encourage him, perhaps to laugh it off, and so the whole series of appointments went through, with results that upon the whole were highly gratifying. It was observed throughout this journey, as often before and afterwards, that Dr. Boyce was habitually a small eater. His large figure, and the fact that he had begun to have occasional attacks of gout, led many people to imagine that he ate very freely. But it was never so, at any time of his life. Even Kentucky hospitality did not tempt him beyond a decided moderation.

This journey and subsequent events brought out a noble trait of character in a leading private member of one of the Kentucky churches. Nimrod Long, Esq., of Russellville, was a devoted friend and liberal supporter of Bethel College. He believed that to bring the Seminary to Louisville would damage the College; and so from the beginning he frankly opposed the movement, even visiting Louisville to urge that his kindred and old friends should not contribute. When he saw the announcement that the series of appointments was to include Russellville, he wrote at once a most cordial invitation to stay at his house. He said it was well understood that he could not support the movement, as a matter of conviction, but he wanted us to feel sure, and everybody else to see, that personally he was our friend; and so his invitation must not be denied. There was never a more cordial hospitality. He went to hear the sermon and the plea, looked on while the Presi-

EFFORTS TO REMOVE THE SEMINARY.

dent and some of the Professors of Bethel College contributed, and a good many others of the community, and took pains afterwards at home to explain to one of the visitors his position. His frank and brotherly way encouraged the other to assure him that he would find things work otherwise than he supposed, as had been found elsewhere in Baptist colleges having no theological department; that in two years after the Seminary began in Louisville, Bethel College would have more men preparing for the ministry than ever before. "Well," he said, "if that happens I'll believe it, and then I'll change my mind." Only one year after the Seminary came to Louisville, the S. B. Convention met in Nashville; and as Dr. Boyce was presiding, he requested a friend to ask special contributions for current support of the Seminary. The first man that spoke was Nimrod Long, saying, "I'll give you five hundred dollars." The answer was, "I thank you, many times over. I know exactly what that means." "Yes," he responded cheerily, "and that's not all. I'm going to help your endowment before long." Be sure he kept his word. He even came to Louisville to visit old friends, when, some time afterwards, the Seminary was again in a crisis about the endowment, urging that it must be saved. *There* was a man for you, — a man of strong convictions, self-relying force of character, who could push great enterprises and never give way; yet a man entirely free from mere obstinate persistence in a position once assumed, a man ready to change his mind when he saw cause, and to say he had changed his mind, and to act accordingly with high enthusiasm. Oh that among the great and strong men of the world there were more frequent instances of this admirable spirit![1]

Three years longer, making five years in all, Dr. Boyce resided in Louisville before he could effect the removal of

---

[1] Mr. Long's sons also contributed largely, and his son-in-law, W. C. Hall, Esq., of Louisville, who is a Trustee of the Seminary.

the Seminary. Numerous journeys had to be made into all parts of Kentucky, not only to associations and churches, but again and again to the home of some man who was able and possibly might be willing to help largely. Little by little brethren were brought to understand the nature and the aims of the Seminary, and what he considered its unrivalled adaptation to the wants of the Baptist ministry in general. Slowly one and another man came to believe that it was really worth while to have such an institution in Kentucky, and worth his while to help. More and more the excellent Baptist men and women of the city and State came to know Dr. Boyce personally, to appreciate the strength and nobleness of his character, the breadth of his good sense and beauty of his gentlemanly bearing, the sincerity and devotion of his personal piety. In fact, a large proportion of people, even among those of considerable intelligence, can seldom be brought to take lively interest in something still future and distant, in some enterprise of which they have no personal experience, until they come to know and love its living representative. This makes it quite important that corresponding secretaries and other general agents should not be too often changed. Many began to help Dr. Boyce because they loved him and sympathized with his intense desire; others because they saw he would never give up, would keep at it till he succeeded, and would politely keep after them till they yielded. Oh, the long, sore struggle for the high-toned gentleman, the ambitious student cut off from the studies he loved, the man who had devoted himself to teaching, and now, year after year, could not teach at all!

He also found it necessary to make many journeys to other States, with a view to obtain from them the requisite $200,000, which with the expected Kentucky contribution would make half a million of endowment. There is mention in a letter of July, 1875, of such a trip recently made

EFFORTS TO REMOVE THE SEMINARY. 245

to Texas and Mississippi. In the beginning of 1876 he had an agent at work in Texas, Rev. A. J. Holt, and at the same time Rev. G. W. Given began to help him in Kentucky. In the beginning of 1877 Dr. M. B. Wharton commenced an agency of several years in Georgia, Alabama, and other States; and there were various other agents whose names are not recalled. At the Richmond meeting of the S. B. Convention in May, 1876, resolutions were adopted, on motion of Hon. J. L. M. Curry, expressing a deep interest in the Seminary, and a strong desire for the early completion of its endowment, and warmly recommending liberal and speedy contributions, with a view to secure the completion of the requisite endowment, if possible, by the end of that year. And for this purpose the Board authorized the General Financial Agent (Dr. Boyce) to employ as many helpers as he should think proper.

Through all these financial labors Dr. Boyce gladly embraced numerous opportunities for preaching, both in his journeys and at Louisville. In January, 1875, it is mentioned in a letter that he is preaching at Walnut Street, where the church had at that time no pastor. Though frequently interrupted by necessary journeys, he supplied the pulpit for many months. He also preached in the other Baptist churches of the city a number of times, and to several churches of other denominations. With the spirit of a true preacher, Dr. Boyce yearned after the pulpit and the pastorate. No man is fit to be a theological professor who would not really prefer to be a pastor. But think what is thereby involved of sacrifice for every man fitly engaged in such instruction! Once, in 1875, Dr. Boyce wrote to Dr. Tupper that he sometimes felt strongly tempted to let go the Seminary and devote himself to pastoral work.

The internal history of the Seminary, during these years of Dr. Boyce's struggling efforts to prepare for removal, was quiet and fairly prosperous for some four years. The number of students rose to over sixty, and included not a few men of remarkable gifts and promise. Drs. Toy and Whitsitt were putting forth their finest energies in study and teaching. Dr. Williams was making Systematic Theology a delight to the students, while still keeping up his former classes in Church History, and Church Government and Pastoral Duties. But, alas! his health somewhat suddenly gave way. He had never been exactly a vigorous man, was little inclined to exercise, and worked with great mental intensity. The strain of double work, continued year after year, through the impossibility of Dr. Boyce's returning, wore him out more seriously than any of us were aware. He would not think it necessary to give up his country churches, where he was greatly beloved, and found preaching a constant joy. One winter night he slept in a small room with a missing pane of glass. The result was a deep cold, and a throat ail to which he would not yield, and which steadily worked its way downward. He had an indomitable spirit, and could not bear to acknowledge himself unable to go on with his loved work, until at last he stopped through sheer necessity, and all too late. The Board at Richmond in May, 1876, authorized the faculty to employ competent brethren to give aid in the instruction, in consequence of Dr. Williams's ill health, to whom they tendered leave of absence, with salary continued. The faculty arranged that Church History should be taught by Assistant-Professor Whitsitt, and Latin Theology by Professor Toy. In the general or English Theology class Dr. J. L. Reynolds, then professor in Furman University, gave three lectures a week, and in Church Government and Pastoral Duties two lectures a week were given by President James C. Furman. In Homiletics, Dr. James C. Hiden, then pastor in Greenville, gave aid in the instruction, and especially in correcting the written exercises, as the professor in that department had to resume the Junior Class in Greek, previously taught by

Professor Whitsitt. The faculty were very thankful that three gentlemen were on the ground so remarkably competent to give aid in these several schools.

At the same Richmond meeting of the Board of Trustees, the new degree of "English Graduate" was established. This meant, and has continued to mean, that when a student has been graduated separately in every school or department except the classes in Hebrew and Greek and the Latin class in Theology, he shall receive a general diploma as an English Graduate of the Seminary. It should be observed that this is not a separate course, pursued by those only who do not study the learned languages, but these men have studied all their subjects in the same classes with the men who also study Hebrew, etc.

Dr. Williams made conscientious efforts, going to the mountains in summer, and down the country in winter, to resist the fell ravages of consumption. But the movement was sadly rapid. He died at Aiken, S. C., Feb. 20, 1877, a little less than fifty-six years of age. He was buried at Greenville, and Dr. Boyce came from Louisville to take part in the funeral services. The text for the funeral discourse by Dr. Broadus had been indicated by Dr. Williams himself: "My times are in thy hand." It is vain to attempt any fitting eulogy of William Williams. Besides the high intellectual powers which have been several times referred to in this narrative, his character was such as to command profound respect and warm affection. While undemonstrative in manner, and scorning all pretence, it needed only to know him fairly well, and you would love him warmly. Whoever knew a man more completely genuine, more thoroughly sincere, more conscientious in all his doings? Through life he continued to exhibit those qualities of mind and character which he had shown already in college days, and which are so well stated by Dr. J. L. M. Curry, who was his younger fellow-student in Franklin College, Georgia, now the University of Georgia: —

" In his classes he was easily first, and the first honor which he attained at his graduation, was the proof of his industry and attainments in the College course. The qualifications of mind which gave him success in the class-room gave him success in the debating society, and at that period the debating societies were conducted with an enthusiasm, an interest, a devotion, an emulation that I have not known elsewhere or since. His power of analysis, his keen and thorough perception, his clearness of statement, his discrimination between the true and the false, the genuine and the specious, his apt and concise language, his honesty of thinking, made him a master in debate. I recall a public speech which he made during his Senior year, on temperance, — a dry subject, unless illustrated by anecdote and eloquence. It was short, simple, compact, argumentative, conclusive; and I heard no speech during my college days which elicited such favorable comment. In personal intercourse he won respect and regard by quietness of manner, unvarying courtesy, frankness of speech, uprightness of conduct, and independence of thought. No one who knew him in college life was surprised at his remarkable career as a lawyer, a preacher, and a teacher."

Dr. Williams liked best to prepare his sermons by carefully writing them in full; then, leaving the manuscript at home, and making no attempt at recitation, he spoke freely. By this means he secured the condensation and terseness in which he so delighted and so excelled; and yet the delivery was living speech. This method of preparing and preaching has great advantages for those with whom it never degenerates into recitation. It would be a good thing for our ministry if a volume of Dr. Williams's sermons could be published and widely scattered.

It proved impossible for Dr. Boyce to secure pledges for the entire three hundred thousand dollars in Kentucky and two hundred thousand in other States by the end of 1876, or by May of the following year. But the work had

EFFORTS TO REMOVE THE SEMINARY. 249

so far progressed as to give assurance that it would ultimately succeed. Very encouraging was the gift, by Dr. and Mrs. J. Lawrence Smith, of a tract of land not far from Louisville, which seemed likely to prove extremely valuable; and we know that other important gifts came afterwards from the same source. There were not a few, in the city and State, who by this time had given quite generously. Dr. Arthur Peter made at the outset a large gift in land. Messrs. George W. and W. F. Norton had begun what proved to be a series of noble contributions. Messrs. Joe Werne, J. C. McFerran, J. B. McFerran, John S. Long, W. C. Hall, Theodore Harris, and C. W. Gheens had given five thousand dollars each, twelve persons had given one thousand each, including three who were not Baptists; and many of the smaller contributions were in fact extremely generous. There had also been some very gratifying donations elsewhere in Kentucky, and in other States. And now the conclusion was reached that the removal should no longer be deferred. It appeared necessary that Boyce should resume teaching, as Williams had been taken away; and yet he could not let go his hold upon the endowment work of which Louisville was the centre. The number of students in attendance at Greenville had for four years stood still at sixty-six to sixty-eight, and was not likely to increase without some forward movement. All concerned were growing weary of the long delay and the apparent uncertainty. Something was needed to give a new impulse to the whole enterprise. So the Board resolved, in the meeting at New Orleans in May, 1877, that the Seminary should be removed at once, — a proper understanding being reached during the summer with the General Association of Kentucky, so as to leave no hitch as to the pledges for endowment.

The idea of immediate removal was favorably received. Friends in Louisville and Kentucky felt cheered and assured. The long-cherished idea was about to descend from the clouds and become an accomplished fact. To be sure, there was as yet but little of endowment actually invested and yielding income. The annual receipts upon the five-year bonds of 1874 were in considerable part needed to support agents in different States, in order to make further collections for endowment. But necessary progress is true prudence; and although the Seminary suffered great financial difficulties a few years later, no one has ever questioned that it was wise to effect the removal without further delay.

CHAPTER XV.

TEN BUSY YEARS IN THE SEMINARY AT LOUISVILLE, 1877-1887.

IT was physically no great task to remove the Seminary from Greenville to Louisville. There was nothing to move, except the library of a few thousand volumes, and three professors, — Broadus, Toy, and Whitsitt, — only one of whom had a family. We all loved Greenville warmly. We had found the climate healthy, and the community remarkably agreeable. We were strongly attached to the Baptist Church, the professors in Furman University, and many other valued friends, of all persuasions and pursuits. The Seminary had existed there for eighteen years, gathering many valued associations, and we had to leave behind the tomb of our cherished colleague, and other sacred spots. But there was no doubt in any mind among us that the removal was wise, and all felt hopeful that the results would vindicate the decision which had been reached. There was at once a considerable increase of attendance, the whole number of students for the first session at Louisville being eighty-nine, while sixty-eight had been the largest number before.

The session opened Sept. 1, 1877, and on the previous evening, in the Public Library Hall (now the Polytechnic building), Dr. Boyce devoted the usual Introductory Lecture to an outline of the Seminary's history, and its peculiar plans of instruction. This lecture was published in the "Western Recorder." Some extracts from it will indicate the views and feelings with which he now looked back upon his years of toil and trial, and onwards to the

Seminary's prospects and hopes. The first extract merely alludes, in passing, to opposition which he had encountered in various ways, sometimes unkind, and personally painful.

"I do not propose to recount the history of this enterprise. That history, so far as it ever can be written, must await the full fruition of all our hopes, and should come from one less intimately associated with it than I have been. It never can be written in full; it never ought to be thus written. It is only God's inspiration which dare speak of evils and faults and injuries and calumnies proceeding from men whom we know to be good. That inspired Word alone can make these simply the shadows which bring out more gloriously the brightness of the character of the good. Human prejudice and passion would make hideous deformity of all by the excesses which its pencillings would exhibit. Let all such evil be buried in the silence of forgetfulness. Let the history, when written, tell only of the toils and trials and sacrifices, and wisdom and prudence and foresight, and prayers and tears and faith, of the people of God to whom the institution will have owed its existence and its possibilities of blessing. And God grant that it may go down to succeeding ages to bless his cause and glorify his name when all of us here have been forgotten in this world forever! In the establishment and endowment of this Seminary we think we have solved a problem of interest, not to Baptists of the South alone, but to all who are interested in the ministry of Christ as an instrumentality for the salvation of souls and the edification of his saints."

He then traces the series of movements, ending with a meeting in Louisville twenty years before, which had issued in the establishment of the Seminary at Greenville.

"The wise course pursued in the adoption of the constitution and manner of working of this Seminary, to a great degree made final success certain. Men who had objected to previous plans of theological education yielded readily to this. By it all the objections formerly urged seemed to have been removed. The means of convincing the masses had already thus been attained. From the beginning the work of endowment was popular. The funds were readily contributed. In less than six months nearly one-half the amount needed had been pledged in South Carolina, and within two years the remainder had been subscribed in the other States of the South."

But up to that time only the Atlantic Southern States and some of the Gulf States had shown much interest in the movement. The calamities of the war were overruled for good. Losing the endowment, and compelled after the war to seek aid for temporary support wherever it could be found, the Seminary had enlisted a wide sympathy, and had thus become what it was intended to be, — the common Seminary of the Baptists of the South.

"The influence it has to-day in the entire South is marvellous. No enterprise of Southern Baptists lies nearer to their hearts, or is more liberally contributed to of their means, than this. Signal proofs of the facts could be given, were they necessary."

After speaking warmly of Greenville, — the place and the people, — he goes on, —

"But the disadvantages of a location in a small town were soon realized. There was not room enough for practical work. Our object had been practical training as well as efficient study. This could not be done there, and the opportunity of doing both of them is admirably secured here. To recount the circumstances under which we have been led to Louisville would be to give an interesting chapter in the history of God's providence. Suffice it to say that the calamities of the war forced us to remove from South Carolina. The first endowment having been lost, it was necessary to secure another. In that other, South Carolina could not give the amount necessary from the State in which the Seminary is located, scarcely able, as its Baptist population now is, to complete the endowment of the Furman University, which they had previously established. In seeking a home elsewhere, we have been fortunately brought to this city. Its vast extent and large population, with the thousands here who need the instruction which Sunday-schools and small preaching places can afford, furnish every facility for exercising our pupils in the practical work of pastor and preacher. With its extensive railroad facilities we are put in immediate connection with all portions of the South. . . . Beginning with Maryland on the northeast, and extending to Missouri on the northwest, thence to Texas on the southwest, and to Florida on the southeast, . . . in connection with the Southern Baptist Convention there are one million one hundred thousand church-members, and five million five hundred thousand, persons associated with Baptist congregations, seven thousand ministers, and thirteen thousand churches. From these we must expect large numbers. I have been accustomed to estimate the possibility of five hundred students in attendance after a lapse of some years. I see no reason why this should not be so.

"Our chief difficulty lay in the varied degrees of cultivation and knowledge possessed by our ministry. They are as far from being homogeneous in this respect as they well can be. The vast multitude have had but the advantages of English education, and many of them even in this respect are very defective. A large number have attained the education afforded by our ordinary colleges. Some have been trained in institutions which will compare with any in the land. The variety of natural gifts is as diversified as that of educational development. These are facts in our ministry which must be considered in the solution of this problem. How, then, shall provision be made for all classes of such a ministry?

"We cannot prevent this diversity, if we desire to do so. Many of us think it just the kind of ministry we should have. We believe that what appears to human eyes a source of weakness is in reality a source of strength. But our time to-night forbids the attempt to argue this question at length. Suffice it to point to the extensive use made by the Romish Church of just such instrumentalities, and to the further fact that the two largest denominations in this country, which have entirely under their influence twenty-five of the fifty millions of its population (I mean the Methodists and Baptists) are the two which alone foster and rely upon men of such a variety of learning and ability. The humblest and most untaught of this ministry are not necessarily ignorant of the Word of God, though these may sometimes present it in a rough and uncouth form. They may also be, and commonly are, full of faith and prayer and zeal in the preaching of the simple gospel. . . . That God has blessed this ministry of varied classes we cannot doubt, as we remember the abundant proofs it has brought forth. Standing here to-night amid the cultivation and scholarship of the ministry of this favored city, and among some, doubtless, who disagree with the opinion I express, I freely state my own personal conviction that it is the kind of ministry which God has ordained for the conversion of the world and the edification of his people. . . . I believe that no denomination can exert a widespread influence throughout all classes of the people which does not receive its ministry from classes as varied as the membership it contains.

"For us, at any rate, this ministry of varied classes is an existing fact. The very structure of our church polity renders it impossible to rid ourselves of it. What, then, shall be done with this ministry, so far as theological education is concerned? Shall we make no provision for it? Shall we have schools for mere English students, and others for those of classical culture, or shall we combine in one common Seminary instruction for them all?

"Some have proposed separate schools for men of collegiate and non-collegiate attainments. Others have admitted the mere English students to pursue in an imperfect and desultory manner, at such times and in such classes as were possible, such studies as they might pick out here and there from a course arranged especially for men of collegiate education. Our plan has been to arrange equally for these and for those of higher culture, — even the highest, — in the one common theological seminary. Which is the wiser course? Which best solves the problem of the varied ministry? Looking back at the past from the standpoint of to-night, we believe that ours is the true solution. In it, at least, we give to men of merely English culture all the advantages they would gain by having a separate school. Every subject which could be taught is as clearly and fully presented to them as though it were to be comprehended by no other minds than theirs. A wide range of study has been made accessible to them. At the same time, we have not lowered the standard for men of the highest culture, but, on the contrary, have from the very arrangements necessary for our merely English students been able to extend the course of the better-educated beyond what we could otherwise have done. Neither is there any omission of any study, or any part of a study, usual in theological institutions, but, on the contrary, we add to the usual curriculum. If at any time and in any respect the teaching falls below what is elsewhere given, that is due, not to the fault of the system, nor to the training and attainments of the students, but to the difference of ability and learning which one instructor possesses as compared with another. In other words, the same professor will teach more thoroughly and completely under this than under the usual system.

"The first change we make is in dropping the form of classes arranged according to the number of years of attendance, and adopting that of separate classes, completing each study within the one session in which it is taken. The other system goes upon the mistaken supposition that all students can advance equally over a given study in the same time. This is not true even of college graduates. Wherever students are arranged in curriculum classes, the amount of study must be adapted to the average capacity of the class in all the studies pursued together, and not to that average in one study only, as in separate schools. The consequence is that men of better minds and preparation are retarded, and those who are below the average are unable thoroughly to master the subjects of study. But if each one selects such a number of studies as he can successfully pursue, some may take only two, others three, others even four or more, and the difference in capacity and training is compensated by the greater or less amount of work undertaken. This is to the common advantage of all. No one is kept back by the incapacity of others, and no one forced to learn imperfectly for lack of time to do the work thoroughly. . . . The simple division into schools of subjects, rather than into classes of men, gives the needed condition of successful work for all.

"A second equally simple arrangement has been to have a separate hour for each study, so that no two classes are reciting at the same time. It matters not, therefore, what subjects are taken, the student finds his recitation hours entirely distinct, and not conflicting with each other."

Dr. Boyce then goes on to show how these arrangements enable the student to spend in the Seminary one year, or two, three, or four years, or even more, selecting for each year the subjects best adapted to his wishes and preparation, and completing each subject within the session. He shows that this plan has not only great advantages for the students, but also for the professors.

"I think I speak in reason when I say that under this system any professor can accomplish twofold as thorough work as he could under the arrangement usually made. . . . From this review of the course it is manifest that by our system no student suffers any detriment, but that both kinds of students are the rather benefited by the arrangements for united study. It may be stated that this result was unexpected. We had believed that no injury would accrue. We had not dreamed of the greater extent to which, in this and in other ways, the studies of the college-bred students would be extended by a plan, the primary object of which had been to make provision for the better instruction of the mere English students."

Here again, in Louisville, as when opening the Seminary in Greenville, Dr. Boyce suggested that the Seminary should abstain from erecting buildings until adequate provision should first have been made for supporting the instruction. He rented lecture-rooms and a library room in the third and fourth stories of what was then known as Public Library Hall, now the Polytechnic. A hotel of moderate size was rented, with additional rooms in a building not far away, to supply the wants of students. Such continued to be the Seminary's local habitation for a number of years. A theological school draws almost all of its students from a distance, and therefore is less dependent than other institutions upon the local attraction of large and handsome buildings. These are very desirable, to interest the general community, to gratify the friends in general, and to carry on the teaching with full convenience and advantage; but they are not indispensable in attracting students. Many a struggling institution has been long hindered, some have been even ruined, by the erection of costly buildings before the time. The main thing in any educational establishment, and especially in what are called professional schools, is always the teaching. Sooner or later, good teaching is recognized, and bad teaching is detected.

It was found, to an even greater extent than had been anticipated, that the students could live more cheaply in Louisville than they had done in Greenville, because Louisville is a provision centre, and almost all supplies could be procured at wholesale rates. It was of course otherwise with professors having families, for whom life in a large city is in many ways expensive; and being unable to provide dwellings, the Seminary made a special provision for house-rent. The professors and their families were most cordially received by leading Baptist families of the city, and many citizens of various denominations. The hearts of Kentuckians are big and warm. The social life of Louisville was at once seen to be of uncommon excellence and attractiveness. One of the professors had stated some years before, at the General Association of Kentucky, that if he had to leave South Carolina and could n't go back to Virginia, he had rather remove to Kentucky than anywhere else; and that they ought to take this as a compliment, — which many heartily said they did. There has never been occasion to abate this admiration of Kentuckians.

It was a great pleasure to Dr. Boyce himself and to his colleagues that he could once more resume the work of regular teaching, from which he had been cut off for five weary years. For the first two years at Louisville he was still called the Professor of Ecclesiastical History, but in fact taught Systematic Theology, of which there was nominally no professor. Professor Whitsitt had begun to teach Ecclesiastical History after Dr. Williams's health gave way, and he continued to do this provisionally at Louisville until he was finally made professor in that department, to which in the course of the years he has given a quite extraordinary attractiveness. Dr. Boyce was earnestly urged by his other colleagues to resume the teaching of Systematic Theology, to which he was far from averse, if satisfied that such an arrangement was best. The sacrifice he had made in giving up that department had turned out to be on his part only a matter of feeling, as he never had opportunity to teach Church History at all, and could now resume the subject to which he had always been devoted. His colleagues expressed to him the full conviction that while few men in all the world could equal Dr. Williams in *lecturing* on theology, and the students had unspeakably enjoyed his clear and vigorous statements of doctrine, yet Dr. Boyce could do still more towards giving them a profound personal acquaintance with doctrinal truth by that system of thorough drill in recitation which he had derived from President Wayland, and had developed in his own fashion.

The number of students for the second session at Louisville rose to ninety-six, and it was evident that the attendance would continue to increase. The financial situation was not entirely satisfactory, as will hereafter appear, though Dr. Boyce was still hopeful of carrying through the existing plan.

But at the end of the first Louisville session, and throughout the second, the Seminary was found to be involved in a new and painful difficulty, which weighed heavily upon Dr. Boyce's heart. Certain views in the historical and literary criticism of the Old Testament, which in later years are popularly described by the misused term "higher criticism," were found to have been adopted and taught by our justly honored and dearly beloved colleague, Dr. Toy. As this became a matter of notoriety, and yet a good many failed to understand Dr. Toy, on the one hand, or Dr. Boyce on the other, it may be proper to give a plain statement of the facts, which are believed to show nothing in the least discreditable to the character and motives of either party.

Dr. Toy had entered upon the study and teaching of the Old Testament with the idea that it was very important to bring the Scriptural references to physical phenomena into recognized harmony with all assured results of physical science. He had himself been, while chiefly devoted to language and kindred subjects, an eager student of various physical sciences. During his first years as professor in Greenville, he made earnest attempts, upon one or another line of theory, to reconcile the existing views of geology and astronomy with Old Testament statements, and afterwards to bring the tenth chapter of Genesis into harmony with the current ethnological views. None of these attempts were entirely satisfactory to his own mind. Some persons think that such theoretical reconciliation between sciences still inchoate, and interpretations still incomplete, must of necessity be only tentative, and the matters left to grow clearer for men of the future. But our young professor could not be content without every year renewing his efforts. About that time appeared the most important works of Darwin, and Dr. Toy became a pronounced evolutionist and Darwinian, giving once a popular lecture in Greenville to interpret and advocate Darwin's views of the origin of man. About the same time he became acquainted with Kuenen's works on the Old Testament, presenting the now well-known evolutionist reconstruction of the history of Israel, and relocation of the leading Old Testament documents. These works, and kindred materials coming from Wellhausen and others in Germany, profoundly interested Dr. Toy. They reconciled Old Testament history with the evolutionary principles to which he had become attached in the study of Herbert Spencer and Darwin. If the Darwinian theory of the origin of man has been accepted, then it becomes easy to conclude that the first chapter of Genesis is by no means true history. From this starting-point, and pressed by a desire to reconstruct the history on evolutionary principles, one might easily persuade himself that in numerous other cases of apparent conflict between Old Testament statements and the accredited results of various sciences the conflict is real, and the Old Testament account is incorrect. This persuasion would seem to the critic to justify his removing various books and portions of books into other periods of the history of Israel, so as to make that history a regular evolution from simpler to more complex. For example, it is held that the laws of Moses cannot have arisen in that early and simpler stage of Israelitish history to which Moses belonged, but only in a much later and more highly developed period, — all of which might look reasonable enough if we leave the supernatural out of view. Then the passion grows stronger for so re-locating and reconstructing as to make everything in the history of Israel a mere natural evolution; and the tendency of this, if logically and fearlessly carried through, must be to exclude the supernatural from that history altogether. These views would of course be supported by certain well-known theories to the effect that the first six books of the Old Testament were put together out of several different documents, as indicated by certain leading terms, and other characteristic marks of style and tone.

Near the end of the Seminary's first session at Louisville it became known to his colleagues that Professor Toy had been teaching some views in conflict with the full inspiration and accuracy of the Old Testament writings. By inquiry of him, it was learned that he had gone very far in the adoption and varied application of the evolutionary theories above indicated. Dr. Boyce was not only himself opposed, most squarely and strongly, to all such views, but he well knew that nothing of that kind could be taught in the Seminary without doing violence to its aims and objects, and giving the gravest offence to its supporters in general. Duty to the founders of the institution and to all who had given money for its support and endowment, duty to the Baptist churches from whom its students must come, required him to see to it that such teaching should not continue. From the first he saw all this clearly, and felt it deeply. Anxious to avoid anything that might look like an official inquisition, he laid these convictions before Dr. Toy through a colleague who had been the latter's intimate friend from his youth. Dr. Toy was fully convinced that the views he had adopted were correct, and would, by removing many intellectual difficulties, greatly promote faith in the Scriptures. Besides opposing that opinion, it was urged upon his consideration that these ideas could not be taught in the Seminary, and moreover that the great majority of the students were quite unprepared for fitting examination of any such theoretical inquiries, and needed to be instructed in the Old Testament history as it stands. He was entreated to let those theoretical questions alone, and teach the students what they needed. He promised to do this; and in entering upon the next session, of course tried faithfully to keep his promise. It was fondly hoped by his colleagues that in quietly pursuing such a course he might ultimately break away from the dominion of destructive theories. But some students had become aware of ideas he had taught the previous session, which excited their curiosity, and kept asking questions which he felt bound to answer. So, as the session went on, he frankly stated that he found it impossible to leave out those inquiries, or abstain from teaching the opinions he held.

It was hard for Dr. Toy to realize that such teaching was quite out of the question in this institution. He was satisfied that his views would promote truth and piety. He thought strange of the prediction made in conversation that within twenty years he would utterly discard all belief in the supernatural as an element of Scripture,— a prediction founded upon knowledge of his logical consistency and boldness, and already in a much shorter time fulfilled, to judge from his latest works. Some of us are persuaded that if any man adopts the evolutionary reconstruction of Old Testament history and literature, and does not reach a like attitude as regards the supernatural, it is simply because he is prevented, by temperament or environment, from carrying things to their logical results. While not himself perceiving that the opinions he was teaching formed a just ground for his leaving the Seminary, Dr. Toy concluded to send to the Board of Trustees at its approaching session in Atlanta, May, 1879, a statement of the views that he had adopted, and of his persuasion that by teaching them he could do much good; and, in order to relieve the Board from restraints of delicacy, he tendered his resignation.

After due consideration, the Board voted almost unanimously to accept the resignation. The regret at this necessity was universal and profound, and perhaps deeper in the Faculty than anywhere else. Dr. Toy had shown himself not only a remarkable scholar, and a most honorable and lovable gentleman, but also a very able and inspiring teacher, and a colleague with whom, as to all personal relations, it was delightful to be associated. Some of his attached former pupils and other friends thought that there was no necessity for losing him, and that his views were not really in any high degree objectionable, and began vehement remonstrances in private or in the newspapers. This proceeded in a very few cases from sympathy with his opinions; in most cases from lack of acquaintance with the real nature of those opinions and their necessary outcome. Dr. Boyce's personal grief at the loss was shown by a slight but impressive incident. When Dr. Toy returned to Louisville, and had made his preparations to leave, his two colleagues who were here went to the railway station. The three happened to stand for a little while alone in a waiting-room; and throwing his left arm around Toy's neck, Dr. Boyce lifted the right arm before him, and said, in a passion of grief, "Oh, Toy, I would freely give that arm to be cut off if you could be where you were five years ago, and stay there."

After a year or two given to literary pursuits in New York city, Dr. Toy was elected Professor of Hebrew in Harvard University. A letter of inquiry from the celebrated Ezra Abbot had led one of the Louisville professors to send a most cordial recommendation, with the explanation that Dr. Toy's leaving the Seminary was due to nothing whatever but his holding views like those of Kuenen and Wellhausen, — to which there would, of course, be no objection in Harvard.

To the now vacant chair of the Old Testament the Trustees elected Dr. Basil Manly, who, after serving eight years as President of Georgetown College, was willing to resume his former work in the Seminary. This was a great consolation to the other professors, who had never ceased deeply to regret his departure; while the known soundness of Dr. Manly's doctrinal convictions, with his admirable character and abilities, awakened a general feeling of satisfaction and confidence. His Inaugural Lecture, Sept. 1, 1879, was on the question, "Why and How to Study the Bible." He dwelt on the different grades of ministerial education, and urged that "the one central object which should be aimed at by all connected with a Theological Seminary is *a practical knowledge of the Scriptures*. . . . If we are to be mighty in God's work, we must be mighty in God's word."

For several years before leaving the Seminary, in 1871, Dr. Manly had made considerable annual collections for the purpose of aiding such students as needed it in the matter of paying their board, etc. For the ensuing eight years this task had been performed by Dr. Broadus. The increasing number of students demanded larger collections, and also put heavier burdens upon the Professor of Homiletics, in the correction of sermons and other written exer-

IN THE SEMINARY AT LOUISVILLE. 265

cises. So Dr. Manly now resumed the charge of this "Students' Fund," and on this account was asked to teach only in the one school of the Old Testament (English and Hebrew). Professor Whitsitt, who had for three years been the actual teacher of Ecclesiastical History, besides his own schools of Biblical Introduction and Polemic Theology, was now formally appointed Professor of Ecclesiastical History also. This made for him a very heavy burden of work; but he performed the duties with ability and devotion. Dr. Boyce was at the same time formally re-appointed Professor of Systematic Theology, which he had been actually teaching during the two years at Louisville, along with his other school of Church Government and Pastoral Duties.

It was during this period of ten years from the removal to Louisville until his health began to fail that Dr. Boyce most fully developed and exhibited his powers as a teacher. From the tributes paid to him after his death by students of this period the following utterances may be taken. Rev. E. E. Folk, then editor of the "Baptist Reflector," at Chattanooga, said: "He was a great teacher. He could get more hard, solid study out of a boy than any teacher whose classes we ever had the privilege of attending, with possibly one or two exceptions. You had to know your Systematic Theology, or you could not recite it to Dr. Boyce. And though the young men were generally rank Arminians when they came to the Seminary, few went through this course under him without being converted to his strong Calvinistic views." During an informal meeting held at the Seminary upon receiving news of Dr. Boyce's death in Europe, among various brief addresses Dr. M. D. Jeffries, pastor in Louisville, said: "Dr. Boyce was a ceaseless worker. There were doubts and discussions among the students on points of doctrine, which he could most happily allay. To him is largely due the vigorous adherence to the old doctrines on the part of the Baptist ministry." Rev. F. D. Hale, also pastor in Louisville, spoke of Dr. Boyce's "silent influence over him as a student. When he began Boyce's Systematic Theology, it threw him into great perplexity as to doctrine. But he found it all of inestimable value. He had learned to have more faith in God and to take in the system of Christianity as a whole; and he had gained such a firm hold of the old doctrines of grace as he never had before, by studying under Dr. Boyce. He had also learned at his feet to love the work, and to sympathize with lost souls. He had a joy, a zeal, a hope, a faith, and a love for the old gospel he would never have had but for Dr. Boyce." Let us add the following from Dr. J. William Jones, a student of the Seminary's first session (1859–1860): "As a teacher, Dr. Boyce greatly impressed me. I found very irksome at first his system of requiring the student to give a minute analysis of the lesson in Dick's Theology, which was then his leading text-book; but I soon got used to it, and many a time since I have had occasion to thank God and to thank my old professor for the thorough drill he gave us in the doctrines of God's Word." Dr. Jones adds that in later years he once delivered a message to Dr. Boyce from one of his more recent graduates, who was laboring in a region where the so-called "New Theology," "advanced thought," "liberalism," and loose views generally were painfully common. The message was: "Tell Dr. Boyce, with my love, that since I have been here I have thanked him a thousand times for his faithful teaching and thorough drill in Systematic Theology. What I learned of him has proven a healthy tonic in a malarious atmosphere." He says that "the great teacher's face lighted up" on receiving the message, and he replied, "I warmly appreciate this. It is a very high gratification to me that during my life as teacher I have been enabled to do something towards holding our boys in the 'old paths' of God's

Word, and so drilling them in the Old Theology of the inspired Book that they are not carried away by every wind of doctrine that blows in these days of 'Isms." Dr. Jones adds that in his wide travelling as a Mission Secretary, meeting a very large number of former students of the Seminary, hearing them preach or freely conversing with them, he has found them, as a rule, "not only effective preachers and efficient pastors, but sound to the core in their theology. Dr. Boyce has left his impress upon his students, and will speak through them as the years go on."

The method of teaching to which these brethren have referred had been (as we have previously remarked) derived by him from the great President Wayland, many of whose pupils have adopted the same method, developing it with much individual variety. In Dr. Boyce's hands it required that the students should analyze every paragraph of the lesson in the text-book, and be ready when called on, without questions from the teacher, to take up one paragraph after another, and state clearly, in their own words, its line of thought or argument. Numerous students have complained of this rigorous requirement in the early part of every session, but they have very generally rejoiced at a later period, in having acquired such thorough familiarity with Scripture doctrine, and having gained a faculty for like study of other books as they might see proper in coming life. The danger of this method is that it may degenerate into little more than memorizing of the text-book or lecture. The teacher has to resist this tendency. The better-trained students soon begin to show how the thing ought to be done, and the class in general derive from the process a highly valuable intellectual discipline, as well as a thorough and familiar acquaintance with doctrinal truth, with the leading Scripture proofs, and the principal arguments for and against each position, — an acquaintance which cannot fail to prove of very great advantage in all their life-long preaching and study. Dr. Boyce's "Abstract of Theology," of which we are to speak in a subsequent chapter, was prepared as a text-book for this method of instruction. His successor, Dr. Kerfoot, had himself greatly enjoyed and profited by this kind of instruction when first a student of the Seminary, 1869–1870, and continues to follow it with vigor and enthusiasm.

By advice of Dr. Hodge when at Princeton, Boyce had gained some acquaintance with the masterly treatise on Theology by Francis Turrettin, who taught in Geneva, 1653–1687. For one who sympathizes with what we call the Calvinistic, or Augustinian, type of Theology, this work is in certain important respects unrivalled. Many a subject is presented with such exact analysis, such complete statement, such consummate argumentation, as one very rarely encounters in the noblest writings. Some persons call the book dry,— an epithet which not a few apply to all systematic theological discussions; but to Dr. Boyce it was simply delightful. It gratified his taste for analysis, it satisfied his Calvinistic convictions, its energetic and forcible exhibitions of truth awakened in him practical as well as intellectual sympathy. From the foundation of the Seminary it had been his favorite idea that as in the study of Scripture there were separate classes in English and Hebrew, and in English and Greek, so in Theology there should be separate classes, using English and Latin text-books. While the chief instruction in Theology should be brought within reach of intelligent men having only an English education, there should be a separate class for men acquainted with Latin, and desiring to make wider and deeper study by means of Latin text-books. During the first sessions he used Turrettin alone; but soon began to add some treatises from Tertullian and Augustine, with Anselm's "Cur Deus Homo." After getting fairly to work again at Louisville, he transferred such reading of Latin Fathers, etc., to a "special class" of Patristic Latin, such as had long existed for Patristic Greek, and began to combine with Turrettin a good deal of reading in the "Summa Theologiæ" of Thomas Aquinas, who is recognized as one of the foremost philosophical and theological thinkers, and of late years has been recommended anew by the present Pope for Roman Catholic students. A few of Dr. Boyce's students heartily sympathized with his delight in these great authors; perhaps a good many worked through the course in "Latin Theology" only because it was necessary to the degree of Full Graduate. Of late there are signs of growing interest in this department, such as Dr. Boyce fondly hoped would arise in the course of years.

The subject of Church Government he also found quite congenial. Not content with discussing Baptist views of the constitution and government of a church, he took a wide range, exhibiting the great Roman Catholic system, which is one of the most remarkable products of the Roman genius for organization and government; and so as to various other systems. The theory and practice of church government appealed to both sides of his nature, as a scholar and thinker on the one hand, and on the other a statesman and a man of business. In teaching Pastoral Duties, his admirable good sense, good feeling, and good taste availed much, though he had never had experience of a large pastorate. In adding to this branch a course of instruction in Parliamentary Practice, with Mell's excellent little volume as a text-book, Dr. Boyce was at his best, and the course has proved of real value to the students. Not only our Baptist Conventions and Associations, but every Baptist church-meeting must be dealt with as a free popular assembly, and it becomes highly important that our pastors should have such genuine acquaintance, not only with "rules of order," but with the principles involved, as will prepare them to conduct the meetings with easy and quiet movement, and with fairness to all concerned. An arbitrary presiding officer may seem to expedite business, but will inevitably sometimes be unjust to one or another member of the assembly. A "little learning" as to rules of order will often promote only fussy wrangling, and waste of time and temper. The subject needs to be really studied, though it is not difficult, nor very extensive. There has been marked improvement in our Baptist conventions and churches as to this matter during the past forty years, and there is room and hope for a yet more general and thorough acquaintance with the proper conduct of popular assemblies.

Besides his ever insatiable longing for extensive knowledge and varied reading, Dr. Boyce gladly turned his attention to various branches of study which might contribute to success in his own lines of teaching. He went to work at the German language when fifty years old, and was soon able to make some use of German works on Theology. He attended, a year or two later, the full course of instruction in the Senior Greek class of the Seminary, preparing every lesson and listening with steady interest, asking questions and taking notes. He was especially interested in Text-criticism as applied to the New Testament, which an English professor has declared to be nearer an exact science than any other department of theological study. When the second volume of Westcott and Hort's Greek Testament appeared, containing their elaborate system of text-criticism, he went carefully through it, though the style is difficult, and mastered with great satisfaction its scientific method and interesting results. Ah, if only the Seminary's finances had reached a satisfactory condition, if he had not been carried away so often on long journeys still, and burdened while at home with practical difficulties, how eagerly he would have gone on widening and deepening his knowledge with every advancing year!

But the financial situation was far from satisfactory. The plan had been to raise $300,000 in Kentucky for endowment, and $200,000 in other States. For reasons heretofore explained, it was found necessary to make the removal to Louisville before either of these amounts had been fully subscribed. The annual expenses were unavoidably increased by removal to a large city. The students themselves lived more cheaply than before, but the rent of the hotel occupied by them, and of the rooms necessary for instruction and library, cost heavily. House-rent must also be provided for the professors who had families. Several agents had to be supported, who were occupied in efforts to complete the subscription of endowment, and to collect the annual payments already due. These agents must necessarily be men of more than ordinary ability and influence, with good salaries, and their wide travelling added no little to the expense. Meantime, many of the payments due for endowment had not been made. Some persons thought the Seminary was now successfully established at Louisville, and all would be well, so that they need not incommode themselves about prompt payment. It would be useless to attempt searching out, and in fact no one but Dr. Boyce ever knew, the great variety of difficulties and objections that stood in the way of payment. Thus it was impossible in the first years at Louisville to get such a sum invested as would yield anything like an adequate income. There were a good many outstanding five-year bonds for annual support still unpaid, but they also were in not a few cases hard to collect. Moreover, as Dr. Boyce had settled down to teaching again, and could seldom spare time for long journeys and personal applications, many persons took for granted that things were somehow getting on well enough. He still worked hard in vacation. Thus, in June, 1879, he and Dr. Broadus canvassed the city of Richmond. He was just up from a bad attack of gout, and weakened by the medicine that relieved it, so that we had to ride about; yet he was full of energy and courtesy, making earnest and persevering appeals to all who could be reached. But the work as a whole went on slowly. It became impossible to avoid using a portion of the funds designed for endowment in providing for the annual support of professors and agents. This is always a painful necessity for persons devoted to the establishment of a new enterprise. Dr. Boyce felt it keenly, deplored it, but nothing else seemed possible.

So it came to pass that in the third session at Louisville, when Dr. Manly had returned, and Dr. Boyce had been formally reappointed Professor of Systematic Theology, and the way seemed open for happy work and growing prosperity, it became apparent to his business eye that financially the Seminary was going to ruin. The salaries were inadequate, and could not possibly be lowered. The faculty had been cut down to four professors again after the death of Dr. Williams, and some of them were gravely burdened with their work. The agents were indispensable, and so much of the money coming in had to be used for expenses that there seemed no reasonable hope of investing an adequate endowment. About the end of the year 1879 Dr. Boyce explained this situation to his colleagues. The Seminary could struggle on in that fashion for several years, but the generous donors would assuredly have a right to complain if their gifts were used up for current expenses. He saw no hope of effecting a permanent endowment unless some person could be found to give a new impetus to the whole movement by personally contributing $50,000 for the endowment of a chair. He definitely proposed that the professors should make special and frequent prayer that God would raise up some one able and willing to give the $50,000. At a meeting of the Missionary Society, which includes all the students, he asked them to join in this special prayer for what he represented as in his judgment the only thing that could provide for the Seminary's permanent existence and large usefulness. He spoke with deep feeling: his heart was evidently set on the idea, and on the particular sum named. He sent a few lines to two or three Baptist papers, expressing the hope and prayer that God would put it into somebody's heart to make this gift. He would talk about it when meeting any one of the professors, and they would consider whether perhaps this or that person might prove to be the one. "Man's extremity is God's opportunity." He had done all that seemed possible in other ways, and could see no way out but this.

It can never be forgotten with what a radiant and yet tearful face he came a few weeks later into a colleague's study, holding out an open letter, and saying, "Here is the answer to our prayer." The letter was from Hon. Joseph E. Brown, of Georgia, Ex-Governor and United States Senator. It stated that he had for some time been considering the propriety of making a large gift to some institution of higher education. He had wished that one of his sons might feel called into the ministry; and as that apparently could not be, he felt all the more moved to help educate the sons of others for that work. He had seen Dr. Boyce's brief note in the "Index," and would be glad to have him arrange a visit to Atlanta at his expense, and explain the exact financial situation and prospects of the Seminary, so that he might decide whether it would be safe and wise to invest in its endowment. Within a few days Boyce had gone and returned, bringing the $50,000 in cash and first-class securities. Ah, was not that an answer to prayer? For years Providence had been leading the man and the movement, and now Providence had brought them together. The gift was made Feb. 11, 1880.

Now the question was how to secure other gifts, which, united with the funds already invested, would yield the income necessary. At this point Mr. George W. Norton, of Louisville, took the matter in hand, bringing to bear upon it his extraordinary business talent. He and his excellent brother and partner in private banking, Mr.

William F. Norton, had already made generous gifts for the Seminary. The point was to give more in such a way as might insure its speedily obtaining at least $200,000 of invested funds. Mr. Norton suggested an amendment to the charter, requiring that the principal of all contributions for endowment made since Feb. 1, 1880, be held forever sacred and inviolate, only the income to be expended, — and if any part of the principal were used for expenses, then the whole should revert to the donors, — and that a Financial Board of five business men in Louisville should be elected every year to invest the principal, hold the securities, and pay over the income to the Treasurer of the Seminary. Mr. Norton's idea was that no Treasurer or Board of Trustees would be sure always to resist the pressure of urgent need, and it was necessary to arrange so that the principal absolutely *could not* be drawn upon for expenses. Such an amendment to the charter passed the Legislature of Kentucky, and was approved March 31, 1880. Thereupon the Messrs. Norton offered to give each a very generous sum towards the proposed $200,000. New heart was at once put into the Seminary's more devoted friends, and Dr. Boyce began fresh efforts, as far as the pressing duties of a teacher would possibly allow, to obtain new gifts and collect outstanding obligations. One of the professors had done a good deal of summer preaching in New York and vicinity, and now went to seek contributions in that city. The result, after anxious and prolonged effort, was a subscription of nearly $40,000, all duly paid, of course, except about one fourth, prevented by a business failure. These generous gifts of several noble men and women in New York were another special providence in the Seminary's time of peril. In the course of some two years the proposed $200,000 was received and invested, and the institution was no longer in danger of perishing, though a much larger endowment must of course be earnestly sought, and through the toiling years Dr. Boyce continued to seek it.

For several years the number of students was between ninety and a hundred. This made it a laborious task to correct the written exercises necessary in the Hebrew and Greek classes, and still more to deal with the written exercises in Homiletics. Besides, the health of Professor Whitsitt had been seriously impaired by the too heavy burden of teaching Ecclesiastical History, and at the same time Biblical Introduction and Polemic Theology. The treasury could not afford another professor. The Trustees authorized the Faculty to appoint for the session 1881–1882 an assistant instructor in Hebrew, Greek, and Homiletics. The choice fell on Rev. George W. Riggan, of Virginia, a Master of Arts of Richmond College, and a Full Graduate of the Seminary's previous session. His conspicuous abilities, and enthusiasm in learning and teaching, made him a very valuable helper, and he grew rapidly in power and influence till his early death a few years later. After two years he was advanced to be assistant-professor, and on Oct. 1, 1883, delivered a vigorous and suggestive inaugural address on "The Preacher's Adaptation to his Intellectual Environment." Through having Mr. Riggan's help in teaching Hebrew, Dr. Manly was able to resume the school of Biblical Introduction, which he had taught up to the time of leaving the Seminary in 1871; thus Dr. Whitsitt also was considerably relieved, and after some years his health greatly improved.

The addition to the teaching force came in good time, for in the session 1882–1883 the number of students rose to one hundred and twenty-five, — the largest previous number having been ninety-six. Then it fell off somewhat for several years; but in 1886–1887 was again one hundred and twenty-five, and in 1887–1888 rose to one hundred and fifty-seven. Dr. Boyce believed in that last session during which he was present that the number would go on increasing, as it has done.

But the increasing number of students only rendered

more manifest the need of buildings, since the rent of a sufficiently large hotel and other adjacent rooms was costing more and more. The amount invested did not yield enough to support the Faculty and other officials, to say nothing of agents. Large sums were outstanding in old bonds for annual support; but what could be collected upon these seldom amounted to more than enough to meet the deficiency in the account for annual expenses. Every now and then, Dr. Boyce would grow thoroughly indignant at the failure of many persons to make annual payments for which they had given their solemn pledge and their legal obligations. During the session 1882–1883 he made up his mind that such persons ought to be sued at law. He wrote a long letter to one of the agents at that time in the field, setting forth reasons why he thought this ought to be done. Dr. Boyce had a high sense of commercial honor. He did not at all sympathize with the old-time negligent fashion of many planters and farmers, buying on twelve months' credit, settling then if convenient, but feeling that a gentleman ought not to be harassed about pecuniary obligations which he did not at the time find it convenient to meet. The son of Ker Boyce had all the instincts, convictions, and sentiments of a merchant, with whom failure to pay a debt was almost like stealing. It seemed to him an outrage that persons who had given him a bond would coolly go on neglecting to pay it, though reminded again and again. Nobody can question that the widespread practice of pledging contributions to religious objects, and then failing to pay, with little regret and no feeling of shame, is a very great evil. Dr. Boyce had taken pains to put contributions into the form of notes payable in bank, always inserting the name of some particular bank indicated by the contributor. To neglect meeting such obligations at maturity, unless really impossible, seemed to him a point of personal dishonor. So he obtained authority from the Board of Trustees to collect these bonds by process of law, and sent large quantities of them to lawyers, in different parts of the Southern country, with directions to bring suit if they could not otherwise collect. This course led to great complaint on the part of some persons who had given the bonds. Their point of view, on the score of custom, was entirely different from his, and it is probable that each party did the other some injustice. However invested with the forms of legal obligation, and of banking exactness and punctuality, the donors remembered that all this was really a promised *gift;* and if they found payment inconvenient, some of them regarded legal proceedings as offensive and unjust. There were those among Dr. Boyce's most intimate associates who always considered his course in this matter a mistake of judgment. Similar efforts to collect by legal process have been made in the history of several institutions, and they appear to have generally awakened an irritation, if not hostility, among givers, which more than counterbalanced the financial gain. Yet no one who knew Dr. Boyce can ever have questioned for a moment that the measures adopted were in his estimation thoroughly just to others, and required of him by his official duty. And let us not turn away from the subject without remembering how surpassingly important it is to cure, by all judicious representations, the practice of making pledges for benevolent objects, and neglecting to pay.

It was probably in the session of 1883-1884 that Dr. Boyce began to look around for a suitable location in which Seminary buildings might be erected. A committee of fifteen had been appointed by the Trustees, consisting of the Faculty and a number of leading business men of Louisville, to decide upon the best location. Many thought, very naturally, that it would be wise to place the Seminary a few miles out, where one or two hundred acres of ground could be purchased for a moderate sum, and when the city should grow out and around, this land would make the institution wealthy, as has taken place in the history of Columbia College, New York, and several other institutions. A majority of the committee favored the choice of some such location for the Seminary, while others urged very important reasons for preferring to place it in the heart of the city. Here it would be frequently observed by its friends, would seem near to them, and thus more readily command their liberal support. Here the students would not form a community apart, but would attend the city churches and Sunday-schools, and easily visit in the city families, to their great benefit in various ways; and being near the railway stations, they could much more easily strike out on Saturday afternoon to preach at churches in every direction, and returning on the early trains of Monday, go promptly to the lecture-rooms. Some of us were alarmed at the idea of banishing the Seminary from all these present advantages for the sake of a possible financial gain in the far future. In point of fact the honored brethren who favored an outside location could never agree in opinion as to whether we should go out to the east, or the south, or the west, it being quite difficult to foresee in which direction the city would most surely and rapidly grow. The matter hung fire for many months. At length Dr. Boyce ascertained that some lots in the heart of the city, on Broadway between Fourth and Fifth Avenues, could be purchased. Then by judicious inquiry he learned that other lots nearly adjacent, fronting on Fifth Street, might also be bought. Getting the consent of the committee, he quietly purchased these lots from their various owners at moderate rates, explaining to his associates how they could be combined into adequate grounds for the Seminary. This process settled the question of location; and the wisdom and business tact with which he had carried the matter through commanded the hearty approval and admiration of the business men on the committee.

But sufficient land in that central location was going to cost more than fifty thousand dollars. Part of it must be paid at once, and other sums must be collected within a year or two, while still the endowment was far from adequate, and the annual expenses hard to meet. Everybody agreed that the lot was exceedingly well chosen. A prominent owner of real estate in the city, to whom it was one day pointed out, and whose wife was a Baptist, said emphatically, "Why, Dr. ——, you have the best lot for a public building in the city of Louisville; and I'll give you five hundred dollars to help pay for it." One of the most eminent Baptists in the city, known to be very wise in his management of real estate, who had never favored the removal of the Seminary to Louisville, and had never contributed to its support, because doubtful as to the wisdom of theological education as distinct from college education, was yet so pleased with the selection of the location that he spontaneously proffered a thousand dollars towards paying the cost. Several generous friends, who had already contributed largely, took hold again to meet this purchase. But still the money was hard to obtain, and Boyce's soul was often bowed down by financial burdens and anxieties. In June, 1884, he wrote to Dr. Broadus (who was preaching in Brooklyn) with reference to some small proposed expenditure:—

"Besides, we are going to be hard run. I intended to warn you lest you should purchase any books for the Library this summer. I am anxious to cut down Seminary expenses. . . . I have yet made little progress further than when you left. The churches are burdened with all manner of appeals. I tell you 1 fear the people will begin to feel that the preachers and their projects are nuisances."

Yet this was the man whom some people represented as fairly loving to beg for money! A few weeks later he wrote an earnest appeal to his friend William F. Norton,

Esq. (who was temporarily out of town), to start him with twenty-five hundred dollars towards the twenty thousand he had to raise for payment on the lots.

"Getting this sum is really going to be fearful work; yet it is necessary to get it, if possible. If I can do this, then the hope of buildings at no distant future may be reasonably entertained. Without it, I do not believe I shall ever see the day when these buildings can be completed. I do wish before I die to see the Seminary fully equipped and at work. For this I have spent my whole life thus far, and am willing to spend the remainder if I can attain the end. But my heart often sinks within me at the difficulties to be overcome. My faith in the enterprise fails. I begin to think I must leave it incomplete, for some other man to finish. Oh that I could get my brethren to see its possibilities for good, with an ample endowment! I know it could do ten times its present work."

He goes on to explain that the time has arrived for making the titles to the lots, and the payments due are indispensable. "The matter presses, and I am in despair. Sometimes I am right sick that I should ever have allowed myself to be caught in such a scrape." Alas! the great heart scarcely able at times to bear its burden; the noble powers prematurely wearing out through financial exertions and anxieties, constantly hindering the work he so longed to do as student and teacher and author.

There were kind friends to help forward his exertions, not only in Louisville, but elsewhere in the State and country. In November he wrote to Mrs. Governor Robinson, of Georgetown, Ky., thanking her for a contribution, and added: "I know not how the Seminary could ever have been established without the kind help of the women of our churches; and among them I count no two more earnest and self-sacrificing than yourself and Mrs. Thomas. I trust we shall have the pleasure of seeing you here soon. I should like to show you the beautiful location we have secured for our buildings." So we see it is secured, and it is beautiful. But much of the purchase-money was still to be obtained.

Within the next year or two the beloved Dr. Edward Judson preached a number of days in Louisville, at the Broadway Baptist Church, and became acquainted with our Theological Seminary, and interested in its struggles and possibilities. On returning to New York he spoke warmly on the subject to one and another,—particularly to Mr. John D. Rockefeller. Some time later, Mr. J. A. Bostwick passed this way with some other great railroad men, and while driving round in Louisville, a Methodist gentleman, Mr. Carter, pointed out the lots which the Baptist Seminary had purchased, and spoke kindly of the institution. Afterwards Mr. Bostwick called on Mr. G. W. Norton, talking with him about railroads and about the Seminary. These several occurrences suggested that it might be possible to get help in New York for the erection of a building. A professor who was by this time pretty well acquainted in New York went again to seek such aid. Telegraphing was at that time remarkably cheap, especially for night despatches, and Dr. Boyce proposed constant communication.

The sum desired was sixty thousand dollars. Mr. Bostwick, at the first interview, agreed to give fifteen thousand. Upon being told of this the same day, Mr. John D. Rockefeller cheerily added twenty-five thousand. So next morning Dr. Boyce knew that two thirds of the amount had been given, but more than half *on condition* (Mr. Bostwick being averse to conditional gifts) that Boyce should at once raise money enough to finish paying for the land. It was an unpleasant day in Louisville, but he turned out, lame from a recent attack of gout, saw the Nortons and Mr. Theodore Harris and others, and telegraphed that night that he had the money in cash promises,—nearly thirty thousand,—but *on condition* that the remaining twenty thousand for the building should be raised in New York. *Hic labor, hoc opus.* It took nearly three weeks. Many an attempt failed, others dragged, others brought but little. Hope deferred made the heart sick. But one could almost hear Boyce's ringing voice and merry laugh as he would telegraph, night after night: "Don't think of coming back without it. Nobody wants to see you here. Stay all winter, if necessary." Slowly, slowly! A telegram of twenty words was only costing fifteen cents. Boyce knew every important failure or success, and kept exhorting. Several who thought at first they could not help, yet consented to take hold to save a friend from defeat, and a good enterprise from foundering in sight of land. Blessings on all the generous givers and wise counsellors! But for them, and but for Boyce's cheery telegrams, the movement would have proved a failure. Let no one think it easy to obtain large contributions in the great cities. Many applications must necessarily be rejected. Wise and conscientious givers must know what they are doing. If through personal acquaintance and varied information they are satisfied that here is a really promising enterprise, well managed, and heartily supported by friends right around it, why, then they may give,— or they may not; for nobody can be always giving, and every one must judge for himself.

When it was announced that sixty thousand dollars had been contributed in New York to erect a building for the Seminary, Senator Brown, of Georgia, who had endowed the professorship, spontaneously sent five thousand for the building. New York Hall, as it was named, really cost nearly eighty thousand dollars. It furnishes dormitories for about two hundred students (two in a room), with a beautiful dining-room and an ample culinary department, and also professors' offices and lecture-rooms, so arranged that they could in future be converted into dormitories whenever other buildings should be erected. There is also an admirable gymnasium. Dr. Manly and some honored Baptist laymen gave much time and thought to the duties of a building committee. May New York Hall long continue to remind the successive generations of students that the Seminary was greatly aided in its early days by generous gifts from the great metropolis.

In the course of these busy years as student and teacher, and these toilsome and ever-renewed exertions to establish the Seminary's finances, Dr. Boyce was in other ways also quite useful as a citizen of Louisville. He became a director in the Louisville Banking Company, which the President, Mr. Theodore Harris, has built up into the largest establishment of the kind in this part of the country; and his wise counsels as a business man were greatly valued in that and other enterprises. Again, as in former years, he had inviting offers to high business positions in his native State. One invitation was to become president of a bank in Charleston, — the one over which his father had so long presided, — with a salary of seven thousand dollars. During the same year he was asked to become president of the Graniteville Cotton Factory, near Aiken, S. C., in which his father's estate had stock, with a salary of twelve thousand dollars. He might have been pastor of his mother's church in Charleston, or of some church in Augusta, doing much good, and having ample opportunity to recover all that he had lost by the war; yet he declined both offers so quietly that few of even his intimate friends ever heard of them. A year or two later, one of Boyce's colleagues was riding in a buggy with a friend in the Blue-grass, who remarked, "Folks in our neighborhood think that your Seminary professors get entirely too big salaries." The other, in reply, mentioned the above two offers, and asked what his folks would think of Boyce's having declined such invitations. The old gentleman said, with great naïveté, "Oh, they would n't believe a word of it." A good many well-meaning people think that ministers are always ready to go where they can have a larger salary, and little do they know of the invitations often declined.

Dr. Boyce was a Trustee of the Slater Fund, from its original establishment, — a fund now exceeding a million, the income of which is to be used perpetually for the promotion of higher education among the colored people of the South. His practical wisdom and life-long interest in the negroes admirably adapted him to this position, and he greatly enjoyed the annual meetings of the Trustees, a distinguished body of gentlemen.

In the Broadway Baptist Church of Louisville, Dr. Boyce was a very earnest, faithful, and useful member. For some years he taught a large Bible class in the church at the Sunday-school hour, composed of students and many other persons, and took much pains to prepare the lessons, which became really lectures to quite a considerable congregation. He of course gave a very hearty support in every sense to the pastor and other officers, as a resident minister who is not a pastor ought always to do. On one occasion he thought it his duty to oppose earnestly the wishes of the beloved pastor, Dr. J. L. Burrows. A highly esteemed gentleman, whose father had been a Baptist, had himself been baptized by a Christian (Campbellite) minister, and after a good many years wished to join the Broadway Baptist church, but did not wish to be now baptized. Dr. Burrows was disposed to receive him upon his former baptism, as a good many brethren would do, in some parts of the country. Dr. Boyce resisted this, steadily and successfully, and took pains in many ways to show at the same time his hearty good feeling towards the pastor, who in turn acted with characteristic magnanimity.[1] Some years later, the honored gentleman in question was received into another Baptist church of the city, and baptized.

---

[1] This noble, eloquent, and widely useful minister died in January, 1893.

IN THE SEMINARY AT LOUISVILLE.

In 1885, April 14th, Dr. Boyce and his colleagues were greatly saddened by the death of Assistant-Professor Riggan, who had now been their colleague for nearly four years. His remarkable ability, his splendid zeal as a student and a teacher, with the purity and unselfishness of his character, had greatly endeared him to professors and students. In the Blue-grass church of which he had been pastor for some years, there were intelligent persons who thought him the ablest preacher they had ever heard. His sermons often contained an amount of profound thought and closely linked argument which most people would not have listened to but for the kindling enthusiasm with which he spoke. His memory will long continue to be an inspiration. One of the Full Graduates of that session, and previously a graduate of Howard College, Rev. John R. Sampey, of Alabama, was appointed assistant instructor for the next session; and as the increasing number of students kept demanding additional help, Rev. A. T. Robertson, of North Carolina, also a Full Graduate, and a Wake Forest man, was appointed two years later. Each of them, after two years of service, was advanced to be assistant-professor, the former in Old Testament and Homiletics, and the latter in New Testament and Homiletics. Unable to appoint additional full professors, through lack of means for support, the Seminary was exceedingly fortunate in securing young men of rare ability and rich promise.

In 1885 Dr. Boyce was cheered by a bequest from D. A. Chenault, Esq., of Madison County, Ky., of $15,000, the interest of which was to be used for helping to pay the personal expenses of needy students. A like bequest of $10,000 was made by W. F. Norton, Esq., of Louisville, who died in 1886. These generous gifts made a permanent and highly valuable addition to the Seminary's financial strength at a point of constantly increasing pressure; but this did not relieve Dr. Boyce's solicitude as to procuring additional endowment for the support of the instruction.

In all the latter part of his life, as we have heretofore noticed, he was so burdened with the business of the Seminary, as well as the care of his father's estate, that his correspondence was mainly restricted to business letters. Yet in the copies preserved in letter-books appear many letters to his sisters and his nieces, — often accompanying birthday gifts, — apt to be quite entertaining, and sure to overflow with simple and earnest expressions of personal affection. Some of these letters, or extracts from them, may now be given: —

To his Sister, Mrs. Burckmyer, Jan. 13, 1880.

Thank you for the book; it is very nice. Every now and then, yesterday afternoon, while I was answering some letters in my wife's room, F. would exclaim, "This is so good!" "How nice this is!" "How beautifully this is executed!" etc., etc., as she looked over the pictures of the book, which, after looking at it awhile, I had to lay aside because of necessary work. When I had simply said, "The homes of England," F. said at once, "'The stately homes of England,' is by Mrs. Hemans." You see she is somewhat informed in literature. The fact is, the young folks are getting ahead of me. I was badly caught last night. Hearing L. referring to Green's "History of the English People," which the women-folks had been reading until they came to Harold, and then stopped at my wife's suggestion to read Bulwer's "Harold." and hearing her speak of Beda, I said, "Bede" (one syllable). She said it was Bæda in the book, and I laughed at her, thinking she had been carried off by mispronunciation, and said, "Well, bring me a place where it is spelled *Bæda*, and I will give you a quarter." In five minutes she came with Green, and I had the quarter to pay. You see the love of the extreme old is leading even historians to take Latin names for their English equivalents. You will see some of these days, when the encyclopædias begin to mention your brother, that he will figure as Boethius, or Boecius. But the learning of the day is getting ahead of us old folks. I have long had to stop trying to teach grammar to the children. The names of moods and tenses and cases, etc., etc., and the characteristics of various parts of speech and the relations between them, are to-day designated by such extra scientific terms that I cannot talk with them. Think of my being thus caught on the Venerable Bede, and through the instrumentality of one as " green " as that historian! The girls all laughed at me because I had made so extravagant an offer, for they said L. would have worked an hour for the chance of making ten cents. L. is the financier and banker of the family. It is said that her purse is like the widow's cruse of oil. Put a dollar in it, and she will be the extravagant purchaser of all she wishes, will have loaned to every one some part of that dollar, and yet, with all her loans outstanding and her purchased possessions on hand, she will have her dollar still. F., on the other hand, will not spend, but puts away her money, often in unknown places; yet when demanded she has nothing to show, — has spent nothing, has given away nothing, has loaned nothing, and still has nothing. It is well that L.'s honesty is established, or the open mouths of astonishment which these two sets of developments cause in the family would break forth into fearful accusations.

But what a race a wild pen will lead one, if he give it flight! Well enough this would have been in the days when pens were feathers, and could be presumed capable of developing " airy trifles ; " but that an old steel pen should thus fly off into sparks would seem impossible until you realized that it has come into contact with an old flint rock like me. Seriously, however, I do thank you heartily for the book, but greatly more rejoice in my knowledge of the love which has prompted it, and the good wishes as to my birthday which accompanied it.

To Mrs. Burckmyer, Oct. 16, 1880.

I thought a great deal of you on the 14th (your birthday), and asked many blessings upon you. God bless you, my own dear sister! I always did love you dearly. There has been a peculiar drawing of us two together, and it has extended to my wife. During these later years of your deep sorrow — in which I so strongly sympathize with you, and in which I was also so deeply afflicted — I have felt that I must come to you in my own place, and also as far as possible in that of your dear husband. And I have learned that my love for you was not so great as could be, from the fact that it is daily increasing. I could not, but for this experience, have supposed that possible, for I had thought no sister could be loved by brother more than I loved you. Would that I were more worthy of your love, and more worthy to pray for you! It is a great trouble to me often to know how much worse I am than I am supposed to be. Hence I do not suffer, as some do, when persons think or speak disparagingly of me, for I get too much love. But if to love you is to be fitted to pray for you, I yield to no one in fitness. The truth is, I often think with wonder and gratitude of the deep love that all of us brothers and sisters have for each other.

In June, 1881, he writes to Mrs. Burckmyer a long description of the new house which, by the authority of the Board of Trustees, he had purchased as a residence for the Chairman of the Faculty, on the corner of Chestnut and Brook Streets. He had bought it from the widow of Henry Clay, son of the famous statesman. It was a very large house, with numerous and spacious rooms. He had never in Louisville had room for his books, the greater part of them being packed away in boxes; but here there would be a noble library, and a private study besides. He could now entertain her and her family, and other kindred and friends. He hoped also to give receptions to the professors and students and friends of the Seminary.

To Mrs. Burckmyer, Oct. 12, 1881.

You will get this on your birthday. I congratulate you. I wish you as many more birthdays as God may see to be best for you, and then a peaceful rest and joyous life where life is not measured by such paltry periods as years and centuries, and where as we grow older we are only made brighter and more fit to live.

To Mrs. Burckmyer, Jan. 10, 1883.

Your very kind note of January 6 received. I wonder how many brothers in this world have such a sister, not to say sisters, as I. Truly, in some things, God has blessed me to overflowing; and I appreciate it. No one delights to be loved, and loved for himself, and not so much his profitableness to others, as I do. I think one reason why we ought to love the Lord so much is because we know as well as he does how unprofitable we are, and that we are loved, not even for what we are, but simply because we are his. It is so delightful to be owned. There is at least that pleasure in being a slave, and I think our slaves of old felt this, and a great nearness it made between them and their masters and mistresses. I know I have never been able to love my best hired servants as I did my more indifferent ones whom I owned. I think it is not so with the hired ones; that until long service makes such an indissoluble attachment that in a sense they seem to belong to us like our children and relatives, we never learn to love them as much as we may.

But I must not make a homily of my letter. The books will probably be here to-day or to-morrow. I have not yet bought Hayne's poems, and so I shall have the pleasure of reading them as your gift to me.

I see you are to have the Princess Louise in Charleston for the winter. Well, of one thing I am sure, that, though poor, and not now capable of showing the hospitality and courtesy of the past, Charleston is, of all the places in the country, that in which she will find that people know how to treat a royal princess, with honor and respect due to her station, and without any vulgar toadyism. I trust that through the British consul she will fall into the right hands. It is funny that she should have asked whether Charleston is safe. It is as bad as two years ago when she declined in the fall to come through Louisville for fear of yellow fever. I wonder if any of our educated ladies would ask for a military escort to go to Dublin, or fear to visit London, lest they should have the leprosy; yet probably we are as ignorant of Mexican matters as the English of America. The Star of Empire goes westward; but still it is always eastward that our eyes are directed with especial interest and knowledge. Is this an evidence of blindness, or of want of foresight?

To Miss Charlotte B. Holmes,[1] *Jan.* 10, 1883.

I received your card to-day, and your mother's and your grandmother's books, and as you are the smallest of the three, I write

---

[1] Granddaughter of Mrs. Burckmyer.

to tell you so, and to get you to tell them. Take care they do not find it out before you tell them. I am glad you like the book I sent you, and the jointed doll. By it you will find that all children are good in their places; even ugly ones may not be stiff-necked, and may have active legs and arms. Then you will find that the jointed doll cannot cry, nor roll its eyes about, nor get its hair rumpled, nor break its nose, nor lose its earrings, as some dolls can. Perhaps you can find out some other excellent qualities in it before I see you. To-morrow is Uncle Jimmy's birthday. He will be fifty years old. How many times is that older than you? Find out, and tell me when I see you.

To Miss Charlotte B. Holmes, Jan. 22, 1883.

You must get mamma to make you understand that a grand-niece, instead of being larger than only a niece, is apt to be much smaller. Your mamma is only my niece, and you are the grand-niece. I am afraid to try to explain, unless I could talk with you and hear your dear little questions, and find out just what you would wish to know about it. . . . We are having such cold weather here as you never see in Charleston. Tell grandma that the thermometer last night was below zero. She will know how cold that is. Yet we have a heap of fun. The little children run out and slide on the ice all along the sidewalk, and every day I see them going out to the big pond with skates in their hands, to skate upon the ice. Then we have had ever so much snow, and the ground has been as white as iced cakes for a week at a time. The big river is not yet frozen over, but sometimes it is, and the people can walk or drive over on the ice from one side to the other. Do you think you would like to see the water frozen from the Battery away over to the opposite shore of the island, and the people driving carriages over, as they do in the streets of Charleston? Some of these days, when you get large enough, you must come and see all these and other sights which you cannot see in Charleston. But you must not think this is a nicer place to live in than Charleston. Your Aunt Lizzie is groaning over the prospect that when the pit is opened after this cold spell, all her flowers will be frozen up and killed. We can't have them here as you have in Charleston. . . . Don't you think grand-uncle suits your big Uncle Jimmy?

To Miss Charlotte B. Holmes, December 21.

Your nice letter of December 18 was received this morning. I am very glad you are so pleased with your little watch. It was the prettiest of the kind I could get in Chattanooga, but not near so pretty as I should have liked to have it. Your mamma guesses right. The lesson is punctuality, which I think one of the most important lessons in life. Add to that, promptness to move and act at once, not to dawdle and wait to be told several times. It also teaches when to go to bed, so that you will not need to have mamma urge you. One thing else : Be careful with the watch ; don't wind it up, or move the hands, except when necessary ; use the watch, but don't abuse it. I shall see when next I meet you what good care you have taken of it. I should not have given it unless I had thought you would take good care of it.

We may add two or three specimens of the numerous kindly letters he wrote to namesakes.

To Master R. Boyce Given (of Kentucky), Jan. 10, 1883.

MY DEAR LITTLE NAMESAKE, — I received your nice little card and letter. The letter was very nicely written. I fear you have begun too well. A few years from now, I am afraid the handwriting will not be so good, nor the letter so elegant in its language. But do not fear to write me because of that. I shall love the little things you may say, and the crooked letters in which you will write them. I want you to be a good man first, and then a wise one. To be either, you must begin while you are young. Try to be good, and when old enough study very hard.

To Boyce Broadus, Dec. 25, 1884.

MY DEAR LITTLE FRIEND, — Many thanks for your kind remembrance of me, and for your presents, — the one so beautiful and fragrant, and the other so useful. I shall wear the former to-day in my coat, and hope that my little friend is all day as happy as his love to me has made me; and the other I shall use every day for a long time, and every day think of the kind thoughtfulness you have shown. God bless you, my dear boy, and give you every kind of happiness now and evermore.

We turn to specimens of the letters he wrote to former students who were living far away as foreign missionaries. The following was written April 6, 1883, to REV. P. A. EUBANK, Baptist Mission House, Lagos, West Africa:

I am sitting at my desk in my lecture-room, conducting the Final examination in Church Government, and my mind naturally reverts to my pupils of last year. I therefore have taken the letter you wrote the Missionary Society, Sept. 25, 1882, and shall proceed to answer some of the questions you put in it.

Probably some of the students have already written you that we have decided to forward the money contributed at one of our mission Sunday-schools in the city — the one with which you labored — to the Board at Richmond, for the special purpose of a training-school in Yoruba. And now as to your questions.

1. "There is no church at Abbeokuta: should the Lord's Supper be administered to the people who have been baptized, and then identified themselves with the mission?" My reply is, Yes. But this needs some explanation. (1) If there are several persons at Abbeokuta, why cannot a church be formed? The building, the pastor, the deacons, are not essential to a church, but only two or three members. If you say that there is no one capable there of conducting worship, and therefore no use for a church, I ask, Are there not persons there who can pray together, who can form a social meeting, and who can watch over each other? If so, why not have a church? Look into the New Testament alone, without prejudice from present custom, and see if it is not the fact that the Apostles formed their new converts into churches, or even more likely that a number of these together became thus a church by virtue of being the only persons in the place who had become disciples where there had been none before. (2) If for any reason the persons at Abbeokuta can have no church there, and such a church may seem to those of you who are present not to be essential, the persons there baptized should become members of some other church, and that church can have the ordinance of the Lord's Supper administered to its members at

Abbeokuta as well as at the more general home, by simply resolving that the said church will hold a meeting at Abbeokuta and partake of the Lord's Supper, which of course will only be done by those who are there. (3) Any doubts as to such questions are to be determined in favor of the most extensive privileges being given. As a matter of course, when we are practically certain a thing should or should not be done, we must follow that certainty. But when we cannot decide whether a privilege should be given or not, we are bound, I think, to grant it. This is on the principle our Lord laid down with reference to the Sabbath, when he said, "The Sabbath was made for man, and not man for the Sabbath." Why should brethren be deprived all their lives of the blessing of partaking in remembrance of him according to his commandment, because they live at such a distance from a church as to make this impracticable? Would it not seem, in the absence of any provision of Christ by which this exigency may be met, that our decision should be that it is better that Christ's command to eat the bread and drink the wine should be obeyed, even without an assembly for that purpose of a constituted church, than that we should stickle for the partaking of it in this way, which we infer to be right, and that to such an extent as to prevent obedience to the command? And most of all, does it not seem that our Lord, when he spoke of the two or three, intended to show that of so small a number even as this could a church be, and therefore that there need never be a celebration of it otherwise than as a church, because so easily would that number be gathered wherever there are disciples. Is not the essential idea of the administration of the Lord's Supper rather the idea that it is not a private meal, which any one can partake of at any time, and thus overlook Christ's relation to his people as a collected body, and not individual members only, than that it is a regular church meal, which can only be partaken of by a church in regular session? In other words, is not the point to prevent individual partaking, rather than to secure a union of the brethren in the partaking?

Question 2. "Is it right to baptize a believer with a view to his becoming a member of a church not yet organized?"

Answer, certainly. Did not the Apostles do this constantly? Your doubt arises from the common practice among churches at home, where churches are convenient, and where the consultation as to whether a person shall be baptized, takes place before the baptism. This finds an Apostolic example in the case of Cornelius. But the authority of the minister to baptize without consultation with the church is seen in the baptism of the eunuch by Philip. If the brethren are present who propose to enter into the proposed new church, I should consult them as to the baptism; but if none are present, I should baptize at once, without consultation. This I believe was the universal custom of Apostolic days.

Your third question seems to me to raise issues which can only be settled in each individual case. You refer to the refusal to testify against each other from fear, and to the case of a woman who terrified a church by saying she had come to see who would raise a hand against her. I see no other way to do in each case, however, than to instruct in the truth, and to use moral suasion. What else can you do? You have no authority over a church. You can only exercise influence through the esteem they have for you, and use effective moral suasion by the power of your words. But I think, in general, the other members should be warned not to allow superstitious fear to keep them from doing right; and this offending woman should be taught that there is nothing in becoming or being a Christian where there is no genuine religion. Why should she wish to be in the church at all? I think all you can do is to follow Apostolic precepts, — watch, warn, exhort, rebuke, always recognizing the authority of the church and its independence, and exercising in your own person no right, real or pretended, by which you would attempt to rule.

Your fourth and fifth questions I will answer together. "Should converted polygamists be received into the church without being required to give up their wives, except one? If we receive polygamists, and thus have some in the church, what should be done with a member who takes a plurality of wives after being received?"

I think this matter may be arranged if you will follow what I think was the plan in Apostolic days. (1) Christ was outspoken as to the necessity of monogamy. (2) So likewise, so far as they are known to us to have spoken, were the Apostles. These two facts settle, therefore, the Christian opinion on the subject. (3) But Christianity, unlike Judaism, always interprets law with regard to a merciful dispensation of it. Consequently, when persons were found with more than one wife, they were (a) doubtless admitted to membership, (b) but with such teaching as showed that polygamy, though tolerated, was only tolerated from mercy towards those already married, where the annulling of the marriage relation of any one or more of the wives would be cruel and unjust to her. (c) This would be accompanied, not by a stigma upon those thus placed, but by some evidence that their position was undesirable. (d) This is found in the requirement that the offices of the church should be confined to those who have one wife only. "A bishop must be the husband of one wife."

Now, it seems to me that such action would settle the questions you ask. You will show from it that polygamy was discountenanced, was allowed because of peculiar facts, and yet blamed so far as to become a disqualification, and consequently that it is not possible that polygamy should have been allowed to take place by a man's adding to one or more existing wives.

To your sixth question, as to the judgment of moral questions according to the Bible, or with regard to the moral weakness of the heathen, I reply: (1) That we ought not to lower the standard of *instruction* on moral questions. These should be set forth in all their beauty and elevated character. (2) That we should be tender and merciful in their application. While we teach rigidly what Scripture teaches, and thus raise up the banner aloft, we should yet recognize the low standard with which these have been familiar, and make allowance in dealing with them. "A bruised reed shall he not break, and the smoking flax shall he not quench." Our Lord's treatment of the woman taken in adultery is a lesson of such treatment, even when the standard of moral teaching was not low, but highly elevated.

I shall not ask your pardon for my long letter, because I have tried to meet your own wishes. It has been a pleasure to me to state thus briefly such points as I hope may either give satisfaction, or set you to thinking, and perhaps lead to the attainment of wiser conclusions.

We have had a prosperous session. We have regularly matriculated 117 students, and have had in addition two who left before matriculation, besides three or four others who have attended lectures. Two ladies also have attended lectures, both of whom will go to China, one being Miss Blandford, whom you know, and the other Miss Morris, of Missouri. The Faculty will recommend to the Board that the sessions hereafter be opened in October, instead of September, and close June 1, instead of May 1.

We think of you and our other dear students in foreign lands very frequently. At every missionary meeting you are all spoken of and prayed for, and others exhorted to go out and help you. You may be sure of our continued love. Please give my best regards to your wife.

To Rev. E. Z. Simmons, Canton, China, April 6, 1883.

As you were informed by my secretary, your letter of October 14 was received, with instructions as to the bonds of yourself and Mrs. Simmons; but I laid it aside at the time, intending to write you a friendly and not a business letter at some leisure moment. Unfortunately (or fortunately?) such moments of idleness are not common with me. I find myself very much overburdened with work, because my cares are various. Sometimes I feel like cutting myself away from everything except my professorship work; but so many are dependent upon me that I cannot do so without injury to them. My own family is small, as you know, and it is not to them that I refer.

Our Seminary has greatly prospered this year. Last year we had ninety-six students; this year we have had over one hundred and twenty, besides two ladies, who propose to go to China as missionaries, namely, Miss Blandford and Miss Morris. Only to-day Dr. Manly came to me to arrange for a meeting next Tuesday afternoon to examine, in behalf of the Board at Richmond, another lady, of whom Dr. Manly speaks most highly, — a Miss Roberts, sister of Rev. H. C. Roberts, one of our last year's students, and pastor of a Baptist church in this city. Our students seem to be imbued very generally with a missionary spirit. The fact that Pruitt and Walker went to China last year, and Eubank to Africa, has moved them deeply. A number are contemplating some foreign field, with various degrees of interest and purpose. I trust the time has already come when we shall send some fruit every year to China and Africa, to Italy and South

America. Our missionary meetings are held monthly, as when you were here, and are full of interest. The ladies in the various churches here are active in the Woman's Mission to Woman work, and I think are doing much good, more especially as they seem to be very judicious and modest. I had the pleasure of reading the secretary's report of the society connected with Broadway Baptist Church, because the lady said she could not rise before a mixed audience and read it. I told her I so much admired such modesty and true womanliness that I could not refuse, and would read any number of papers for such societies upon those conditions.

The churches here are all raising money for city purposes, — Broadway to pay off a debt of $15,000, and the other churches to help Dr. Weaver, and East Church, Green's old place. The Seminary Missionary Society is also doing a large work in this city, for which the funds are given by members of city Baptist churches. The students have engaged in this with great zeal. It was begun two years ago last November, and has constantly developed, until we now have about one thousand children in eight mission Sunday-schools.

To Rev. W. S. Walker, Shanghai, China, Dec. 1, 1883.

Will it be too late for congratulations when my letter arrives? If not, please accept them for yourself, and present them for me to your wife. My dear fellow, I am so glad that you are married, and especially that you have a wife so sweet and amiable as I see she must be, from the photograph of her you sent Dr. Manly. I don't think you would have done as well at home, had Dr. Tupper and the Foreign Board given you three months longer to find one. I was greatly relieved that you did not get a wife in that way, and that you have obtained one in the way of natural (I don't mean Darwin) selection. You have always had a very dear place in my heart, and I shall always look at your work with very peculiar interest. May God continue to bless you greatly in it! Your wife, I understand, is a sister of Dr. Mateer, the senior missionary of the Presbyterian mission at Tungchow. I understand that to marry you, she had to begin to twist her mouth to a new dialect. I did not know before that such wry faces must be made in swallowing my old pupil. I judge, however, from what I have heard of her brother, that she, if like him, is capable of all things. . . . You heard last year of our increased numbers. We shall do as well this year. There are already one hundred and four students. Our classes are doubly as large as when you were here. The students are a noble set of young men, — some not so very young, — and every year we see that we are producing an effect which cannot be measured, upon the South. There never was so much missionary spirit in the Seminary, never so much in the churches at large. I do not venture to attribute all of this, under God, to the Seminary; I know that other causes are at work. But I know that the Seminary has been a potent factor in the past, and must be still more so in the future. . . . We hope to send you other men from time to time, to help you brethren abroad, in China, in Africa, in Mexico, in Brazil. The more we send, the more we shall find ourselves able to send, — consecrated men, of devoted piety, filled with the missionary spirit, and as well cultivated and educated, especially in theological and Biblical lore. The more we send from the Seminary, the more will the other students be filled with zeal for missions, and the more will their churches give; and as these increase in giving, they will become still more willing to give, not money only, but men. The fact is, I believe we have begun a round of spiritual power which will be like a whirlwind, and will gain force as it goes, sweeping forward with resistless power unto the end of the world, — that is, if we shall prove faithful. God keep us so; for all force will soon be at an end, unless He help.

I trust your own work becomes increasingly interesting, as day after day passes, and you grow better able to preach the blessed gospel to the perishing. We have felt much troubled at the dangers to which our brethren at Canton have been exposed, and we have not known whether or no there was any possibility of danger at other points, but supposed that there was. In such peril our hearts go out towards all of you with much apprehension, which is only allayed by our faith that the heart of Jesus also goes out in like manner, with greatly more tenderness. It is well for all of us always to remember that the commission was connected by a "therefore" with the "all power" intrusted to his hands. He then can take care of his own cause. . . . Blessed be

God, we can get into no situation in which we may not have the sympathizing pity and prayers of Jesus!

Give my best regards to Dr. Yates. I wish I could once more see him. His sympathy for my work here has been a great consolation, his opinion of its value a very great and constant encouragement. I believe he is justified in his belief as to the value of the Seminary to Foreign Missions; but it is a great pleasure to know that this is his faith.

To Rev. M. T. Yates, D.D., Shanghai, China, Jan. 10, 1884.

Yours of November 21 received. . . . I trust what you have written to Herring and the "Recorder" and Tupper may be effectual to prevent any such idea from controlling the going-out of missionaries as would dispense with the most thorough education possible. I am very sure that all should be thoroughly educated, although I know what good work men have done without such opportunities. You may be sure that we shall do all that we can in this direction. While we are devoutly attached to the cause of missions, — indeed, because we are thus attached, — we would not increase the number of missionaries by an addition of incompetent men. I had rather send out men defective in physical than in mental strength. I trust if you have not known before, you know, through what Brother Walker can tell you, how much of the missionary spirit pervades our institution. If we cannot overcome the tendency of many to remain at home, we do at least destroy all anti-missionaryism, and build up such genuine interest as will give the mission cause some chance to have its claims presented before all the churches these students will serve. I believe, indeed, that thus there will be awakened a true spirit everywhere. How otherwise than through our work can it now be accounted for that South Carolina, in its present condition of comparatively deep poverty, so far excels what it did for missions in the days of its wealth? In Kentucky we have a soil to work upon not so long nor so well cultivated as that of South Carolina was when we began in 1859. But I venture to say that here also we shall do, with the help of God, a great work; and as fast as we can get hold of the students of the Southern States, or others, you will see a revolution. Had I the use of a million of dollars to-day, I could in twenty-five years make this whole Southern country so full of missionary Baptists that unless the devil could devise some other means of weakening or retarding the kingdom of God, we should support thousands of missionaries. Had I such a sum, or the half of it, I would from its annual interest support all who would attend the Seminary and needed help, and I would send out agents to "compel" them to come in, and have one thousand students here each year. But, after all, all in God's good time. I think we ought to say this, *in contentment*, relying on him; while in discontent, as long as the work is not done, we should bend every effort towards it with all the means we have. I am deeply grateful for the interest you have taken in our work. Pray for us.

We add the following miscellaneous letters: —

To Professor John L. Lincoln, LL.D., Brown University,
Jan. 2, 1885.

Your letter from Charleston, S. C., was indeed a surprise, but none could be more pleasant. It delights me to know that you have been in the old city so dear to me as my boyhood's home. I only regret that I was not there with you, for there is so much that is not only characteristic, but quaint and worthy of special notice, about the city, and which is not apt to be seen in a hurried visit, that I wish you had had some native guide, and above all I wish for the pleasure it would have given me to be your guide. I am especially pleased to know that while there you remembered me, and to such an extent as to be moved to write me your kind letter. The four of us who were under your charge on the same floor with yourself while I was in college, were always your admirers, not merely as our Latin professor, but chiefly as our friendly monitor and guardian. And I confess that one of the chief pleasures of my life has been the friendship of my former instructors at Brown. Your letter therefore has brought me more than ordinary pleasure. I read it with much pride to my wife and daughters, who seemed also fully to appreciate your kind greetings.

Rev. C. H. Toy, D.D., Harvard University, April 28, 1885.

I have received your kind letter of the 25th, sympathizing with us in the loss of Dr. Riggan. He died on the 18th, about 11 A. M. His disease was meningitis. He had really worked himself down; and this, with the recent loss of his child, had put him in a bad condition for an attack. He was sick about twelve days, the immediate cause being over-fatigue in preaching, and riding three miles after it at night, when he had been thrown by preaching into a profuse perspiration. His symptoms were at first like those of typhoid fever, but afterwards so developed meningitis as to leave no doubt about the disease. His loss is a sad one to us. He was doing well, and we looked forward naturally to a long and useful life. Nevertheless, God knows what is best, and does what he wills.

From a Letter to Rev. W. T. Lowrey, of Mississippi, April 28, 1885.

I thank you for your quotation from Brother Trotter, and for your own kind expressions. It is very pleasant to know that I have the affection of my pupils. I often fear that it must be otherwise; and such words as you wrote are worth to me far more than you can imagine.

To William E. Dodge,[1] Esq., New York City, Sept. 21, 1885.

Yours of 17th received. The copies of Dr. Mayo's address were also received. I have carefully read the address, and am obliged to you for sending it to me, and I will give the extra copies to various parties who will appreciate them. I think the South indebted to him for his candor and kindness, and to you for your liberality in printing and distributing the address. I do not think he fully appreciates the efforts for common school education which were made in the South prior to 1860; they were much more extensive and successful than has been generally supposed.

[1] He and Dr. Boyce were together on the Board of Trustees of the Slater Fund.

Unquestionably they were not what they should have been, nor are they now what they ought to be. They were also confined to the white race. Yet I know that in many, and I believe in all the Southern States, appropriations were annually made for free education, or to supplement what was privately done by payment for free scholars on the part of the State. The present system also has not proved an unmixed blessing; for while more ample provision is now made for the masses, it has destroyed the numerous private schools by which good education was then afforded the better classes. Pardon my mentioning these facts, I know you wish the truth; and I say these things in full appreciation of the advantages of common schools, which will remedy these evils when they are brought to the perfection existing at the North.

The following extracts will illustrate Dr. Boyce's ups and downs about the Seminary:—

To John A. Broadus, July 20, 1885.

I confess I get sick at heart when I see brethren so unwilling to help, and so perfectly indifferent to the position in which they leave me. I am like a man sinking in a quagmire or quicksand, and seeing others to whom he cries for help walking off quietly to eat their supper.

To his Sister, Mrs. Mary C. Lane, of New York, Nov. 3, 1886.

I find on my return that my friend William F. Norton, one of our most liberal contributors, and whose death is a great loss to us all, left $10,000 in his will to aid indigent students for the ministry in our Seminary. Only last spring he gave us $7,500 to pay off our debt for the land, his brother giving us $10,000 at the same time.[1]

---

[1] They had both also given liberally for the endowment. Since Dr. Boyce's death the two Norton families have expended $60,000 in erecting a large and handsome building for lecture-rooms and offices, which the Faculty have named Norton Hall.

To a Baptist Minister in Kentucky, Nov. 5, 1886.

Yours received. I regret very much to have to decline answering your question. I should be glad to furnish you my opinion on the subject, but for the fact that I have made it an invariable rule never to give an opinion even on the simplest subjects where they have been made a matter of discussion in a church or among its members. I do not in any sense think that we are to be governed by what is called "baptistic," but only by the New Testament rules, and that Baptist usages are only matters of convenience and opinion when universal, and not opposed to the Scriptures. I should always follow Baptist usages where the New Testament was not opposed to them. The great difficulty in doing so, however, is to find out what Baptist usage is. In some places and some ages it differs from other places and other ages. All the advice I can give you is to go by the New Testament always, Baptist usage to the contrary notwithstanding. But when there is nothing in the New Testament bearing upon a case, follow the usage, unless other circumstances make it unwise to do so. Baptist usage has only the power of an opinion; the New Testament's direction or usage is law.

In concluding this chapter, we may state as the full conviction of Dr. Boyce and his colleagues, after years of experience, that a Theological Seminary gains greatly from being established in a large city, and at a central point in the city. And Louisville has proved a highly satisfactory location. It is easy of access, a growing city, with the Baptists numerous and rapidly increasing, and all friends of the Seminary. More than half of the students are occupied every Sunday as teachers in Mission Sunday-schools or as preachers, and quite a large proportion of them have some pastoral charge in the city, or among the churches of Kentucky and Indiana, within a hundred miles. A few may neglect their studies for such preaching, but in general it contributes to prepare them for future usefulness.

CHAPTER XVI.

PUBLISHED AND UNPUBLISHED WRITINGS.

WE have already spoken (chap. ix.) of Dr. Boyce's "Three Changes in Theological Institutions,"— an address which produced very notable results, because it interpreted to Southern Baptists one of their profoundest wants, and because it was backed by the convictions and energies of a man capable of bringing something to pass.

About 1872 he issued "A Brief Catechism of Bible Doctrine." This was published first in Memphis by the Sunday-school Board of the Southern Baptist Convention, the Board established during the war, and removed from Greenville to Memphis. This Board not long after ceased to exist. In 1878 a revised edition of the Catechism was published in Louisville by Caperton & Cates. It consists of twenty short lessons, full of instruction for the young. It was the author's "desire to promote catechetical instruction in the family and Sunday-school." The attempt was made "to simplify, as far as possible, without sacrificing important truth." It is an excellent little work, which has been a good deal used, and deserves to be used very widely.

Dr. Boyce's chief publication was his "Abstract of Systematic Theology," printed for the use of his class in 1882, and revised and enlarged for publication in 1887. His text-book in the general or English class of Systematic Theology had for the ten first years of the Seminary's operations been Dick's Theology, gradually substituting for this or that portion a lecture of his own. When

Dr. Charles Hodge's great work appeared, in 1872, Boyce hailed it with delight, — so broadly comprehensive, complete at all points, surpassingly able and satisfactory, and expressing the consummate life-work of his own revered teacher. Though the three large octavos made a treatise too extensive for his method of instruction, he immediately introduced it as a text-book, — of course selecting, and still substituting his own dictated lectures at various points. He would doubtless have continued to use this great work. But the next year Dr. Williams became Professor of Systematic Theology, and preferred to take simply Dick as the basis of his own course of lectures. When Boyce resumed the subject, in 1887–1888, he tried Van Oosterzee's "Christian Dogmatics" for one year; but it proved somewhat cumbrous, and not very strong or inspiring. Then for two years he used Dr. Hovey's "Manual of Systematic Theology and Christian Ethics." This he found to be a clear, sound, and vigorous book, but designed to serve only as the basis of fuller discussion in a course of lectures; while Boyce wanted a more analytical and complete treatment, to be recited by the students in his peculiar method. In 1880–1882 he used A. A. Hodge's "Outlines of Theology," which appeared in 1860, and an enlarged edition in 1878. This excellent volume was based on his father's instruction, but everywhere shows independent thought and decided ability. Here also, however, there was a lack of adaptation to the precise wants of Dr. Boyce's class. Having accumulated a good many lectures, which he had been giving at various points, he finally undertook to prepare a work of his own which should be suited to his lecture-room wants, — a work comprehensive, but analytical and condensed, presenting all the points necessary to a complete discussion of every subject, but usually in a brief statement, while elaborating where it seemed specially requisite. His duties as Chairman of the Faculty, and all the heavy burden of meeting the Seminary's annual expenses, and toiling to secure adequate endowment and buildings, occupied so much of his time and energies that he could not carry the work through as completely as he desired, and as rapidly as was necessary. So, in 1882, he printed one hundred and fifty copies of his existing lectures, and such others as he could prepare. This volume of lectures was not published, but used exclusively as a text-book for his class. It contained 514 octavo pages, and, though hurriedly brought out, proved for the next five years well adapted to its design. The classes, however, were steadily increasing in number; and being anxious to re-work the book thoroughly before publishing, he began to purchase back the copies which had been furnished to students, in order to keep the class supplied year after year.

Meantime he went on with studies looking to the revision and enlargement of his Abstract. But the financial and other business distractions were very serious. He was also working much at the course in Church Government, wishing to make a complete exhibition of the Roman Catholic and leading Protestant forms of church organization and government, and to discuss the principal creeds, using Dr. Schaff's book and many others. Dr. Boyce's study of any subject was sure to be planned on a large scale, and pushed with great resolution. Before he was ready to publish the matured and completed "Abstract of Theology," the increasing number of students demanded more copies than he could recover of the unpublished volume. Moreover, his health showed marked signs of decline. So, in 1886–1887, he carefully revised, and in many parts re-wrote, the existing work. Enlarging upon some subjects, he condensed elsewhere, so as to keep the volume within about the same compass as before, and not too large for his course of instruction, embracing about one hundred lessons. The work received his closest attention. Every paragraph was the result of life-long studies, now faithfully renewed, and the treatise presents his mature convictions. But some parts of the volume were written down rapidly, though after long thought, and so the sentences are not always clear. Yet the reader who will consider with some patience need never doubt as to what is meant, and he finds the thought itself to be in a very high degree clear and strong. The work was published in Baltimore in 1887 (H. M. Wharton & Co.), and is now published by the American Baptist Publication Society, Philadelphia.

Dr. Boyce omits several important topics which are often embraced in treatises on Systematic Theology, because in this Seminary those subjects are taught in other departments. Thus, Canon and Inspiration are taught in the school of Biblical Introduction, Church Constitution and Ordinances in the school of Church Government and in that of Polemic Theology. His work could therefore devote itself entirely to the statement, discussion, and defence of the *doctrinal contents* of Scripture.

Like his preceptor, Charles Hodge, Dr. Boyce was much influenced as to general method by the great treatise of Turrettin, which he was teaching every year to his smaller class in "Latin Theology." But, like Dr. Hodge again, he based everything upon laborious collection and conscientious examination of Scripture passages. No one better knew that the theologian and the exegetical student are interdependent. His colleague who was Professor of the New Testament once said to him, in some pleasantries of conversation, that students of exegesis might have some freedom if it were not for these dreadful theological people, who know beforehand what every passage ought to mean, in order to suit their creeds and systems, and who have not a proper respect for philology and criticism. Boyce replied that a student of theology might have some peace if it were not for these dreadful teachers of exegesis and all sorts of criticism, who are constantly snapping up his favorite proof texts, and declaring that this is not the correct reading, or that is not the correct translation. Yet, of course, the systematic arrangement of revealed truth is constantly dependent on the critical and exegetical study of the inspired writings; while the uncertainties of exegesis and criticism may often be quieted — and its over-confident wanderings should often be restrained — by a due regard to the general teachings of Scripture upon the question involved.

The chief emphasis in this work is laid on the doctrine of God rather than on that of Man. Much that some theologians would treat exclusively under the doctrine of Man is here presented, or the way prepared for it, in the doctrine of the divine nature, attributes, and purposes. Thus the book is truly a Theology, in the strict sense of the term. Besides, the later portions, on Man, were more rapidly written, and therefore less full than they might have otherwise been made.

We give extracts from two notices which this work received at the time. The "Standard" of Chicago, a singularly able and judicious paper, points out carefully and correctly the peculiarities of the work, as designed for a text-book in class instruction, and as omitting certain subjects commonly included in theological treatises. It then proceeds as follows: —

"We find the book, as respects its specific purpose, deserving of high praise. It does not attempt too much, yet aims at and accomplishes enough. Its analysis, in the case of each topic, is remarkably helpful, alike for the student and for the general reader. In statement, in argument, in the expanding of the thought, where this is called for, there is great clearness. We judge that it may be taken in hand by the student, by the pastor, or the general reader, and made available for theological instruction in a way to be a most effective guide in all the great matters included.

"As a theologian Dr. Boyce is not afraid to be found ' in the old paths.' He is conservative, and eminently Scriptural. He treats with great fairness those whose views upon various points discussed he declines to accept, yet in his own teaching is decidedly Calvinistic, after the model of 'the old divines.' Difficulties, as connected with such doctrines as the Federal Headship of Adam, Election, and the Atonement, he aims to meet, evidently, not so as to silence the controversialist, but so as to help the honest inquirer. We offer no opinion as to the correctness of his theological opinions, this being beyond our province; but we have this to say, that the remarkable steadiness of the Baptist ministry and the Baptist churches, in this age of theological drift, is unquestionably due very much to the firm Scriptural attitude of our theology as taught in the theological schools, South, West, and East.

"We take pleasure in expressing our very high appreciation in all respects of this very able work. If in a few cases we should prefer a different form of statement, we still hesitate to urge a preference, where the criticism, if ventured, would imply difference from one who in his whole cast of mind is a theologian, and in his many years of service has proved himself entitled to rank with the eminent teachers of the land."

Another remarkable commendation was given by "The Independent," of New York. This paper strongly objects to the theological views presented in the work, because they involve decided "Calvinism;" but this sets in contrast the strong statement of its merits as a text-book.

"For the purpose of a teacher, it is an admirable piece of work, compact, well-arranged, and with a good critical statement of the various forms of doctrinal opinion under each topic. The whole is done in a clear, strong, and manly way, with no evasion of difficulties, no sentimental coloring or softening, but everywhere bold, honest thinking, expressed in plain, vigorous, and excellent English. Young men drilled in such a manual, and theological students in any grade who bend their minds to the task of mastering it, will have here a robust and fundamental schooling that must invigorate their philosophy, even if subsequent thinking is to introduce great modifications into the theological system learned from it."

The critic then proceeds to object to the book as Calvinistic, but in so doing says: —

"There is a great deal of close, strong thinking and keen theological criticism in the chapters on the Atonement, Election, Reprobation, and particularly applied to the question of the Extent of the Atonement. . . . We doubt if the Calvinistic doctrines of Election and Reprobation can be put better than they are in this volume."

Dr. Boyce's work is, indeed, as these newspaper notices have said, thoroughly in accord with the system of theological opinion commonly called Calvinism. This is believed by many of us to be really the teaching of the Apostle Paul, as elaborated by Augustine, and systematized and defended by Calvin. It is a body of truth that compels men to *think*, — in itself a great advantage. The objections to it are believed to grow out of either misapprehension, or misapplication through wrong inferences. Men assume predestination and election, and then deny human freedom and responsibility; or they assume freedom and accountability, and then deny predestination and election, — in either case because they cannot fully reconcile these two sides of theological truth; thus making our capacity to harmonize things the limit of possible truth, and the criterion of Scripture interpretation. The world of matter is kept in equilibrium by the antagonism of physical forces, and the world of truth in like manner through countervailing facts and principles. Whatever theoretical position may be held, no truly devout man actually lives in practical neglect of either divine sovereignty or human responsibility. The blindest "Hardshell," who has "no message to the unconverted," does not neglect to plough his corn; the most ultra and heated Arminian believes in the doctrines of grace whenever he grows earnest in prayer.

This "Abstract of Systematic Theology," designed as a text-book for classes, is in like manner well suited to careful private study. Nothing is more useful to a thorough-going student than to take some first-class book on a great subject, and master it completely, chapter after chapter, paragraph by paragraph, so that he can state the exact line of thought in any portion to himself or to some patiently sympathetic friend. The writer remembers to have thus studied in his early ministerial life Butler's "Analogy," McCosh on the "Divine Government," and several other works, and can see as he looks back how the thought of those great books went into his blood. The class-room presents great advantages; but through life a man must be his own teacher, his own pupil, and his own fellow-student, and bring all the energies of his being to bear upon the persistent effort to fill each of these positions worthily. Besides, the Abstract will be found quite convenient for consultation when preparing sermons. If your text involves some doctrine, you may easily turn to the chapter treating that subject, and find its main thought separately and pointedly stated, so that you may readily seize upon the matters that are wanted. If now to Boyce's Abstract a minister will add such a copious work as Strong's "Systematic Theology," he will possess a very admirable theological apparatus, — and both works from American Baptists.

A volume ought to be published of Dr. Boyce's sermons and lectures. One of his most delightful practical sermons (heard twice by the writer) was on the text, "This man receiveth sinners" (Luke xv. 2), as illustrated by the three parables of the Lost Sheep, the Lost Coin, and the Lost Son. The difference in color of the light thrown by the three illustrations was depicted with delicate taste and deep feeling, and the practical impression was wholesome and powerful. Another of great interest was on "Behold, I stand at the door and knock" (Rev. iii. 20). It opens with a beautiful description, which represents a door long closed and rusted, overrun with weeds and cobwebs, while one stands before it and knocks; and the sermon well sustains the interest thus excited. In 1873 he prepared a sermon of uncommon vigor on "The Place and Power of Prayer" (1 John v. 14, 15), suggested by the proposition then familiarly known as "Tyndall's prayer-test," which became a favorite sensation with the newspapers, and was much talked about for several years. Some disciple of Tyndall had proposed that two patients suffering from the same disease should be treated in the same hospital, with exactly identical remedies and surroundings, and that one of these should be made the subject of widespread prayer for his recovery, while the other was not prayed for at all; and the result would show whether prayer has any real efficacy. Of course no really devout and thoughtful Christian could join in applying such a test; for to experiment upon God's promises through a manufactured occasion is exactly what the Saviour was refusing to do when he quoted the words, "Thou shall not test the Lord thy God." Dr. Boyce did not dignify this fantastical proposition by any extended answer, but merely took it as the occasion for a thorough-going discussion of the topic indicated. Here his powers were at their best. His intellectual force was exerted in establishing and defending fundamental truth, his interest in practical things was awakened by the practical issues raised, and his fervently devout feeling was deeply stirred by dwelling on the privilege and the duty of prayer; so that the whole man was fully enlisted. This is probably the foremost sermon to be found among his manuscripts. It was preached at various points throughout the Southern country, and a number of times in Louisville, being repeated by special request at Broadway and Walnut Street churches, and given also at Chestnut Street Church and at several Presbyterian churches; and it was spoken of by many as in a high degree satisfying and helpful.

A number of other sermons may be found among the

manuscripts that would be read with decided interest and great profit. One is on The Unjust Steward (Luke xvi. 9); another on Mary the Mother of Jesus (Acts i. 14); and another on The Incarnate Word (John i. 14). There is a very pungent and solemn sermon on the Danger of Refusing the Son of God (Heb. xii. 25). One of special interest to ministers treats "The Value of a Complete and Accurate Knowledge of the Doctrines of Grace to the Successful Preaching of the Gospel" (Titus iii. 4–8). Two of the latest sermons he wrote in full were for the Broadway Baptist Church in 1884, on John vi. 66–71, "To whom shall we go? Thou hast the words of eternal life." But there is a later, written for Broadway in 1886, on 1 John iii. 2. We have heretofore mentioned and quoted from the excellent funeral sermon on Dr. Basil Manly, Sr.

Dr. Boyce's Lectures on Systematic Theology were of course mainly incorporated in the published Abstract; but his earlier lectures on Polemics, and those in later years on Church Government and Pastoral Duties, present several of permanent interest and value. Especially notable is the Lecture on Mormonism, and a popular Lecture given at a church on "The Local Visible Ecclesia." Before a literary club at Greenville he read an Essay on Eve, as conceived and represented by the poets, which was extremely pleasing. Nothing interested him more than to ransack libraries on some particular theme, and bring together all that he thought valuable. Besides Milton and Mrs. Browning ("Drama of Exile"), he found not a little in earlier and later poets as to Eve, and exhibited and discussed the different poetical conceptions with much taste and feeling. One side of his gifts and culture is probably better shown in this Essay than in anything else that remains to us.

CHAPTER XVII.

DECLINING YEARS AND DEATH.

THE gout began to show itself as early as 1871, being inherited from his father. After curing an attack, through the powerful specifics employed (sometimes relieving the pain within twenty-four hours), Dr. Boyce's vigorous constitution would rally with wonderful quickness, and in a few days he would seem thoroughly well. It is frequently true in other cases as in his, that a person fleshy from childhood and through life is never a very large eater. Probably most of us eat too much, especially some who have bad digestion, and remain comparatively thin and even gaunt. Several years after the first attacks of gout, Dr. Boyce began to apprehend other and kindred disorders, and was induced to try some proposed means of reducing flesh, chiefly by avoiding certain kinds of food. Making a faithful trial of this for some time, he became satisfied that a reduction of general vigor was the only marked result, and returned to his ordinary simple and healthy diet.

As the years went on, the attacks of gout became somewhat more frequent, and there were increasing evidences of other disorder. In 1882, while working hard on the first (unpublished) issue of the "Abstract of Theology," and quite often during several months writing new sermons for the Broadway Church, — together with all the teaching and financial labors, — he began to suffer seriously. Once after a sermon he complained of a bewildered feeling in the head, and asked if he had said anything unsuitable; for he did not quite know what he had been saying during the last minutes. This was evidently the result of overwork. During that period, and again in 1886, 1887 (while preparing his book for publication), he would often, for weeks in succession, begin work at five A. M., and continue, with variety, but no intermission, till eleven P. M., kept up by excitement and force of will, and not conscious at the time of any serious damage. He also suffered, as did Addison Alexander and Count Cavour, and other famous men of full habit and great mental labors, from lack of bodily exercise. After removing to Louisville in 1872, he never kept a carriage, and so did not have the exercise of driving, by which he frequently profited at Greenville. He had not learned to ride on horseback in youth, and never attempted it after the brief term of service as Chaplain, and as Aide to the Governor. He walked with remarkable ease and grace for so heavy a man; but it pretty soon fatigued him in these last years, and so he rarely walked except to lecture, or down street on business, or to market in the morning,— an early task in which he took special pleasure. He never tried gymnastic apparatus. The frequent railway trips required by Seminary affairs and private business afforded his only considerable means of exercise, and sometimes returned him in manifestly improved health; though in the later years such a journey was often followed by an attack of gout.

The higher ranks of intellectual workers in our cities, including the great business men, now comprise many who need to make a business of taking exercise; and if they only realized the need, and would make conscience of the matter and faithfully try experiments, every one might assuredly find means of regularly and amply exercising the muscles in some proportion to the exhausting and incessant strain he puts upon brain and nerves. The necessity of replacing the worn-out nerve and brain matter by new material derived from food, awakens appetite, and leads us to eat freely. Then, if there be a corresponding break-down of muscular and fatty tissue through exercise, the digested food is all usefully employed in replacing the different kinds of tissue; but without this, more food must be digested than the circulation can dispose of, and the result is either dyspepsia, as so many of us find, or gouty deposits in the joints, or excessive exertion and premature decay of the kidneys, or the like. We *must* all learn to take ample muscular exercise every day, and a little walking or driving is not enough. The hope for most city men of mentally laborious and anxious life is believed to lie in the use of exercising apparatus, at home or in a gymnasium. Great improvements have been made in this respect within a few years. The gymnasium of to-day does not propose feats of strength or agility, but moderate exercise for all the most important muscles. Let us hope that "the athletic craze" will prove to be only the excess accompanying a healthy tendency. Some regularly employ a succession of gymnastic movements, without any apparatus. The late Mr. George W. Norton, of Louisville, was convinced that he had prolonged his life several years through this practice, and similar cases are known elsewhere. One must of course add to indoor exercise such walks and rides and excursions into the country — for which the electric cars are becoming a great convenience — as will give fresh air and change of scene. The great trouble about the whole matter is that every one of us inclines to regard his case as peculiar, and to suppose that he does not need, or really has not opportunity for, such systematic daily exercise. There are, of course, constitutional differences, some men needing it less than others.

When he became conscious of seriously disordered health, Dr. Boyce made every effort to retard the progress of disease, trying the Buffalo Lithia Water, and the Hot Springs, as well as specific medicines. He was both resolute and cheerful by nature, and was "sustained and soothed by an unfaltering trust" in the Providence of his Heavenly Father.

In May, 1887, he requested the Board of Trustees to appoint Rev. F. H. Kerfoot, D.D., as Co-Professor of Theology, proposing that they should divide the salary. His object was to have time during the next session for personal journeys in the interest of the endowment, and, a year later, for making his long-deferred trip to Europe. Dr. Kerfoot, a Virginian, and a graduate of the Columbian University at Washington city, became a student of the Seminary at Greenville in 1869–1870, and applied himself laboriously and successfully to a full half of the course, with the hope of completing it in two years. After protracted meeting work in the summer, he returned the following autumn; but his health soon became seriously impaired, and it was necessary to quit. A year or two later he took the third year at Crozer Seminary, and was graduated. After this he spent about two years in the University of Leipzig and on a trip to Palestine. Returning, he was for some time Professor of German in Georgetown College, Ky., and pastor of two neighboring churches. When the Seminary was removed to Louisville, in 1877, the Faculty desired his accession as an assistant instructor, but yielded to the urgent appeal of friends in the Eutaw Place Baptist Church, Baltimore, who wished him as pastor. In that church, and, some years later, in the Strong Place Church, of Brooklyn, he had a highly useful pastoral career. This was interrupted by an accidental fall from a platform, leading ultimately to protracted lameness and nervous troubles; and, at length resigning the Strong Place pastorate, he returned, after a season of rest, to his old church at Midway, Ky., and entered the Seminary as a regular student for 1886–1887, doing all the class-work with thoroughness and relish, and taking his diplomas in the schools attended. And so it came to pass, in the course of Providence, that he was here to relieve Dr. Boyce's failing strength and to become his successor. Dr. Boyce's letters show that his plan was to let Dr. Kerfoot do all the teaching during the first three or four months of the session, while he should be on collecting journeys, and then to resume some of the classes himself. But in point of fact the business continued to press, and his health slowly failed, so that all the work was necessarily left to Kerfoot, and his own last teaching was done in the session of 1886–1887.

Several letters may now be inserted. The first refers to his birthday.

To Miss Nannie K. Lane, of New York, Jan. 15, 1887.

Many thanks for your congratulations. . . . I feel very young, indeed, except when the gout seizes upon me and fills me with despair. It is very pleasant to me to receive the many greetings I have had, though yours is the first from any of my nieces or nephews. I hope we shall see much more of each other this coming year. What a joy to me was that pleasant Sunday afternoon at the Bartholdi Hotel. God bless you, dear Nannie, for your great love to me.

The two following show how he was painfully toiling on to complete and bring out his "Abstract of Theology:" —

To Messrs. H. M. Wharton & Co., Baltimore, Jan. 24, 1887.

I find the progress of my book very much impeded by my health, or rather want of health. I shall be forced to do one of two things, — proceed as best I may, and leave out much new matter I wish to introduce, or delay as long as necessary to complete what I wish. Sickness and the quantity of proof received and the pressure of engagements greatly hinder me. I had hoped to get the book out by May, but think better now to delay longer, as I shall not need it for my classes until October 1.

To Hon. Joseph E. Brown, Atlanta, June 3, 1887.

I am getting out a book on Systematic Theology, — a text-book for students. I write to ask your permission to dedicate it to you. It is the only way I have ever had of testifying to my high esteem and affection for you, or of showing my gratitude for your many kindnesses to my work, the Seminary. I trust you will allow me to so honor my book as in this humble way to connect it with your name.

The next letter refers to a noble man, who has been spoken of in a previous chapter.

To Mrs. Nimrod Long, Russellville, Ky., April 25, 1887.

I returned to the city this afternoon, and learned as I was approaching it the sad news of the death of your dear husband. I knew that his health was very feeble, but did not think when I met all of you at Chattanooga that the end would come so soon. I sympathize with you very much in your affliction. I had learned to love him very warmly, as well as to esteem him very highly. He was an excellent man, full of zeal for God, and love for his brethren and his faith, and full of liberality and good works. I rejoice to know of his friendship for me, and have felt myself greatly honored by it. His loss to us all is very great, in many respects irreparable. To you and his children it must come home more sensibly than to any others. You have the joy of his intimate fellowship and strongest affections. I know somewhat from my own past afflictions how your hearts must be filled with anguish. But yet we grieve not as those who have no hope. We shall see him again where there will be no parting forever. He has but gone before us to the blessed state of the righteous who die in the Lord. We too must soon follow. May we be as well prepared! May it be to us as great a joy as is his! May this hope of his happiness be a comfort to you, and may God be with you in your trial with his comforting spirit of grace!

In June was held the fortieth anniversary of Dr. Boyce's class in Brown University. He wrote in May to his dear friend Dr. Guild, expressing the hope that he could attend, but wrote again, on June 10, that he found it impossible, without travelling on Sunday, which he could not do. He sent his "best love to each of the dear boys of

'47." The University conferred upon him at that Commencement the honorary degree of LL.D., which he had previously also received in 1872 from Union University in Tennessee. The following letter acknowledges the honor: —

To Rev. E. G. Robinson, D.D., LL.D., President of Brown University, Providence, July 23, 1887.

Your kind letter of July 20 was received yesterday, and the diploma came to-day. You have all been very kind to me at Brown, and I am very grateful. I love the old College, and those associated with it, — only the more because of my distance from it, and the consequent fact that a visit to it is anticipated with hope, and remembered with unfading joy. There is no institution which could give me a degree that would be as highly prized as one from Brown. Thank you for your kind words, and your expression of desire that I may sometimes revisit the cherished spot. I assure you that I shall always be pleased when I can do so.

To Hon. W. A. Courtenay, Charleston, S. C., July 15, 1887.

I have this morning received the copy of the Year Book of Charleston for 1886, which you have been so kind as to send. I thank you very much. I cannot tell you how much I prize these annual volumes. I have taken great delight in reading them. You are doing a noble work in having them prepared, — a work done for no other city, and one which constantly awakens wonder at the richness of the vein of historical research connected with the dear old City by the Sea. It is my pride to have been born in Charleston, and that pride is increased by every volume of the Year Book which appears.

To William E. Dodge, Esq., New York, July 4, 1887.

Your letter received on my return from a protracted absence. I have awaited an opportunity of reading the book of Dr. Josiah Strong, which you were so kind as to send me, before answering the letter. I have been greatly engrossed with the preparation of a text-book in Theology for my classes, which had to be completed before I could take any summer vacation. I finished it only last week, and hope now to get some rest, which I am sadly needing.

I have read the book of Dr. Strong, "Our Country," with much interest. It is very able, and presents an admirable collection and discussion of facts, for which he deserves the thanks of all good citizens. In one respect, however, I think he has made a mistake, which is important in connection with the Catholic controversy. So far from any proportionate increase, there has been a decided proportionate decrease of Roman Catholics. Indeed, if the amount of additions by immigration be taken into account, the decline of Catholicism in this country should be appalling to them; and but for the substitution of so much infidelity for it, would be a matter of congratulation to all Protestants and patriots. To arrive at this, take the population of 1776, and to that add the natural increase as shown by the general population, to that add the immigration of each ten years and its natural increase, and see what the figures would be. The Romanists should have had more than half the population. I speak moderately. I think it would be nearly three-fourths. But they have really to-day not more than one-tenth of the whole population. The mistake of Dr. Strong is in comparing the number which Roman Catholics give with that given by Protestants, when the latter number is that of the actual communicants of each denomination, while the Romanists give that of all adherents. The number of communicants should be multiplied in each case by five, to give the number of adherents. The figures thus to be obtained will be confirmed by the tables taken in 1870 by the Government of the number of church sittings provided by each denomination. I made some figures about ten years since which lead me to say that out of the fifty million inhabitants of the United States at that time, the Methodists and their adherents had twenty-five million, the Baptists fifteen million, other Protestants and Jews five million, Romanists five million. I am satisfied that this small percentage comprises all there is of Romanists in our country. In confirmation, as I have suggested, take the reports in the census of 1870 as to the sittings, or provision made for members of congregations. I only recollect at present Kentucky, and I have no means of access to the tables. But in Kentucky the Baptists have more than one half of the State, having somewhat more than all others, — Protestants, Jews, Catholics, and all else. If Dr. Strong had duly regarded the difference between the way in which the Catholics report members — counting as a matter of course all persons who are adherents of theirs — and that in which Protestants generally count (I am sure Baptists do, and believe all of them do), namely, the actual communicants, his statement of facts would have been far otherwise.

In July, 1887, he took his family on a pleasant journey of two or three months to California and Alaska. As to this tour, his eldest daughter has kindly consented to furnish some notes, which will at the same time illustrate certain traits of his character.

"Father was a delightful travelling companion. He was so accustomed to moving about that he knew perfectly how to make himself and others comfortable. He delighted to have ladies in his charge. Their many trunks and bundles gave him no concern. He seemed to think it was only proper that they should be made comfortable. He always thought out his trips, and arranged everything so that the greatest enjoyment could be had with the least trouble. During the winter months he would make so many plans for the next summer's outing that we would be fairly bewildered as to what we should really do. Of course a great deal of his travelling in the South was when raising money for the Seminary. He learned to eat anything that was put before him, and quite won the hearts of country people.

"Having need of only four or five hours' sleep, he could accommodate himself to any hour of rising, and an early country breakfast had no terrors for him. Considering how constantly he was on the cars, it was strange that he was never in any accident of any moment. He slept as peacefully in his berth as in his bed. Being very closely confined during the winter months, the summer was always looked forward to by him as the time for rest and recreation. As soon as he could get away from his work, he would start with his family to mountains or sea-shore. There he would fairly revel in the lovely views and pure air and the pleasure of unlimited companionship with his family. The last years of his life his trips were more extended. In this his family tried to encourage him, as it was felt that he should get so far from his home that business cares would perforce be too far away to be constantly troubling his mind.

"In 1887 he went to California and Alaska. We all look back upon this trip as most satisfactory in many respects. He had begun to show signs of his health breaking down completely. Being overburdened and overworked, he really prolonged his life by going so far from his home. No letters or papers reached him for weeks, and though he occasionally worried over this deprivation, on the whole it had an excellent effect upon him. He entered with ardor into the trip, enjoyed everything, and soon commenced to look like a different man. Our route was from Louisville to Kansas City, thence to Manitou, through the Arkansas Cañon, returning to the Central Pacific, then to Sacramento and San Francisco (where we remained five days), then to the Yosemite Valley. We entered the Valley from the Cliffs, and had what we considered quite a breakneck ride down the steep path. We were told to allow our horses great freedom, — not to attempt to guide them, but only to hold the bridle lightly, in case they should stumble. We were quite willing to trust ourselves to them as soon as we found how carefully they picked their way, and how sure-footed they seemed to be. This lack of necessity to guide them allowed us to gaze at our leisure upon the beautiful scene before us. It seemed to us impossible that anything could be more beautiful. The snowy cliffs bathed in the last gleams of the sun, the atmosphere of shimmering blue, the magnificent trees, the cascades, the ever-changing vistas, — all combined to make a scene that brought to our minds the description of the mountains from which Bunyan's Pilgrim was said to look on the beautiful land of Beulah. We were so unfortunate as to visit the Yosemite during the dry season, and consequently suffered a great deal from the dust. The dust from the roads poured over the wheels of our carriage like water in a mill-race. It was impossible to keep ourselves respectable. The fine dust settled in our sashes, hair, depressions and wrinkles in the face, until we felt like animated dust-heaps. As soon as we arrived at the different resting-places we were immediately met by an immaculate Chinaman, who dusted us vigorously before we were allowed to take a step.

"We remained in the Yosemite only a day or two, as our time was limited, and then left for a visit to the big trees. As we approached this region the trees became larger, taller, and more perfect in shape; our eyes becoming gradually accustomed to them, we were actually unimpressed when we first saw the great Sequoias, though our large wagonette, holding three on each seat, was driven easily through the hollowed trunk of one still standing, and apparently in flourishing condition. Though we took a cord and measured another, so as to give us an idea of the circumference and to be able to convince our friends at home by demonstration, still we could not take in their great size. It was only on our return home, when in attempting to describe them we unwound and stretched out the string with which we had measured the trunk, that we began to realize how enormous they were. To tell the truth, we began to feel doubtful about the correct measurement ourselves, and were very glad to have our silent witness with us.

"While in California we visited Santa Barbara, where we saw the crimson passion-flower, covering the tall trees as a luxuriant vine; Santa Monica, the seaport of Los Angeles, which was at that time in the spasms of a boom, with every other man a real estate agent, and lots at fabulous prices; Passadena, Monterey, and near Monterey the famous park and grounds of the Hotel del Monti. The old hotel had been burned one year before, and the new building was not completed; but we did not regret our visit there, as we saw the unique and weird Arizona garden, which is such a surprise to the lovers of flowers. The plants were very queer, and many of them never before seen by us. The tennis-courts were surrounded by tall wire screens, over which purple clematis ran in the greatest profusion. The cacti in this garden were so distorted and curious in their growth that they were positively uncanny. On returning to San Francisco we remained a week, and then went by sea to Portland. We passed through the Golden Gate about five o'clock in the afternoon. It was beautiful as a dream, even lovelier than the Palisades on the Hudson, and having a resemblance to them. We had a rather rough trip, and were, with the exception of Father, all sick. We reached Portland, remaining there several days; then went on from there to Port Townsend, where we were to take our Alaska steamer. We were detained there several days, and a dreary little place it was. When we at last got off, we were in the highest spirits and ready to enjoy the wonders of Alaska. We went up as high as the Muir Glacier, then to Sitka, Victoria, Tacoma, and then home, by way of the Northern Pacific, stopping in Minneapolis, St. Paul, and Chicago."

This journey brought marked improvement to his health and hopefulness, as shown by the following letter to his eldest sister: —

To Mrs. Mary C. Lane, New York, Dec. 14, 1887.

Yours of December 12th received this morning. I am sorry you have been troubled about my health. I assure you that I am getting on very well. My health has been very much better ever since I went to the Pacific coast. My girls and wife think that I have also been much improved by last month's agency work. It is true that I am not so strong as I was two years ago, but ever so much better than when I saw you last spring. I shall get to New York some time this winter, and you will see all this, unless I have some reverse. I take great care of myself. It is because I am so careful, and rested so much at Richmond, that Beck supposed me much weaker than I was. I would not work more than five hours each day. What troubled me was that it became evident that the work would take much longer than I had supposed.

My attacks of gout are now much less frequent and much less severe, and I think I am doing very well.

God grant us both better health, if he sees fit; but if not, I am, for myself, more than contented. My work for the Seminary is almost done. I can leave it very soon beyond all ordinary risk, and so that, with God's blessing, all will go well. My Estate matters are in such a condition as will give little trouble to any of you, should I die. My own private affairs need some more attention, and I should like to have sold out all the Estate property and turned it over, by dividing it to the different Trust Estates. I think I can sell it to better advantage than any one else. On these accounts I care to live somewhat longer. Otherwise, except for my love for family and friends, I have no such desire.

Yet, to speak candidly, I think I shall outlive any of you, except Rebecca, and perhaps Kerr.[1]

God bless you, my dear sister. The Lord has been very gracious to you, and I think is drawing you nearer and still nearer to himself. May he spare you to us all somewhat longer! Yet if not, ours will be the grief, and yours the joy.

The day after this cheerful letter was written, there came upon the Seminary a grave calamity. Dr. Manly and his family were boarding in the suburbs of Louisville, beyond the Water Works. At dusk, on Dec. 15, 1887, while walking from the railway station to the house, he and his host were knocked down by robbers with a sudden blow on the head, and it was perhaps fifteen minutes before he recovered sufficiently to go on to the house. He resumed teaching too soon, and had to go away for some time, at the entreaty of his colleagues. The blow served to develop a valvular disease of the heart, besides permanently weakening his excellent constitution; and Dr. Boyce was oppressed with the fear that his valued colleague would not have many added years of usefulness.[2]

Although his health was now considerably improved, Dr. Boyce found himself unable, as heretofore stated, to take any part in the teaching during the session of 1887-1888. For several months he did a good deal of agency work for the endowment, striving to bring it up to the point of furnishing income enough for the annual expenses of the Seminary. During the spring and summer of 1888 his health was steadily declining. In May, at Richmond, as Dr. Mell had passed away, other brethren nominated declined, and Boyce was almost by acclamation elected

---

[1] This was sadly fulfilled in great measure. Mrs. Lane died the ensuing summer, and Mrs. Tupper in the autumn; Mr. Kerr Boyce early in 1892. Only Mrs. Burckmyer and Mrs. Lawrence remain.

[2] Dr. Manly did excellent work in the following years, but never fully recovered, and died on Jan. 31, 1892, beloved and lamented. It is hoped that a Memoir of him will appear.

President of the Southern Baptist Convention once more. He presided in manifest bodily weakness, but with all the high courtesy and cordiality of former years. In the early summer it became manifest that the only chance of improving his condition and living for any further work was to take his family abroad for a long time. At various periods of his life, from early maturity, we have met with expressions of desire to visit Europe. During these last years the desire had been strengthened by the wish to give his daughters the opportunity of gratifying their taste and cultivating their powers in regard to music and art, as well as of visiting with his family the scenes of historic and literary interest about which they had been reading through life. Perhaps only some persons can fully appreciate the great sacrifice he had made through many years in postponing this high privilege for himself and his wife and daughters. Besides the long struggle to establish the Seminary, he had borne many burdens of toil and anxiety in regard to his father's estate, including properties which could not yet be disposed of without sacrifice, and in some cases annual wants which he must assist in supplying. There were also some important investments of his own which had not been in a satisfactory condition, and added much anxiety to his declining years. But in the summer of 1888 the way seemed to open for going abroad. Dr. Kerfoot had shown himself well able to keep up the teaching, and was also specially fitted to continue the work of General Agent, while the duties of Treasurer he could himself perform through arrangements made beforehand and the help of his faithful secretary, Mr. Almond. Kerfoot could remove his family down from Midway, and occupy the Boyce residence. The endowment had not reached the necessary point, but it was possible to keep the Seminary going. New York Hall had been entered, greatly brightening the inner life of the Seminary. The business of his father's estate had come into a more manageable condition, and his own affairs were more satisfactory. So the long-deferred trip to Europe was now practicable.

Let us insert here some further notes, kindly prepared by Miss Lizzie Boyce: —

"At first his attacks of gout were at long intervals, but towards the ten last years of his life they began to be more frequent. About two years before his death he was apt to be laid up every two weeks. The tendency to rheumatism and gout was clearly an inheritance with him, as many of his family connection were similarly affected; two of his brothers used crutches during many of their last years. Father bore his suffering with great patience; his books would be his consolation at such a time. He would have them piled up on the table beside him, and on his bed. He would write letters by the quantity, and seemed to us to accomplish as much in a certain way as when well. As soon as he could manage to stand, he was up and hard at work again. It was useless for the doctor to scold, useless for us to protest. He was pressed in so many ways with important duties that he felt compelled to take up his burden again without delay.

"The task of revising, and often rewriting, his text-book on Systematic Theology, and of correcting the proof, was a great burden to one already overworked and suffering. He would frequently become so exhausted that he could scarcely hold himself erect in his chair. In this last year his malady caused him to to be tormented with unnatural drowsiness, which hampered him greatly in his work,— in truth, he was apt to fall asleep, unless he forced his attention, when conversing with his friends, or at any time. This symptom alarmed us so much that we begged the physician, Dr. Holloway, to use his authority and put a stop to Father's continuing the work upon his book. The doctor warned him that no man could stand the strain he was undergoing without shortening his life, and that he was even then in a very dangerous condition. Father agreed that the work proved more exhausting than he had expected, but he had begun, and now wished to finish it. He added that he had not time to rest, as his business affairs and his duties to the Seminary were more pressing than ever, so that it was impossible for him to pursue any other course. Later on, he had one night a heart attack, the nature of which we did not understand. He entered the room where we were seated, gasping for breath, and with his complexion so ashy that he presented a most alarming appearance. It was nearly midnight, and no servant in the house; but I ran to a neighboring drug-store and telephoned the doctor. By the time he arrived, Father was better, and soon afterwards felt much relieved; but after this attack I noticed that any exertion made him pant for breath.

"We were all so worried over his state of health that we began to urge Father to take a sea-voyage. The doctor said that unless we could put a stop to his working, he would certainly die within six months. This was so alarming that we used every effort to persuade him to take a prolonged trip. He then decided to go abroad, and remain there an indefinite period, until his health improved, returning to America at intervals for attention to pressing business, and yet spending most of his time abroad. This plan of being absent for a long and indefinite time caused him to work more and more ardently in trying to arrange his affairs. I fear that this extra labor proved fatal to the end we had in view. By the time we were packed up and everything arranged, he was in a most alarming condition, and by the time we reached New York to take our steamer, I began to doubt the wisdom of our going at all. We feared to go, and we feared to return. Remembering that he was an excellent sailor, never suffering from sea-sickness, we concluded that we would at least not say anything until we reached Liverpool. If he was then worse, we would insist upon returning at once."

The last days at home were saddened by the death of his oldest sister, Mrs. Lane, of New York, a woman of noble character and deep devoutness, belonging to the famous little Amity Street Baptist Church, with the celebrated scholar, Dr. William R. Williams, as long her pastor and friend.

To Mrs. C. R. Burckmyer, July 29, 1888.

I suppose Sister was either buried yesterday, or will be to-day. I presume you were telegraphed of her death Friday just before noon. It is her great gain, but our sore loss. We shall never know how good she was, nor how much she loved us all. This almost breaks up New York to me. It was my great misfortune not to be able to go on to the funeral, but it is impossible for me to leave before to-morrow (Monday) afternoon. I therefore telegraphed them not to delay on my account. We shall be at the Bartholdi Hotel, Twenty-third and Broadway, and leave *per* "Etruria" on Saturday, August 4th. God bless you and yours. Good-bye.

We have the following letters written during the voyage: —

To Mrs. Burckmyer, Aug. 7, 1888, " en voyage."

I am going to write some letters to be mailed at Queenstown, and I write to you first of all. You will be astonished to learn that none of us have been sea-sick, except a slight qualm or two on the first day for two of the girls. My wife has not been sick at all, for which she is occasionally very grateful. Our vessel is a very fine one, steady and fast, and our accommodations are very good. The food is not extraordinary, but it is well cooked, and abundant of its kind. There is no large crowd, and we are therefore the more comfortable. I do not see where the steamer-chairs could be placed if we had double our number. I know none of the passengers. . . . Looking over the above, I fear you will not be able to read it. I am writing on a book, contrary to my habit of using a table. I sit on the lounge in my state-room, and write the best I can. It will be your business to read the letter, mine simply to write it. I am trying a new food for my wife, bovinine, which Sister used for several months, and which was strongly recommended to me by Amanda Lane and Lizzie Lawrence. My wife thus far consents to take it, and I trust will continue. If I find I can get it in London, I shall try it myself. We expect to be at Liverpool on Sunday. We have changed our plans. I had intended to go through Ireland first, and then Scotland, and then England. But as I do not feel very strong, and the trip through Ireland would be rough, we have decided to go to Liverpool, and then probably branch off into Scotland, finally reaching London, — thus leaving the Irish travel for some other time. At the end of this journey we shall either stop in London for a few weeks, or go to some quiet place, like the Isle of Wight, unless the doctor you get me should send me to Carlsbad or some other springs. . . . We have had a slight rain almost all the time from Sunday morning, and the temperature has been so cool that I have enjoyed winter flannel, with blankets and wraps. I shall hope to get a letter from you soon after my arrival. I do so much wish that we could have had the company of your family. The trip would then have been a perfect pleasure, and I am sure if anything could make me well it would be to have you with me always. The feeling of sadness natural to our starting off to be absent for so long a time has naturally been increased by the condition of my wife's health and my own, and by the death of our dear sister. But I try to rest myself entirely upon the care and protection of our Heavenly Father, knowing that he not only knows what is best, but will assuredly will what is best.

The other letter, written at sea three days later, is to Mrs. Arthur Peter, of Louisville. During the first year of his residence in Louisville, before removing his family, he was long the guest of Dr. and Mrs. Peter, and formed with them a cherished friendship.

"Among all the friends whom I have left in Louisville, there is no one I have thought of so often since leaving as yourself. You have always been so kind to me that I have felt myself somewhat nearer to you than to a mere friend, so much so that I could not have loved you more, had we been blood relations. . . . We have had a delightful voyage thus far, and we are fast nearing its end. When the reckoning of the ship was taken to-day at noon, we were only three hundred and thirty miles from Queenstown, and we shall be there to-morrow morning, and reach Liverpool in the afternoon. My wife has been greatly surprised. She felt sure she would be sea-sick. But no one of us has missed a single meal, and we have been able most of the time to be on deck. I am sorry to say that we cannot report any improvement of health thus far. I am very weak, and can hardly crawl up on the deck. Walking even a short distance, with the uncertain footing one has on the boat, is very fatiguing. But I look forward to a change in this respect as soon as we land. My wife also is able to eat but little, though complaining bitterly of hunger.

"You will pardon me that I have written thus exclusively about ourselves. This is due to the fact that I have nothing else to write about, and to the further fact that I flatter myself I could write to you at present of nothing more interesting to yourself and your dear husband. You will at least have the satisfaction of knowing that I have not crammed up from the guide-book for the materials of this letter. No one can tell whether he will not be tempted sometimes to do so, in trying to tell of interesting matters to distant friends.

"My wife and girls send their best love to you. Mine you already have, and I can send no more than has already been bestowed. Give our love to your husband and all your family."

We may now proceed with the notes of Miss Boyce:

"We remained in Liverpool five days. During this time Father ran down to London to see about his money arrangements before starting on the trip to Scotland. I shudder now when I think how great a risk he ran on this occasion. We doubted at the time whether he should go alone, but he insisted that he needed no one, and as his trip was to be a flying one, we yielded. When he reached London, he took a cab to the Bank. While passing along the crowded street, his horse fell, and he was precipitated to the ground. He told us this with much amusement upon his return to Liverpool, and laughingly described the way the crowd scrambled to get the pennies he threw them for having helped him up and raised the horse. But all this time he was in danger of sudden death from heart-failure, and the doctors consulted in London a month later told me it was a miracle that he had not died at that moment. Remembering that we were alone in Liverpool, without friends or money, I doubt if we should ever have been able to have traced him. Happily he was not in the least hurt, and returned to us looking better than he had for some time past.

"Our first move was to Chester. This place was so exceedingly quaint and interesting, with its cathedral, the first specimen of the lovely architecture we had read so much of, that our stay was an unalloyed pleasure.

"In Scotland we went to Glasgow, arriving in time to see the Exposition opened by Queen Victoria. We had difficulty in geting rooms at the hotels, owing to the large crowds in the city. Our hotel was near the station, and we had a fine time watching the putting up of decorations all around. Seats were erected on the principal streets, and we got a comfortable place to see the procession. We had an excellent view of Her Majesty, with Princess Beatrice, Princess Alice of Hesse, and other notables. The Queen impressed us as a haughty-looking woman. She bowed constantly, but coldly, to the enthusiastic crowd. The younger ladies really seemed to be enjoying themselves, and dispersed bows and smiles right and left. While waiting for the Queen we enjoyed the passing of the Highland troops, all the clans being represented. We heard the bagpipes for the first time really well played, and found the music quite stirring and impressive. At the Exposition we saw the Jubilee presents to the Queen, and noticed how even the poorest gift was well displayed.

"Then we went to Edinburgh, Stirling, and so forth. At Abbotsford Father was particularly interested in the collection of arms and curios, as his much-prized Abbotsford edition of the Waverley Novels has numerous illustrations made from drawings of objects in this collection. He was also pleased with Melrose, Dryburgh, and Roslyn Chapel. In the Highlands and elsewhere, Father enjoyed coaching through the country.

"After visiting the English lakes, we went to London, as he was far from looking improved, and we thought it best for him to see his physician before undertaking a further trip. Throughout this sight-seeing he was only able to get glimpses of the places and things he had so often anticipated visiting. He would sit patiently in the carriage, waiting for us as long as we wished, and only occasionally venturing to move about a little when feeling particularly bright and well. It was positively heart-rending to see him. Many of the objects we looked at through blinding tears, as we thought how entirely he was cut off from everything. He said he was content if we would only enjoy ourselves; but how could we under such circumstances?

"At the National Gallery in London he got his first view of the English masterpieces. On Sunday we went to Spurgeon's Tabernacle. Mr. Spurgeon was seated, and apologized for not standing while he preached, saying that he was unable to stand any length of time. We were much struck with Father's likeness to him. Father noticed it himself, and said he wished he was as much like him in preaching power. After the service we went to Mr. Spurgeon's room in the rear, and received a warm welcome. Mr. Spurgeon did not then seem near so much like Father as we had thought, as he had not the breadth of brow, and his face was more seamed. He asked Father to speak at the Pastor's College. When told our errand in London, — that we had come especially to consult Sir —— Garrod, who was described to us as 'the greatest authority in the world on gout and kindred diseases,' — he smiled, and said, ' Well, perhaps he may do you good; he has a great reputation; but as for me, I believe in none of them, — none have helped me.' He was at this time just recovering from a severe attack of gout.

"Father was so much excited by this interview with the great preacher that he became pale and exhausted, and began to pant for breath; so we had to cut short our stay, and leave for the hotel. Much moved by this meeting, his eyes filled with tears as he went away, and he said to me, 'How little I have accomplished, compared with that man! If I can only get well and live a few years longer, I'll make greater efforts.'"

On Monday, September 3, he wrote to Mrs. Burckmyer, telling of various things which have been narrated above, and added: —

"I have been singularly struck by the great resemblance between England and South Carolina. I had no idea that Charleston and its surroundings had borrowed so much in its early days, nor that the two distant places had continued to preserve the same old fashions. I have found everywhere houses of the same kind of dark brick, walls like those around so many Charleston places, — Judge King's, for instance, — farm-houses just like those on the old plantations in South Carolina, built of brick. In the homes you see the same kind of papering, like tapestry, that I used to see at Aunt Henry's house in Anson Street, and the old-fashioned Venetian blinds everywhere that were in all the houses when I was a boy, with the same wooden, carved cornice-work that is seen in old Charleston houses. Every day as I have travelled I have had cause to call attention to these resemblances."

Miss Boyce proceeds: —

"Monday morning we went to the British Museum, and Father went to see Dr. Garrod, but found him absent, and was examined by his son and associate in the profession. About an hour afterwards, as we were standing in one of the great rooms of the Museum, we saw him approaching, with a pale but quiet look, and when we anxiously questioned, he said that the doctor thought him in a dangerous condition, and had told him to go to bed at once. We returned to the hotel, and presently Dr. Garrod and another physician arrived. They examined him carefully, and then, in a private interview, told me plainly that he might die at any moment. I entreated them to help me get him home; but they objected, saying that he would probably die at sea. The horror of this overcame me. Dr. Garrod advised a change to a quiet boarding-place, and after visiting several places which he recommended, we chose one pleasantly situated on Conduit Street, near Oxford Circus. The doctor brought his own carriage, and assisted Father to make the removal. He was as tender and careful as if he had been an old friend. We found the place exceedingly comfortable, and much more cheerful than the hotel. Father was confined to his bed for weeks, as the doctor had given orders that he must move as little as possible, and must not attempt to write. Day after day passed while he lay there very quietly, bearing his long confinement with infinite patience and cheerfulness.

"Dr. Garrod visited him daily, and seemed much gratified with his continued improvement. He told me he had never seen any one with greater vitality, and added that Father must have been endowed with a wonderful constitution. After some weeks he was allowed to take short drives, which he enjoyed greatly. His sanguine temperament made him feel as if he were in a fair way to perfect recovery, and he began to talk of his plans for the Continent. I entreated him to return home, and begged the doctor to order that he should return to America. But he refused, saying that he thought we had best go to some quiet place for the winter, and return home in the spring. He added that with great care, and abstinence from mental exertion or worry, Father ought to live at least a year longer."

During this confinement in London, with a frightful attack of dropsy in the chest, connected with his gout and kidney troubles, and of course embarrassing the heart and lungs, Dr. Boyce was visited by Mr. W. S. Jones, assistant-cashier of the Louisville Banking Company (in which Dr. Boyce was a director), and by Rev. W. E. Hatcher, D.D., of Richmond, Va. Both were greatly pained to find him so feeble and suffering, and with so little prospect of recovery, but reported afterwards that he was patient and cheerful, sustained by submissive trust in Providence. Hearing, on Mr. Jones's return, of this prostrating and alarming illness, and thinking of his wife and daughters alone with him there in a distant land, one of his colleagues wrote, and urged him, if he should grow strong enough, to return home, in order to be within reach of his kindred and friends in case of similar attacks. He replied as soon as able to write, and explained his plan. He felt unable to stand a return voyage at that time, but hoped that by spending a winter in the south of Europe in the quietest way, he might escape gout and rheumatism, and be able to return in the spring. His only remaining earthly concern was to settle up finally his father's estate, which could be done after the following January, when the youngest grandson would be of age. He added that there must be no illusions about the fact that he could never hope to teach again in the Seminary; and if he should come back at all, he would resign at the end of the session. He said that the professors ought to be considering whom they would be prepared to recommend as Professor of Theology, in case of his death or resignation. A letter was at once sent, asking, in behalf of the professors, whom he would himself suggest; and he answered, from Paris, that he had no disposition whatever to dictate, or to volunteer suggestions, on that subject, but that if the Trustees should ever care to know his opinion about the matter, it was that the best appointment would be that of Dr. Kerfoot.

His last days in London were saddened by another case of profound family affliction, the death of his admirable sister, Mrs. Dr. H. A. Tupper, of Richmond, Va.

To Mrs. Burckmyer, from London, Oct. 19, 1888.

Allen telegraphed me the news of Nannie's death. The bare fact is all I know as yet, and I feel anxious to hear. I suppose there are letters on the way which will tell all about it. What I already know is enough in one sense. When the despatch came, I was just stunned. I sat and looked at it, and wondered that a little piece of paper could so utterly crush one by a few words. It was so unexpected! When the news of Sister's [Mrs. Lane's] death came, I was partly prepared for it; but this news was like thunder at noonday from a cloudless sky. I saw then how it was that my poor dear wife felt so dreadfully the death of her sister Sally, whom she had not thought of except as of one in perfect health. . . . My last letter from Richmond came from Nannie herself.

We have been greatly blessed by the preservation of the lives of so many of us to a good old age. But the circle, once broken, has again been broken in a very short time. Two deaths in three months! How soon may we not look for others! And we owe gratitude not only for life continued, but for continued affection and love among us all. A happier family in this respect it would be very hard to find. May we only be brought more closely together as we are diminished in numbers!

To Miss Amanda B. Lane, from London, Oct. 22, 1888.

It is not often that a family so long preserved together loses two of its most valued members within three short months, nor do I know a family anywhere out of which two such women could have been taken. I write this soberly, feeling that none who knew them will doubt its truth. Not even in our eyes, much less in their own, were they perfect; but I think even their faults were but the outcropping fungus of their virtues. They differed very much, yet was each a type of excellence. Dear to me as will always be the homes and families they have left, on account of those now in them, they will be rendered still more so by the memory of these two dear sisters, with whose love God has blessed me for more than half a century of intimate fellowship.

Dr. Boyce and his family left London for Paris at the end of October, designing to spend a month there, and then seek some pleasant seaside resort for the winter. He had procured a light wicker rolling-chair, so that he might be carried about without walking, which the doctor was anxious to prevent. During the two last weeks in London he had driven out every day, and gained strength rapidly. Again he was hopeful of recovery. He greatly enjoyed the ride from London to Dover, delighting in the beautiful scenery. His daughters remember how he would call their attention to the fields and hedgerows, the simple cottages here and there, or some novel sight that would arrest his attention. The day was sunny and the Channel smooth, so that they crossed most comfortably. He was much fatigued by the time they arrived in Paris, at twilight, but brightened up as they drove through the brilliantly lighted streets. Their Paris abode was at the Hôtel des Deux Mondes. For several days he came down regularly to his meals, and delighted to drive, and sometimes walk a little way, with the family, in the mild and pleasant weather.

Soon after reaching Paris he received a letter that gave him great pleasure. Mrs. J. Lawrence Smith, of Louisville, daughter of Hon. James Guthrie, and widow of the celebrated scientist, had in the middle of October privately expressed to the acting Chairman of the Faculty her intention of giving to the Seminary fifty thousand dollars for the erection of a Library building, as a Memorial of her departed nieces and nephews, Sarah Julia Caperton and Mary Caperton, William Beverley Caldwell, Jr., and Lawrence Smith Caldwell. To the spontaneous and confidential intimation of this purpose she added, "But you may write to Dr. Boyce about it. He is sick and suffering abroad, and it may give him pleasure to know that the work of his life is making some progress." A letter to that effect was of course gladly written at once, and this was his answer: —

To John A. Broadus, from Paris, Oct. 31, 1888.

I received last night yours of October 17. I think we have both of us more to learn of the duty of faith and confidence in the working of God for our Seminary. With all our anxiety and hopes and fears, how true it is that in our agony of trouble as to what will occur, we find that God has found us ways of which we have never dreamed! Witness the gift of Governor Brown. We were praying for help, and crying out in our despair; and almost without our lifting a finger, it came from a quarter to which we had never looked for such a sum. So, also, your letter of to-day tells me of a generosity not exceeding what might have been expected for worthy objects from the generous donor; but we have already had so much from that source that we had no right to expect more, — so much so that I have felt almost ashamed of having asked and received the five thousand dollars last given; and certainly the help now proposed was beyond all possible conception, except by the generous heart which proposes it. . . . Please express to your friend my most hearty thanks, both personally and officially, for this contemplated gift. I know not what words to use; none could express too strongly my gratitude and thanks. May God reward her, for He alone can do so worthily of her generosity and noble purposes![1]

He proceeds to speak, in the same letter, of arrangements he was about to make for transferring his own noble theological library at once to the Seminary. In May, 1887, he had indicated to the Trustees his purpose of doing this, — a purpose long known to his older colleagues, — but on the condition that twenty-five thousand dollars should be raised as a special endowment for the Library of the Seminary. In this letter he makes no condition, but says he has expressed to his wife and

[1] The Memorial Library building was opened in May, 1890. It was carefully planned according to the best recent ideas and examples, and is one of the most beautiful, convenient, and every way satisfactory library buildings in existence. Its "book-room" will hold sixty thousand volumes, and can be easily enlarged to more than double that space when necessary hereafter.

daughters his wish that all the theological books in his collection should, in case of his death, be transferred to the Seminary Library. These books had been chosen with constant care since his early life, and were regarded by him with the greatest affection. As the institution had always been limited to a small annual sum for the purchase of books, he had taken pains not to procure the same work — with some necessary exceptions — for his own library and that of the Seminary. Thus his noble collection came into the library as exactly complementary.[1]

On November 3 Dr. Boyce wrote from Paris to his colleague, Dr. F. H. Kerfoot, about various practical matters connected with his residence and the Seminary, and then added as follows: —

"Thanks for your prayers and kind wishes for my health. I could not deny my willingness to live for further service, but I think the days of such service are nearly over, and that there is not much to live for when one is really rusted out. The Lord knows better how long to use me. I am even willing He should keep me useless, but I am thankful to believe that such is never His will as to any of His servants. He often uses us for nothing as

[1] It is proper to state that his wishes in this regard were of course very carefully carried out. The following year his daughters selected all the properly theological works, to the number of some five thousand, and took great pains to complete the collection and classification of the immense mass of pamphlets and periodicals which he had gathered with loving care through life, and which are a treasure to the Seminary collection. The Seminary Library now amounts to over twenty thousand volumes, and greatly needs a special permanent endowment, as well as particular gifts of money and books. Some persons have wondered that Dr. Boyce's noble collection was not kept separate. Yet his older colleagues were quite sure that he would himself have chosen to have his books distributed throughout the library, according to subjects. Separate collections may be a pleasing memorial, but in that way the books are not worth half so much for actual use. Dr. Boyce had himself distributed the books received from the libraries of Professor Bailey, Dr. Manly, Sr., and others.

DECLINING YEARS AND DEATH.   341

well as for something. I wish only to be His and to serve Him, He helping me to do so in humility and faith. God be with you and yours!"

We now extract again from Miss Boyce's narrative.

"We had not been in Paris more than a week, before Father began to show signs of a return of his malady. The Paris physician who had been recommended by Dr. Garrod did not, I think, understand the case. He was much alarmed at Father's condition, and gave medicine that was powerful and dangerous, — as afterwards explained to us by others, — and without benefiting his patient in the least. Each day Father lost strength. At first he did not seem discouraged at his relapse, and thought he had exhausted himself by too much exercise. But when after a few days of rest he failed to grow stronger, I think he began to see that no care on his part could strengthen the enfeebled heart, and that he could not live many more months. Still, he was as patient and bright as possible. He would always be much distressed if we showed any reluctance to leave him, telling us that he was only contented when he knew that we were seeing all we could of Paris. The windows of his bedroom looked out upon the Avenue de l'Opéra, and during the first days of his sickness, when he was able to sit up in his chair, he would sit at the window and wave his hand and smile to us as we passed across the avenue below in going and returning. But after a few days he had no longer the strength to do this, but had to recline on a couch drawn before the fire; for the weather had become cold, it being now December. He was much troubled at this time with insomnia; his nights were turned into days, though fortunately he slept much during the day. He read during these weeks in Paris a great number of French books. We had two tickets at the Circulating Library, in order that he might have plenty to read. But afterwards there came days when no book would interest him, and no conversation could entertain beyond a few minutes. He was feeble, and off and on during the day would be drowsy.

"After a while he began to dislike the physician, and refused to take his medicine. We were overcome with fright, and anxiously urged him to try further treatment. I asked the doctor how much longer he thought he would live if he remained in Paris, and being told a week or ten days, we determined on a desperate effort to get out of the city, though privately warned by the doctor that he might die on the road.

"Dr. Garrod had recommended that he should go to Pau, in the south of France, and we found it possible to get a *coupé à lit* from Paris to Pau without change of cars. We left the city at night, Father being taken in his chair to a carriage, and lifted into the train. Our night was fearful, as we were in great anguish of mind for fear he might die at any moment. He seemed much exhausted, and for hours before we got to Pau he was asking if we were not nearly there. We arrived at Pau on time, but there was much delay in securing the physician whom Dr. Garrod had recommended. But in a few days Father began to improve. This, however, did not last long, and we soon realized that the end was near. Only once did he rally sufficiently to talk with me on business, and then it was only a few words. He was out of his head a great deal, and in his wanderings his talk was nearly always of the Seminary. We would constantly catch the names of the different professors, and perhaps the last words we distinctly heard were something about Seminary and students. The day before he died he was conscious for several hours, but could not talk, as his tongue was much swollen. He recognized us, and pressed our hands or returned our kisses, but did not attempt to speak. An English clergyman, whom we asked to visit him, saw him for a few moments that morning, and prayed and talked with him. Father tried to say a good deal to him, but it was impossible to understand what he was saying. He soon became unconscious, and remained so until the end. This was on Friday, Dec. 28, 1888."

The news of Dr. Boyce's death was cabled by Miss Lizzie Boyce to Louisville, and received with great concern by a wide circle of friends in the city, and especially at the Seminary. An informal meeting was held that afternoon of the Faculty and students, together with such Trustees and others officially connected with the Seminary as were within reach, including members of their families and some friends. Brief and loving addresses were made by Professors Whitsitt and Kerfoot; by Drs. Weaver, Warder, Eaton, Jeffries, and Hale; and by Messrs. George

W. Norton, Arthur Peter, and Theodore Harris. Extracts from some of these utterances will be given in the concluding chapter.

When the family returned, bringing with them the mortal remains of James Petigru Boyce, to rest in the Cave Hill Cemetery at Louisville, funeral services were held at the Broadway Baptist Church on Sunday afternoon, January 20th.[1] There were many visiting brethren from different parts of the country. The pall-bearers included representatives of the Conversation Club and of the Confederate Association. Drs. Tichenor, Burrows, Weaver, J. M. Pendleton, and Kerfoot took part in the worship. It had been hoped that Dr. Manly would make the opening address, but he was sick with pneumonia. Addresses were made by Dr. Broadus, by Judge Alexander P. Humphrey, of Louisville, and by Dr. J. L. M. Curry.

We add some stanzas of a hymn prepared for the occasion by Professor Marcus B. Allmond, and sung in opening the service: —

> "Deal gently, Lord! For we are weak;
> The archer, Death, has smitten low
> Our Leader, and we pray Thee speak
> And cheer us in this hour of woe.
>
> "Deal gently, Lord! Thy mighty ways
> Are not as ours. O blessed name,
> Teach us in sorrow still to praise
> Thy goodness, and Thy love proclaim!
>
> "Deal gently, Lord! Our dead shall be
> New cause to fill our hearts with love;
> New peace and joy in man and thee;
> New hope and faith in heaven above."

At the ensuing annual meeting of the Southern Baptist Convention, in Memphis, a Memorial Service was held on

---

[1] The Florida Baptist Convention was in session at the time, and through telegraphic communication held a Memorial meeting at the same hour.

Sunday afternoon, May 12, 1889, with reference to Dr. Boyce, who had for several previous sessions (and for seven in all) been President of the Convention. Dr. J. L. Burrows presided over the memorial meeting, Dr. W. E. Hatcher told of his visit to Dr. Boyce in London, and addresses were delivered by Dr. H. H. Tucker, who was James Boyce's Sunday-school teacher in Charleston fifty years before, by Dr. J. H. Luther, who was his fellow-student at Brown University, and by Dr. E. C. Dargan, representing the Seminary students and South Carolina.[1]

[1] Use will be made, in one way or another, of all the addresses on these funeral and memorial occasions, in the concluding chapter, and some have been drawn upon heretofore. Dr. Tucker, a man of consummate ability, has since died. Dr. Dargan is now a highly valued professor in the Theological Seminary.

CHAPTER XVIII.

GENERAL ESTIMATES OF CHARACTER.

JAMES P. BOYCE was in character thoroughly genuine. The better you knew him, in all relations and amid all experiences, the more plainly you saw that here was a man made of good timber all the way through.

He was remarkable for good judgment, having clearly inherited this high quality from his father. His faculties were well balanced, and acted in harmony. Of course he was sometimes mistaken as to men or measures, but very rarely. This sound judgment, exercised to an extraordinary extent from early life upon business matters, and accompanied by wide and varied practical knowledge, constituted that high business talent which was known to all in a general way, and most fully recognized by his most eminent business associates. Let us extract from two of the many tributes paid after his death. The first is from the stockholders of the great Cotton Manufacturing Company at Graniteville, S. C., which was founded by his father, and of which he was a Director from his youth:

"A minister of God's holy gospel, called especially to preside over things spiritual, he was yet a safe counsellor and guide in things temporal; and to his clear perceptions of business transactions and their relations, so rare in one of his calling, this Company is indebted for some of its most fortunate ventures and investments. . . . In his death the business world, and especially the Graniteville Manufacturing Company, with which he was so long identified as a leading Director, sustains a loss almost, if not quite, as great as that spiritual world in which he shone a bright particular star. In every relation of life he was true and loyal to duty, and lived his life nobly and well."

In the first meeting held at the Seminary after the telegraphic news of Dr. Boyce's death arrived, the remarks of Mr. Theodore Harris, President of the Louisville Banking Company, in which Boyce had for years been a Director, were reported as follows: —

"Intimately associated with Dr. Boyce in business relations, he knew him as a gifted man in business. He was a great man; the most perfectly rounded character Mr. Harris had ever seen. On one occasion Dr. Boyce presented him a business paper; and, deeply impressed with the great wisdom and ability of the paper, he lost sight of other things, and asked who was its author. As modestly as a maiden, Dr. Boyce confessed the authorship."

He was a man of strong convictions and decided opinions; and, as a kindred quality, a man of strong will and tenacity of purpose. This also was hereditary, and developed by lifelong exercise. He knew why he thought a thing was right, and knew why he was determined to do something. Yet it was never impossible to convince him if he was wrong, — sometimes quite difficult, but never impossible. There was no pride of pertinacity, no reluctance to consider other men's views and weigh their arguments; but he was decided of opinion and tenacious of purpose because he saw good reason for it, and as long as he saw no sufficient reason to the contrary. At the funeral service in the Broadway Church, Judge Alex. P. Humphrey, whose father had been an eminent Presbyterian minister and Dr. Boyce's friend, alluded to the fact that a certain class of would-be practical people look upon ministers as a feeble folk, wanting in vigor and virility, and said: —

"This man illustrated at once the manliness and the devotion of the Christian Minister; no one came in contact with him without observing at once the force of his personality, the strength of mind, the sagacity in business, the far-seeing wisdom; but they found it all the time and always dominated by the one single-minded devotion to the service of his Maker. . . . A Calvinist must necessarily have a clear mind and a courageous mind. Dr. Boyce had convictions that were sure, and a speech that was direct and to the point. He believed that before the foundations of the world were laid, God had fixed what part he should take in the great drama of the universe, that his calling and election were sure, and that he must live worthy of the high vocation wherewith he was called. Viewed in such an aspect, a human life ordained to the honor of his God, set in the orbit that was accomplished by the revolution of the few years allotted to him, appears to my mind a creation sublimer than a star."

On the same occasion Dr. J. L. M. Curry spoke of Dr. Boyce's life as covering "the most eventful period in the world's history," and said that the questions of such an age —

"demanded breadth of thought, sagacious and comprehensive action, and Dr. Boyce was abreast of the times. He was a student, a scholar, a teacher, a financier, a philanthropist, and a parliamentarian; in all these and other branches he was not simply mediocre, but he was remarkable and distinguished, — not a follower, not a mere floater on the surface and current of thought and affairs, but a leader, a seer, a thinker, a born ruler. . . . In intellect Dr. Boyce measured up with his compeers; self-reliant, courageous, broad in his convictions and in his teachings, he was the willing servant of a quick conscience, purified and elevated by love of God. He was no trimmer, no coward. Tolerant of difference, broadly catholic in his views, he nevertheless asserted and acted upon the right of private judgment in the light of the New Testament."

Shortly afterwards a glowing tribute was paid to Dr. Boyce by Rabbi A. Moses (a member of the Conversation Club), in the Jewish Temple on Broadway, and we extract from the newspaper report: —

" This deep humanity and sympathy made Dr. Boyce, as nearly as a mortal man can be, an absolutely just man. . . . He was a perfect gentleman in the highest, broadest sense ; the ideal of chivalry. He could not have been rude to any one, even if he had tried, for his ever-wakeful sympathy would not permit him to inflict pain. . . . Had he turned his attention to politics, what a Senator he would have made! What a President! If he had been thrown among savages, he could have tamed and civilized them, for he was a born leader of men. So much gentleness and kindness, mingled with a determined and unconquerable will, — his character was builded on a solid rock, while beneath it welled a fountain of living water. He was a God-fearing, a God-seeking, and a God-loving man. Before I came to Louisville, I knew Christianity only in books, and it was through such men as Boyce that I learned to know it as a living force. In that man I learned not only to comprehend, but to respect and reverence the spiritual power called Christianity. . . . God grant that Christianity may long continue to produce such men; for men like Dr. Boyce ring heart to heart, and draw us all towards that goal of which we have only glimpses, — that is, God, and the Kingdom of Righteousness forever."

The systematic arrangements and habits of a business man were carried by Dr. Boyce into all his affairs, and into the conduct of his daily life. The letters received were carefully labelled, with date of reception and date of answer, and laid away in dated packages. The letters written, in all his last years, were copied in letter-books. Many of the newspapers he took were carefully preserved and put away year after year, and the more important ones annually bound. The pamphlets were distributed into a great number of paper boxes, marked with the subject, and often with the year. These and the bound newspapers are now a treasure to the Seminary's library. He once said before a Historical Society that any man who would destroy a pamphlet ought to be hung. That his many thousands of books should be systematically arranged according to subjects and sizes, was a matter of course. His wife and daughters heartily sympathized with this love for the books, and after their removal to the large house on First and Chestnut, the great Library was a delightful place to enter.

Along with this love of system was a remarkable punctuality. Some of his associates learned to bestir themselves, from observing that lack of punctuality caused him real pain. We may here extract, as in a former chapter, from some notes which Miss Boyce kindly consented to furnish: —

"I do not know whether punctuality was a special characteristic of my father in his youth, but every one who knew him in later years knew that he was most particular in this regard. In his anxiety to be always on time, he would start say fifteen minutes earlier than necessary for a city engagement, to allow for any interruption or other detention on the way; and he never failed to be at an appointment some minutes before the time, watch in hand, ready to pounce upon the tardy comer. This was the only drawback to our pleasure when travelling with Father. He would often have us at the station an hour or more before the time for the train to start, until we would be exhausted. I think he felt a keen enjoyment, when meeting his classes, to see the tardy ones among the students come slipping in after the hour, with dismay expressed on their faces. He loved to tease them by pretending to be quite angry, and would then tell us, on coming home, how sheepish they looked, and how they would apologize after class."

He was a strong and deep thinker. Very rarely do you find a man so widely acquainted and actively occupied with practical affairs, yet so delighting in the profoundest thought. He really loved to follow out a close-linked and vigorous line of argument. He took pleasure for its own sake in the elaborate analysis, exposition, and vindication of some great theological theme. In our hurriedly practical age many talented men imagine that they have no time for calm and prolonged thought; yet not only ministers, but lawyers and business-men and teachers, might well observe the examples in which the reflective and the active powers of a strong man reinforce each other.

Unlike some deep thinkers, Dr. Boyce was remarkable

for wide general knowledge. We have repeatedly had occasion to notice his extensive and thorough acquaintance with practical affairs, due to original talent and early training, and to the necessity of supervising through life the varied investments of his father's estate. It was curious to see how much he knew about merchandizing, how thoroughly at home he was in banking, how familiar with the management of a great railway line, how keenly attentive while at Greenville to the details of farming. He knew also the national and State legislation connected with these and other departments of business. The love of wide reading which he had shown in boyhood was cherished through life. He had a good general knowledge of history, and was quite at home in the history of American politics, and several other departments. He was exceedingly fond of poetry. One summer he read Wordsworth solidly through, and greatly enjoyed the "Excursion," in which many readers fall by the way. The newest English and American poets he promptly read, and in many cases knew their works intimately. He had also a wide acquaintance with prose fiction, both the great English novelists of earlier and later times, and the great French novelists, — always read by preference in the original. He was an adept in reading newspapers and other periodicals, — which is one of the chief arts of modern intellectual life. Reading aloud to any sympathetic listeners was with him a favorite pastime, while his wealth of varied feeling and rich tones of voice made it very pleasant for the listeners. Miss Boyce says: —

"Poetry, romances, books of travel, comic sketches, — everything he entered into with keen enjoyment. One of my earliest recollections of Father is of his reading to us the 'Pickwick Papers,' and his fruitless efforts to control his laughter. Tears would roll down his cheeks, and his voice would fail him, as he strove to take us through the trials and scrapes of Mr. Pickwick. He always read with easy rapidity and varying expression. His voice was pleasing, and under good control. He could read for hours without any apparent fatigue. I think he was fonder of poetry than prose. Mrs. Browning was a special favorite; Christina Rossetti's poetry and her brother's were also very dear to him. He was quite successful in reading negro dialect. A man of more extensive reading it would be hard to find. At one time he subscribed for nearly twenty religious papers, besides several secular ones, and half-a-dozen current magazines. At home he often had very little time to spend in reading, but he read a great deal when travelling. While soliciting funds for the Seminary before it was established in Kentucky, his travelling-bag would be packed, not only with books of general reading, but with text-books and writing materials, and he would often prepare a lecture on the train. It troubled him no little that these constant trips took him so much from home, and that his literary work had to be pursued in such a desultory way. He was a great reader of French literature, and neglected no opportunity to improve himself in reading and speaking the language. He took French lessons with his family a few years before going abroad, and also German. He enjoyed these lessons exceedingly, was highly amused at the mistakes of the others, and in his turn received with great amiability their jokes and laughter at his own mistakes. I think this was a very noteworthy thing in Father's character, — his perfect friendliness with his children, and the *camaraderie* of his intercourse with them. Our French teacher was sometimes quite overwhelmed by our jokes at his expense, and would inform us that French demoiselles would never think of being so disrespectful. But Father only laughed, and said that he quite understood us, and did not mind it in the least."

Let us add, from the same source, as to his general love of books: —

"His library was a source of great pride and enjoyment. At one time it bade fair to be a remarkably large collection, for a private individual. Most of his books were bought before the war; in after years he could buy little beyond those necessary for his studies, and could seldom afford to indulge any longer in lovely bindings and rare editions. I consider this one of the greatest trials that loss of fortune brought upon him. He still indulged himself occasionally, but then only for our benefit. At New Year he always presented each member of the family with either the complete edition of some author's works, or single works well bound and illustrated. I have seen him sit for hours with a book catalogue in his hand, marking the books he would like to buy, and really seeming to get great enjoyment out of merely seeing what was to be had if he could afford it. He was charmed to show his books to friends. He and Colonel Durrett[1] were constantly in each other's libraries, and often exchanged books. I have heard him say that it caused him positive pain to see beautifully bound or illustrated books, and not be able to possess them. He seldom went down town without going to a book-store where he could indulge himself in glancing over the new works. He bought his theological books with a view to giving this part of his collection to the Seminary. He was devoted to children's books, would read them with interest, and was greatly given to making presents of them to his little namesakes and other child friends. The last gift he gave was a book bought at Pau, and sent to a little grand-niece. He gave his oldest daughter when a child the prettiest and the best books suitable to her age. In fact, she was really possessed of quite a little library when only a baby. The Nightcap Stories, Rollo Books, Grimm's Fairy Tales, the Arabian Nights, and even some French books, were provided for her long before she had learned the alphabet. He took great pains to have only good illustrations in a book he purchased, believing in this way he might cultivate the taste for good drawing and painting."

For nothing was Dr. Boyce more remarkable than for taste, in all the high senses of the term. His face would glow with delight as he gazed at a beautiful flower or tree, or surveyed an inspiring landscape. His home at Greenville was bright with a rich collection of flowers, common and rare, including a great variety of choice roses, and the spacious lawn was finely shaded by noble forest trees. All around Greenville, extending far westward to the glorious Blue Ridge, was much delightful

[1] Colonel R. T. Durrett is the foremost citizen of Louisville as to historical and antiquarian matters, and founder of the Filsson Club, and has a noble collection of books.

scenery. These things he left with a keen sense of loss; and it is only since he passed away that the electric cars are showing us how many a fine landscape may be enjoyed within reach of Louisville. Miss Boyce says: —

"In Greenville flowers are easily cultivated, and were therefore a source of much pleasure to persons fond of cultivating them. Mother's devotion to flowers amounted to a craze, and she was ably upheld by Father. Many winter evenings were pleasantly spent reading the catalogues, and long and earnest were the discussions indulged in as to what they should order for the spring planting. These flowers were called by their botanical names, which sounded very learned to my childish ears; and much it astonished me to hear the tremendous Latin terms with which even the tiniest flowers were named. When I learned many of these words it was a source of amusement to Father and Mother to hear me use them. When the boxes would arrive from the North, with all the newest plants beautifully packed in them, we all had a holiday. Father would put his books away, and lay aside his pen for a trowel, and would follow Mother around with the watering-pot, glad to do his share towards the planting. Every morning the plants would be visited and examined with interest for the first sign of leaf or flower. Mother had a collection of over four hundred pot plants when she left Greenville for Kentucky. This taste for flowers awakened a renewed interest in their cultivation among the ladies of Greenville. Quite a number of them began a pleasant rivalry as to who should have the greatest variety and the newest plants. Mrs. Beattie and Mother would compare notes whenever they met, and a visit to each home was soon adjourned from the parlor to the garden. Father's greatest ambition was to have his lawn covered with blue-grass. He had already made several visits to Kentucky, and brought back wonderful accounts of the beauty of the grass. He spent a great deal of time and money, had the lawn ploughed and enriched, and carefully sown with blue-grass seed, but was unsuccessful in obtaining any steady growth."

This recalls a slight incident that gave pleasure. At Dr. Boyce's instance, the writer had a carefully cherished little plot of blue-grass at his home on Main Street. Once during the war some of John Morgan's cavalry encamped near Greenville. One summer morning two tall and handsome young Kentucky officers came walking gayly by, with bright regimentals and sabre, and one of them suddenly started and said, "Hi, Tom! Blue-grass!"

Among works of art, Boyce's greatest delight was probably in pictures. He kept the *entrée* to every private collection in Charleston, and delighted in taking a friend to see this or that painting. He knew where anything of superior excellence was to be found in the public collections of New York and Philadelphia. At the Centennial Exposition in 1876, the writer remembers to have gone round the picture-galleries with him and his family, and to have been greatly impressed by the unwearied enthusiasm with which he and his wife surveyed every good picture, as well as the promptness with which they singled out the really good pictures in a room. It was one of his most cherished hopes, as to the long-deferred visit to Europe, that he and his might enjoy the world-famous paintings; and we have seen that, though with failing strength, he visited collections in London and Paris, and wrote of hearty pleasure in beholding them.

As to music, Miss Boyce remarks: —

"He always took every opportunity when in New York to attend the best music, in Symphony Concerts, Oratorios, etc. He had heard most of the great singers that have been in this country. On one occasion he went from Greenville to Charleston for the purpose of hearing Carlotta Patti. I remember his telling many times of the exquisite pleasure he had in hearing Jenny Lind sing 'I know that my Redeemer liveth.' The most difficult and classical compositions were as much enjoyed by him as music of a lighter character. He spared no expense in the selection of music-masters for his children, and always showed delight in their progress, often laughing, and telling them that they had inherited from him their great fondness for music. This he would prove sometimes by showing them a small tuning-fork which, when a boy, he received as a prize for being the most promising pupil in a small singing-class in Charleston. He had carefully kept the prize, and would insist that it showed some latent talent on his part, which ought to come out in them."

We have alluded in earlier chapters to his remarkable taste in regard to ladies' dress. On this point the daughter says: —

"He was always interested in pretty dressing, encouraged us to purchase good materials, and never objected to the size of the bills presented. In early married life he bought nearly everything worn by his wife. On the trips to New York which he made two or three times a year, he purchased for her dresses and bonnets, laces and jewelry, and often undertook shopping for his sisters-in-law and other lady friends.[1] He always showed excellent taste, was of course extravagant, — being a man, — and was quite up in all the dressmakers' technical terms. He bought things only in the latest fashions. In later years he often objected to our selections of goods, usually because he considered the material not sufficiently handsome, and would tell us that he could buy better things. This was no doubt true; but our bills would then have assumed pretty proportions. He was exceedingly fond of jewelry, selecting very tasteful and appropriate presents. He would have given Mother many a costly jewel, had it not been for severe injunctions on her part that he must not buy such expensive things."

Mr. William G. Whilden says that soon after the war, when it was hard to tell whether any property was left, Boyce remarked to him, "I do not regret the loss of my means, except for two things. I like to have means of giving freely, and I like to see my wife dress handsomely."

He took a similar interest in all the furniture and

---

[1] It may be remembered that he was once a partner in a great dry-goods house in New York.

furnishings of a home, down to the least details. It may be remembered that when first setting up his home in Columbia, his fancy was to have the entire house completely furnished when his young wife entered it. When he took a house in Louisville, the family were absent; and on arriving they found all things ready, and entirely suited to their wants and their taste.

On a kindred matter, Miss Boyce relates: —

"He gave us many a talk, as we grew up, in regard to our behavior. He was most fastidious in his notions about the deportment of women. He thought they should always have themselves under perfect control, no matter how awkward the situation or how amusing the circumstances. If it was not the time or place for mirth, a lady should be able to be quietly dignified. It was difficult to make him believe that ladies could do anything out of the way. He believed all they said; and although we sometimes tried to make him see that he was being deceived, he never could be convinced. He was always deferential to any woman. Even a young girl was treated with marked respect. His own daughters received many a courtesy from him which, probably, most men would never think of showing their home people."

The humor and wit for which we have seen that John Boyce and his son Ker were remarkable, descended in unabated inheritance to the grandson. He would often tell an amusing anecdote with contagious hilarity, and never with unkindness towards any one. In some moods his jests were very frequent and striking. He did not share the modern disposition to belittle puns, which the great ancient peoples used so freely, and which by a sort of affectation are expected to be now received with a pretended rebuke. When introducing speakers at a banquet, and elsewhere whenever he felt like it, he would play upon men's names as freely as is so common in Hebrew and Greek. A former student, I. P. Trotter, recalls how in the class of Latin Theology one day, a brother who was called on to translate a difficult sentence said, "Doctor, this looks right blue to me." "But I want it *read*," was the quick reply; and one can see how such a slight pleasantry would greatly relieve the situation. If we may judge from frequent results, men inclined to witty speech must be often tempted to raise a laugh by irreverence, indecency, or sarcastic severity. Each of these is a very cheap thing. Dr. Boyce was entirely free from them all. In all respects he was a good converser, never engrossing the conversation, but listening with lively sympathy and ready for quick response; while his quiet good-humor and easy dignity would be diffused over all the scene. Like his father, he would put aside business troubles in the family circle. Once, after middle age, he mentioned to his wife a very heavy financial loss through sudden disaster to a house in which he was a partner; yet in ten minutes he was reading aloud from "Pickwick," and laughing most heartily.

Akin to the love of art and literature was a fondness for writing occasional verses, to accompany gifts, or on any special occurrence. He called them doggerel, but took real pleasure in making such rhymes, and was glad when people liked them. He would frequently translate also from little French poems, turning the phrases neatly, and sometimes with marked felicity.

James Boyce was the soul of honor, and felt an instinctive scorn of everything base and mean. Until ill-health made him sometimes irritable, his friends never saw him manifest great impatience, except where some one had seemed ungentlemanly in speech or action; that he could not bear. He loved truth, and delighted in candor, and felt pained at the opposite of these in others. Dr. H. A. Tupper impressively says:—

"This love of truth was not only one of the chief ornaments of his character, but the best qualification for a professorship of

Theology. . . . It was hard for him to understand how people could do mean things and tell lies. His first impulse was to go to such persons and show them that they had done wrong, — never imagining, apparently, that they well knew their conduct to be ignoble, and their lips untrue. He was not unfrequently checked in such a purpose, as utterly useless. Hence he sometimes did not notice things which were infinitely offensive to him, and had given him infinite pain. And his simple, generous, and magnanimous character sometimes administered the needed reproof, and converted the evil-doer into a eulogist. Little as it may be thought, while the whole country rises up to do him honor, he had good reason to understand what Thomas à Kempis meant in these words : 'It is good for us sometimes to suffer contradiction, and to be badly or disparagingly thought of, even when we do and mean well. These things often aid us in forming humility.'"

And with all his high sense of honor, his dignity and self-respect, Dr. Boyce was marked by true humility and modesty. In the Memorial Addresses before the Southern Baptist Convention, both Dr. Tucker and Dr. Dargan spoke of his meekness. There are many who will understand how high a compliment it is when we say that James P. Boyce was a South Carolina gentleman; and it ought to appear something still more exalted and complete to call him a Christian gentleman.

With a high-toned self-respect ought always to be connected a delicate consideration for others. This was certainly true of Dr. Boyce, and Dr. Tupper says was strikingly true of his mother. He delighted to recognize merit in others, and loved to give credit to his associates in any undertaking. If he ever seemed extravagant in speech, it was when praising a friend. If a student grew sensitive or restless under any requirement of the institution, he would manage with delicate sympathy and quiet steadiness to relieve the strain of the situation. For example, John Stout tells that during his first session in the Seminary, 1868–1869, he was prevented by illness from making special preparation for the examination in Systematic Theology, and went to the room simply to explain his failure to undertake it. The professor urged him to stand the examination, if for nothing else, for the sake of good discipline, to promote the conviction that the examinations are important. That idea touched the soldierly element in the quiet student, and he "sat down to help keep up the *morale* of the institution." When he presently brought up a paper, the professor again urged him, with a look of deep personal interest, to return to his seat and keep on writing. He did so, just to gratify his instructor; and when they met that evening at prayer-meeting, Dr. Boyce took him aside and said, "Your paper was better than you thought. It has passed you. I knew you could pass if you would try." Mr. Stout adds:

"I am sure he saw at a glance that morning how keenly I felt my disappointment, and he determined to save me, in spite of myself. I fancy he saw just where to touch me to stir my dormant energy, and his kindness suggested to him to give relief at the earliest moment that evening to the sensitive fellow who was suffering the mortification of failure."

E. J. Forrester mentions in like manner some specially kind dealing with him. In the years following the war, when few people in Greenville had means of purchasing books, Dr. Boyce had lent his books very freely to students and families, until the losses were so heavy, especially in breaking up sets, that he was compelled to make a rule against lending. In the first session at Louisville, Mr. Forrester wanted to write an essay in Church History that required examination of many books, and asked Dr. Boyce to lend him a number of works. He told him of the necessary rule, but invited him just to come into his library, and work there as long as he pleased, as he himself would be absent from the city for several days. The student keenly felt the personal kindness and personal confidence. He further mentions that finding himself appointed one of the speakers at the Commencement, he tried in various ways to escape from the task, and tells with what prompt firmness, mingled with good humor and delicate kindness, the Chairman of the Faculty overruled all his excuses, and made him stand up to the rack. H. A. Bagby writes that at first he looked upon Dr. Boyce as an austere and exacting man, and was greatly frightened when asked to preach before him in the Broadway Church, which the professor attended, sitting there with a face that seemed to the young man severe and critical. But at the close he called on Dr. Boyce to pray; and the prayer was so devotional and tender, so thoroughly sympathetic with what he had been saying, that his own heart went out at once in warmest love towards the man he had so dreaded. Often afterwards he was struck with the sweetness and simplicity of the professor's prayers. It is related that some student re-entered the Seminary after an absence of several years; and upon being asked by a friend what made him come back, he said, "I want to attend Systematic Theology, and hear Dr. Boyce pray."

At the same time Dr. Boyce was by no means wanting in sternness, where that seemed necessary. In one of his last years of teaching, a worthy student, who was making quite a poor recitation in "Latin Theology," at length chafed under the professor's helpful suggestions, and went on without adopting them. Dr. Boyce simply became silent, and let him go forward till he wound himself up in a sentence, and could not go at all. Then another student was quietly requested to translate; and the former, who was really an excellent man, felt it so keenly that he almost fainted. Upon this incident a student remarks in a letter that Dr. Boyce could be patient as long as patience was a virtue, and as soon as sternness became a virtue he could be stern. Many other instances might be given of his wise and kind dealing with students.

Several ministers and others have testified to the exceeding kindness with which Dr. Boyce would answer letters of inquiry about questions of doctrine or of church discipline. He always declined to discuss a question which had already been brought before a church; but outside of this limit he was willing to take great pains in setting forth his views at the request of a brother who had difficult questions to decide. In the case of a man widely known, such correspondence often becomes extremely burdensome. It was really among the wonders of our age that up to a few years ago Mr. Gladstone answered every letter that was addressed to him upon the greatest variety of subjects, political, literary, religious, and all this by writing with his own pen. Dr. Boyce wrote with great facility; but it makes one sigh to look over the many long letters he had to produce, even in his years of failing strength, in order to answer the inquiries or meet the wishes of numberless correspondents. Many men in like position are simply unable to keep up such a vast correspondence without neglecting nearer and more pressing work.

In every direction Dr. Boyce showed a generous and unselfish nature. Dr. T. H. Pritchard, who was for some years his pastor at the Broadway Church in Louisville, has declared that Boyce was the most unselfish man he ever knew. On one occasion he added, "except the sainted Wingate," who was Pritchard's predecessor as President of Wake Forest College. A gentleman who was long Boyce's business partner says: —

"I never had advice from him which could be construed in any manner to have been given from interested motives, or for the furtherance of his own interest to the detriment of mine. . . . His liberality in business arrangements, his genial kindness of nature, and his gentleness of manner even when suffering pecuniary loss, was unequalled in my observation. He would speak mildly even of men who had grossly wronged and defrauded him."

His considerateness and generosity, and his noble qualities in general, awakened a very hearty affection on the part of men who acted in the capacity of private secretary for him. Mr. E. N. Woodruff, his secretary for six years after the Seminary came to Louisville, says:—

"He was careful to test the capacity of those who came into his service. He withheld much from me at first, and little by little would intrust me with more extended work. When work was done to his satisfaction, he never failed to commend, and always with great delicacy."

A later secretary, Mr. Almond, cherishes his memory with unutterable devotion.

It is widely known that Dr. Boyce was very generous in the way of giving money, both as to general religious contributions and for the relief of individuals. But the extent of his varied beneficence was far greater than any but his most intimate associates could imagine, and was fully known to no one person. Dr. H. A. Tupper tells us:—

"One who well knows what he affirms has said that Dr. Boyce gave away more than he spent on himself and family, and that his beneficence would be represented, in a material way, only by hundreds of thousands of dollars. And yet this was the smallest part of his generosity. The freeness and fulness with which he forgave offences, the lovingness with which he cheered persons who were in distress through evil-doing, and the wealth of tearful and heartfelt sympathy with which he comforted the afflicted, transcended all the other gifts. When he conferred favors, he made the recipients feel that he himself was favored; and while he had many applications for help to which he delighted in responding favorably, it was his peculiar delight to anticipate the necessity of application, to respond to heart-anxieties as yet unexpressed in words or acts, and to answer for the Lord prayers only made in secret. During his last illness, there were striking illustrations of this thoughtful charity, but too sacred for the page of history. Much as he was to public view, he was vastly more in his family, among intimate friends, and under the eye of God, alone with the subjects of his Christlike kindness."

We may add a slight incident which is suggestive. A little boy, ten years old, who bore his name, had received so many proofs of his loving remembrance that one day, generalizing as children will do, he said to his mother, "People are very kind to their namesakes." Maybe it would be well for us all to generalize as children do, and judge human nature by something good and great, rather than to judge people in general by the selfish and the wicked.

Dr. Richard Fuller once said, "The Lord gave Boyce such a big heart that it was necessary to give him a big body to hold it." Yet to all that we have said it ought to be added that he took the greatest pains to give only to deserving objects, thus making a wise investment of means which he held as a steward of the Lord. As far back as 1859, during the S. B. Convention in Richmond, when he was overwhelmingly busy with efforts to get the Seminary afloat, and at the same time actively participating in all the work of the Convention, he took the writer aside to inquire about the young Baptist church at Staunton, Va., saying that Mrs. Linda Peyton had asked him to give a hundred dollars for the church, and he wanted to be sure that it would be well bestowed. This was characteristic of him through life; and even those of us who can give but little should in like manner be very careful to invest wisely what we hold in the Master's service.

One other matter must be mentioned in connection with Dr. Boyce's kindness and generosity. His daughter says: —

"My father was always exceedingly kind to his servants. He never failed to greet them pleasantly when returning home after an absence. His manner towards them was always considerate and kindly. On some of his visits to our old home at Greenville, the negroes who had been his former slaves would sometimes come many miles to see him, and he always appreciated this very highly. One amusing incident was that of his being entertained at dinner in Memphis by a woman who had formerly been his servant. She had been my mother's maid, being a gift from her father on the eve of her marriage. She married the servant of another gentleman in Greenville, who had trained him very carefully as a carpenter and house-builder. When the master died, Mother was unwilling to give up her maid, and the married couple must of course not be separated; and so Father paid the very high price of 3,500 dollars for the husband, whose services he did not at all need. Then he bought the man a large box of very expensive tools, and let him take contracts for work, as he was intelligent enough to manage the entire building of a house. At the end of the war this man, with his wife and children, went to Memphis, and Father gave him the tool-chest as a parting present. He did well as a builder, and their children received a good education. Once when Father and Dr. Manly were in Memphis attending a convention, Fanny came and invited them to dine with her. They accepted, and she received them with pride and joy, seated them at a well-laden table, and waited on them herself."

It may be added that when Dr. Boyce's death was announced, this woman telegraphed to know the time of the funeral, and came to Louisville to attend it. Mrs. Arthur Peter, of Louisville, and Mrs. Dr. Wise, of Covington, have each stated that the servants in their homes always expressed great pleasure whenever it was mentioned that Dr. Boyce was coming for another visit.

A man such as we have thus far described would be likely to show very warm affection to kindred and friends. This has already appeared to some extent in letters to his sisters and other kindred. But these deepest and dearest affections are never fully revealed to the persons most closely connected, and become but slightly manifest to the outside world. We extract again from Miss Boyce's notes: —

GENERAL ESTIMATES OF CHARACTER. 365

"He was an ideal father, in whom supreme tenderness was mingled with great firmness, who showed utter self-sacrifice and tireless care and love towards his children. Even when we were very young, and could but little realize how much he studied our every desire and need, there were a thousand proofs of how his thoughts were centred in our childish interests. In the selection of gifts for us at Christmas he took the keenest pleasure, never allowing any one to take this matter off his hands. He always showed a remarkable faculty in the choice of beautiful and unique presents. Every doll, every game or book, was selected for us by him, and him alone. It seems to me a remarkable fact that amidst all his duties these little things, about which he need never have troubled himself, were claimed as his special pleasure. He entered into the joys of the Christmas season with all the delight of the children. Christmas was a time of great enjoyment in our home, and to my father a time dearer than any other part of the year, I think. From our earliest years he was the first, the best, the truest friend. His letters written to us are filled with expressions of love, and sweet assurances of his perfect confidence that we would always do what would be pleasing to him. These letters were charmingly adapted to our childish years. He had the rare power of entering into the little things that please and interest a child. Sometimes his letters were quite merry, abounding in all kinds of pleasantry; others were full of serious talk in reference to our characters and aims in life. He sometimes wrote to his small namesakes when babies, with comical messages for the baby to tell Mamma, etc. When it is remembered that these form a part of an enormous daily correspondence of a man who often wrote late into the night, not daring to postpone to another day the answering of letters, which if allowed to accumulate would have become an insurmountable task, one cannot but wonder at his never neglecting these little things, as many might have felt justified in doing under similar pressure.

"His sweetness of temper was most remarkable. Only in the last few years of his life, when all the time more or less unwell, was he ever irritable; and then so rarely that it was only noticeable because it came from one whom we had long known as amiable at all times and under all circumstances. When I was a child, I do not remember that my father was ever cross or ever scolded; and I recall my surprise when he said on one occasion that he considered himself to have a very quick temper, and that he had to exercise great self-control very often when others least suspected it. And when sometimes he found it necessary to admonish us, it was always done with so much tenderness that we loved him more than ever, and were all the more anxious to atone for anything that did not meet with his approval. In sickness, no mother could have been more tender in her devotion, or more wise in her ministration. His cool, soft hand upon the heated, aching head, his loving sympathy, his thoughtfulness shown in so many little ways, — it was no wonder that we thought him the ideal of parental love.

"As his children grew older, they became his companions. He interested himself in everything that interested them, — their pleasures, their friends, their studies. He was the first to appreciate any taste of ours in any particular line, and was most anxious to give us every chance of improving any supposed talent. When he took lessons with us in French and German, he bought us quantities of beautiful books and magazines to enhance the pleasure of the studies, and to give us every possible help in acquiring the language."

A corresponding wealth of affection was manifested towards friends. Even little children were strongly drawn towards him. Mrs. W. L. Pickard has written of a visit he paid to their home in Eufaula, in March, 1888, and among other things mentions that her little baby girl would cry to go to him, that he would often take her in his arms and bless and kiss her. She mentions also his considerate kindness in another way. She wished to sell a large painting in order to make a personal gift to the Seminary, but he would not hear to it, and insisted that her husband's gift was enough for them both. C. H. Nash, of Kentucky, relates an incident of the session of 1885-1886, showing the warm affection which existed between him and the students. The class in Theology presented him, at the close of recitation one day, a gold-headed cane. The presentation speaker, D. M. Ramsey, closed by saying, as he handed over the cane, "Dr. Boyce, your boys *stick* to you." Mr. Nash proceeds: —

"The Grand Old Man was taken completely by surprise, and was evidently much affected by the slight token of appreciation coming so unexpectedly. I never saw him so moved. His voice was partly choked by his emotion, as he replied somewhat brokenly. He said in substance that he appreciated the token of affection all the more highly because he had felt at times that he was not understood by his classes. His English and Latin Theology he knew must be hard and dry to many, while the method of reciting he required, and his examinations, were difficult. He said he knew that other subjects and teachers were more interesting, and he felt sometimes that his efforts were not appreciated, but that in his love and interest in his students and their success he yielded the palm to none. We were all touched, and tears glistened in many eyes."

When his death was announced, the first brief editorial notice in the "Seminary Magazine" was as follows: —

"No word from us can express what Dr. Boyce was to his students. It was one of those sweet and tender relations that cannot be described, and can be understood only as felt. In behalf of those who studied under him, we have tried hard to say just what we feel, but all in vain; for, try as we may, we unconsciously penned the words, 'He loved us, *we loved him.*' The hundreds of old students who read this will understand it without comment. They are as unable to explain the matter as we are; they can only say, ' *We loved him.*' "

Of the warm affection which existed between him and his colleagues, especially those who had toiled and suffered with him from the beginning, there has been occasional indication in this narrative, and no attempt can be made to speak of it further now. But of the affection which he awakened in all who came into intimate association with him, one slight token must be added. Not long before he left for Europe, his faithful private secretary brought some work which he did not find satisfactory; and being sensitive through disease, he complained in tones of irritation. When the old friend was leaving, one of the family expressed regret at what had occurred, saying, "You know he is sick now." "Oh, never mind!" was the reply; "he scolds prettier than any other man in the world."

It was always delightful to enter Dr. Boyce's home as a guest. His cordial and graceful courtesy, his overflowing kindness, his cheerful and genial disposition, had all been reinforced by lifelong habit; for he had grown up in a home of wealth and hospitality, and had been surrounded in youth by homes of like sort. His wife kept everything around her in superb condition, and was particularly brilliant in conversation; and their daughters were growing up with like dispositions. A day as their guest, or even a single meal, was a thing to be intensely enjoyed and long remembered. He always took delight in seeking to relieve his wife and daughters from any burden of domestic cares. If a friend was to leave early, he preferred to take charge in person of the domestic arrangements, as early rising was with him a matter of course. And yet, though he could manage everything well about the house, and took pleasure in doing so upon occasion, he never seemed in the least hard to please, either in his own home or in the homes of others.

After all, the most remarkable thing in Dr. Boyce's constitution and character was the rich and well-balanced *combination* of notable qualities. Almost every memorial address or article after his death took notice of this fact. Dr. Williams, of the "Central Baptist," said: —

"He had every reason to be self-exalted; and yet, with learning, and wealth, and social position, and everything desirable in life, as the world views it, he had the simplicity and humility of a child, the tenderness of a woman, and the strength of a giant."

Dr. Whitsitt said, at the first memorial meeting in the Seminary: —

"He had a rare combination of qualities. His character was greater than his works. The chief feature of his character was its elevation. He grew up in the golden age of the Southern nobility, in the State and the city where its best types were supplied. This elevation of character deserves emulation. He had also great simplicity, and at the same time a vigorous sturdiness. He had convictions, and the courage of them. He was gentle and accessible; conservative, and yet thoroughly reasonable. Nature made him great, and grace made him greater. He will be one of the landmarks of our denominational history."

Dr. Dargan said, at the memorial meeting of the Southern Baptist Convention: —

"A strong character lay at the basis of all that Dr. Boyce was, and gave effect and worth to all that he did. A strong character is not the gift of accident, nor is it the work of a day. It is not only the condition precedent to greatness of achievement, it is itself achievement, and at the same time the accompanying and ever-developing power to achieve. The fundamental elements of strong character are a clear mind, a pure heart, and a powerful will. All these were notably present in Dr. Boyce. He was a thoughtful man, — capable of thought, and wisely using the capability. His powers of mind were perhaps not naturally greater than those of many others; but he both trained and used them well. It was no way of his to say and do things that had not honest, hard thinking back of them."

And Dr. H. H. Tucker: —

"He seems to have inherited the business talent of his father, the Hon. Ker Boyce, who, many years ago, was the millionnaire president of the Bank of Charleston, and a man of wonderful business sagacity. Oh, it was beautiful to see James Boyce lay his financial talent, which might have brought him millions, on the altar of the Lord! From his mother he seems to have inherited the spirit of meekness; and where was there ever a gentler spirit than his? He was tender as a woman; his artlessness and simplicity of nature were like a little child; yet he was wise, and he was brave, and when some great emergency called for a man, there was Boyce! The lion and the lamb lay down together in his breast, and, in strange antithesis, he possessed the qualities of both. I know no better eulogy for him than this: he was always just what the occasion demanded.

"We have had men, and have them now, superior to him in one particular or another; but where is there another such combination of forces, intellectual, moral, and social, that completely round out the character of a man? There are some — not so very many — who excel him in learning; some — a considerable number — who are more brilliant; none of better-balanced mind, or of better-balanced character, none of more trustworthy judgment, none more soundly orthodox, none of profounder convictions, none truer to their convictions, none more industrious, none more self-sacrificing, none more generous, none more genial or magnetic in personal intercourse, and not one who combines all these qualities in a character so full of power. It was his Washingtonian evenness of development, his perfect poise, and his huge motive force, all sanctified by grace, that made him great."

Dr. Arthur Peter, himself a man of sound judgment and wide experience, when asked what he thought the most notable thing in Dr. Boyce's character, said, "The well-rounded development and perfect balance of all his powers." His wife, the enthusiastic and ardent friend, answered a similar question by saying, "Oh, he was perfect,— the most perfect mortal man I ever knew." Rev. G. W. Samson, D.D., long President of the Columbian College (University) in Washington, and now in New York city, wrote some months after his death: "Dr. Boyce was in every respect the noblest spirit that I ever met."

From all this gathered eulogium he himself would have shrunk in grief and humiliation. But we are not writing for him, but of him,— writing for the comfort of those who loved him, and for the benefit of those who read concerning his character and work.

When John Knox died, in 1573, Beza wrote: "We have been afflicted beyond belief by the death of Mr. Knox; for the death of good men always appears premature." Inscribed on the wall of Knox's house in Edinburgh, this sentiment has no doubt awakened a response in many hearts concerning one good man or another. So we were tempted to feel about the death of Boyce. But it is a nobler and more helpful view that was suggested to us all by Dr. H. H. Tucker, in the address already quoted, and with his words we may conclude: —

"While our great leaders are alive, we cannot do without them. We could not have done without Boyce. But when they die, we *can* do without them. God never takes them away until their work is done. . . . When we need another Boyce, God will give him to us. *Now* the cause needs *us;* and whether we be great or small, it cannot do without us. Therefore, let us renew our zeal and consecration. . . . Blessed be the memory of Boyce! The Lord gave, and the Lord hath taken away; blessed be the name of the Lord! Be still, O smitten hearts! The past is safe, — we can look back and see it; the present is safe, — we can look around and see it; the future is hidden from us, but still we are just as certain that it too is safe, for —

"'Behind the dim unknown
Standeth God within the darkness,
Keeping watch above his own.'"

O Brother beloved, true yokefellow through years of toil, best and dearest friend, sweet shall be thy memory till we meet again! And may the men be always ready, as the years come and go, to carry on, with widening reach and heightened power, the work we sought to do, and did begin!

Other SGCB Classic Reprints

In addition to *A Gentleman and a Scholar* which you now hold in your hands, Solid Ground Christian Books is honored to present the following titles, many for the first time in more than a century:

THEOLOGY ON FIRE: *Sermons from the Heart of J.A. Alexander*
A SHEPHERD'S HEART: *Sermons from the Ministry of J.W. Alexander*
EVANGELICAL TRUTH: *Practical Sermons for the Christian Home*
by *Archibald Alexander*
OPENING SCRIPTURE: *A Hermeneutical Manual* by *Patrick Fairbairn*
THE ASSURANCE OF FAITH by *Louis Berkhof*
THE PASTOR IN THE SICK ROOM by *John D. Wells*
THE NATIONAL PREACHER: Sermons from the 2nd Great Awakening
THE POOR MAN'S OT COMMENTARY by *Robert Hawker* **(6 vols)**
THE POOR MAN'S NT COMMENTARY by *Robert Hawker* **(3 vols)**
FIRST THINGS: *The First Lessons God Taught Mankind* by *Gardiner Spring*
BIBLICAL & THEOLOGICAL STUDIES by *the 1912 Faculty of Princeton*
THE POWER OF GOD UNTO SALVATION by *B.B. Warfield*
THE LORD OF GLORY by *B.B. Warfield*
CHRIST ON THE CROSS & THE LORD OUR SHEPHERD
by *John Stevenson*
SERMONS TO THE NATURAL MAN by *W.G.T. Shedd*
SERMONS TO THE SPIRITUAL MAN by *W.G.T. Shedd*
HOMILETICS AND PASTORAL THEOLOGY by *W.G.T. Shedd*
A PASTOR'S SKETCHES 1 & 2 by *Ichabod S. Spencer*
THE PREACHER AND HIS MODELS by *James Stalker*
IMAGO CHRISTI by *James Stalker*
A HISTORY OF PREACHING by *Edwin C. Dargan*
LECTURES ON THE HISTORY OF PREACHING by *John A. Broadus*
THE SCOTTISH PULPIT by *William Taylor*
THE SHORTER CATECHISM ILLUSTRATED by *John Whitecross*
THE CHURCH MEMBER'S GUIDE by *John Angell James*
THE SUNDAY SCHOOL TEACHER'S GUIDE by *John Angell James*
CHRIST IN SONG: *Hymns of Immanuel from All Ages* by *Philip Schaff*
COME YE APART: *Daily Words from the Four Gospels* by *J.R. Miller*
DEVOTIONAL LIFE OF THE SUNDAY SCHOOL TEACHER
by *J.R. Miller*

Call us Toll Free at 1-877-666-9469
Send us an e-mail at sgcb@charter.net
Visit us on line at solid-ground-books.com

"Uncovering Buried Treasure to the Glory of God"

www.ingramcontent.com/pod-product-compliance
Lightning Source LLC
Chambersburg PA
CBHW021829220426
43663CB00005B/177